THE FORMATION OF
A MEDIEVAL CHURCH

# THE FORMATION OF A

■

# MEDIEVAL CHURCH

■

*Ecclesiastical Change in Verona, 950–1150*

■

M A U R E E N   C .   M I L L E R

■

CORNELL UNIVERSITY PRESS   Ithaca and London

Copyright © 1993 by Cornell University

All rights reserved. Except for brief quotations in a
review, this book, or parts thereof, must not be
reproduced in any form without permission in writing from the publisher. For information, address
Cornell University Press, Sage House,
512 East State Street, Ithaca, New York 14850.

First published 1993 by Cornell University Press.

International Standard Book Number 0-8014-2837-8
Library of Congress Catalog Card Number 92-54971
Printed in the United States of America
Librarians: Library of Congress cataloging information
appears on the last page of the book.

⊗ The paper in this book meets the minimum
requirements of the American National Standard for
Information Sciences—Permanence of Paper for
Printed Library Materials, ANSI Z39.48-1984.

IN MEMORY OF DAVID HERLIHY

# CONTENTS

# ILLUSTRATIONS

# ACKNOWLEDGMENTS

I BEGAN work on medieval Verona at Harvard University, studying with David Herlihy. As he did not live to see this book published, it is dedicated to his memory. I will always be grateful to him for suggesting that I do research on Verona, for thoughtful advice, and especially for constant reminders, in word and example, of just how interesting and enjoyable the study of history is. Thanks are also owed to Frederic Cheyette of Amherst College, whose research seminar at Harvard in the spring of 1985 introduced me to the study of medieval charters and whose encouragement and support since then have helped me immensely. For originally inspiring me to begin the long but gratifying process of becoming a historian, I express my gratitude to Terence R. Murphy of The American University.

The research for this book was funded by a 1987–88 Fulbright Fellowship to Italy and a Frederick Sheldon Traveling Fellowship from Harvard University. I am extremely grateful to both for allowing me a year in *bella Verona*. A 1989 summer travel grant from the Harvard Department of History allowed me to return to the sources once more. Substantial revision was made possible by the generous research support of the Dean of the Faculty at Hamilton College, Eugene M. Tobin. The Financial Aid Office of the Graduate School of Arts and Sciences made it possible to pursue studies at Harvard, and I am especially indebted to the heirs of Vincent Scramuzza for endowing the scholarship that supported most of my graduate education. And, of course, for financial aid when there was no Financial Aid (in addition to lots else), I thank my parents, Archie and Catherine Miller.

The kind assistance of the staffs of the Archivio di Stato (Verona), the Biblioteca Capitolare (Verona), the Biblioteca Civica (Verona), and the Archivio Segreto Vaticano made my research pleasant as well as possible. I owe special thanks to Don Giuseppe Zivelonghi, librarian of the Biblioteca

Capitolare, and to Silvana Morandi of the Biblioteca Civica for their generous and patient assistance. Professor Egidio Rossini made numerous helpful suggestions during my time in the archives and allowed me to consult his typescripts for a new volume of the Codice Diplomatico Veronese (961–1000) and for new editions of imperial diplomata. I also thank Professor Giorgio Cracco of the Istituto di Storia Medioevale e Moderna (Padua) for reading parts of this work in progress and for access to the Institute's library. He and his fine colleague Professor Antonio Rigon provided helpful bibliographic suggestions and much appreciated encouragement. Professor Andrea Castagnetti of the Università degli Studi, Verona, also steered me to several helpful sources. The hospitality of the entire Nicoli family was crucial in the final stages of my research, and I am especially grateful to Valeria Nicoli for both her friendship and her linguistic skills.

The Medieval Academy of America has generously granted permission to reproduce in Chapter 4 substantial sections of an article that appeared in *Speculum* 66 (1991): 27–42. I thank Luke Wenger, Jacqueline Brown, William Bowsky, and the other (unknown) reader for suggestions on that piece. Many other friends and colleagues provided comments, suggestions, and encouragement during the process of revising this work. I thank Thomas N. Bisson, George Dameron, Duane Osheim, and Fr. Boniface Ramsey, OP, for commenting on the entire first draft (Professor Bisson generously taking time during a leave year to do so). I am also grateful to Daniela Rando (Università di Trento), Ronald Witt, Greg Guderian, Tom Head, and the members of the European History Colloquium at Syracuse University for helpful suggestions on individual chapters. The good cheer of my colleagues in the Department of History at Hamilton College contributed much to this process, as did the questions and comments of my colleagues in the AAUP Journal Club at Hamilton. I especially thank Paula Rust for her statistical expertise and my research assistant, Kristina Ferrare, for producing all the maps and graphs, tracking down loose ends, and buoying my spirits constantly. Finally, special thanks are due to my friend Bruce Venarde. His careful reading of several chapters, his cheerful willingness to listen to even the most inchoate ideas, and his impeccable Latin have saved me from several aggressive stupidities.

MAUREEN C. MILLER

Clinton, New York

# ABBREVIATIONS

*Archives and Libraries*

| | |
|---|---|
| *ACV* | Archivio Capitolare, Verona |
| *ASV* | Archivio Segreto Vaticano |
| *ASVR* | Archivio di Stato, Verona |
| *BAV* | Biblioteca Apostolica Vaticana |
| *BC* | Biblioteca Civica, Verona |

*Frequently Cited Works*

| | |
|---|---|
| *AASS* | *Acta sanctorum quotquot toto orbe coluntur*, ed. Jean Bolland et al., new ed. (Paris and Rome: Victor Palmé, 1863–). |
| *AMAV* | *Atti e memorie della Accademia di agricoltura, scienze, e lettere di Verona.* |
| Annales Camaldulenses | Johanne-Benedicto Mitarelli, Anselmo Costadoni, *Annales Camaldulenses Ordinis Sancti Benedicti*, 9 vols. (Venice: J. B. Pasquali, 1755–73). |
| Biancolini, Chiese | G. B. Biancolini, *Notizie storiche delle chiese di Verona*, 8 vols. (Verona: A. Scolari, 1749–71). |
| CDP | *Codice diplomatico padovano*, ed. Andrea Gloria, 3 vols. (Venice: Deputazione di storia patria per le Venezie, 1877–81). |
| CDV | *Codice diplomatico veronese*, ed. Vittorio Fainelli, 2 vols. (Venice: Deputazione di storia patria per le Venezie, 1940–63). |
| Chiese-terr. | *Chiese e monasteri nel territorio veronese*, ed. Giorgio Borelli (Verona: Banca Popolare di Verona, 1981). |

| | |
|---|---|
| Chiese-Ver. | *Chiese e monasteri di Verona,* ed. Giorgio Borelli (Verona: Banca Popolare di Verona, 1980). |
| DDC | *Dictionnaire de droit canonique,* 7 vols. (Paris: Librarie Letouzey et Ané, 1935–65). |
| Ederle, Dizionario | Guglielmo Ederle, *Dizionario cronologico bio-bibliografico dei vescovi di Verona* (Verona: Vita Veronese, 1965). |
| Fliche, La réforme | Augustin Fliche, *La réforme grégorienne,* 3 vols., Spicilegium sacrum Lovaniense, Études et documents 6, 9, 16 (Louvain: Spicilegium sacrum Lovananesis, and Paris: E. Champion, 1924–37). |
| IS | *Italia Sacra,* ed. Ferdinando Ughelli, 2d ed., 9 vols. (Venice: Sebastianus Coleti, 1717–22). |
| Kehr, IP | *Regesta pontificum romanorum: Italia pontificia,* ed. Paul F. Kehr, 10 vols. (Berlin: Weidmannos, 1906–). |
| Mansi | *Sacrorum conciliorum nova et amplissima collectio,* ed. J. D. Mansi, 53 vols. (Florence and Venice: Antonius Zata, 1759–98). |
| Meersseman, L'orazionale | *L'orazionale dell'arcidiacono Pacifico e il Carpsum del Cantore Stefano: Studi e testi sulla liturgia del duomo di Verona dal IX all'XI secolo,* ed. G. G. Meersseman, E. Adda, J. Deshusses, Spicilegium friburgense 21 (Fribourg: Editions universitaires, 1974). |
| MGH Concilia | *Monumenta Germaniae historica, Legum sectio III: Concilia* (Hannover and Leipzig: Bibliopolius Hahnianus, 1906–24). |
| MGH Const. | *Monumenta Germaniae historica, Legum sectio IV: Constitutiones et acta publica imperatorum et regum,* 5 vols. (Hannover: Bibliopolius Hahnianus, 1893–). |
| MGH DD | *Monumenta Germaniae historica, Diplomatum regum et imperatorum Germaniae* (Berlin: Weidmannsche Verlagsbuchhandlung, 1879–). |
| MGH SS | *Monumenta Germaniae historica, Scriptorum* (Hannover: Bibliopolius Hahnianus, 1826–; rpt. Stuttgart: A. Hiersemann, New York: Kraus, 1903–). |
| Muselli, Memorie | Giuseppe Muselli, *Memorie istoriche, cronologiche,* |

|  |  |
|---|---|
|  | *diplomatiche, canoniche, e critiche del Capitolo e Canonici della Cattedrale di Verona, ACV,* buste DCCCXXXII–DCCCXLVIII. |
| Pighi, "Cenni" | "Cenni Storici" [1145 bull of Eugene III], ed. G. B. Pighi, *Bollettino ecclesiastico veronese* 6 (1919): 150–57. |
| PL | *Patrologiae cursus completus,* Ser. Lat., ed. J. P. Migne, 221 vols. (Paris: Garnier, 1844–64). |
| Ratherius, *Briefe* | Ratherius of Verona, *Die Breife des Bischofs Rather von Verona,* ed. Fritz Weigle (Weimar, 1949; rpt. Munich: Monumenta Germaniae historica, 1977). |
| Ratherius, *Op.min.* | Ratherius of Verona, *Opera minora,* ed. Peter L. D. Reid, Corpus Christianorum, continuatio mediaevalis 46 (Turnhout: Brepols, 1976). |
| Ratherius, *Praeloquia* | Ratherius of Verona, *Praeloqviorvm libri VI—Phrenesis,* ed. Peter L. D. Reid, Corpus Christianorum, continuatio mediaevalis 46A (Turnhout: Brepols, 1984) |
| Ratherius, "Urkunden" | Ratherius of Verona, "Urkunden und Akten zur Geschichte Rathers in Verona," ed. Fritz Weigle, *Quellen und Forschungen aus italienischen Archiven und Bibliotheken* 29 (1938–39): 1–40. |
| RIS | *Rerum italicarum scriptores,* ed. Lodovico Antonio Muratori, 25 vols. (Milan: Typographia Societatis palatinae, 1723–51). |
| VerST | *Verona e il suo territorio,* 7 vols. (Verona: Istituto per gli studi storici veronesi, 1960–69). |

# NOTE ON
# NAMES, MONEY, DATES,
# AND ORTHOGRAPHY

## Names

I have used recognized English forms of personal names whenever possible. When no English equivalent could be found, I used the nominative singular Latin form. Thus, "Iohannes" has been rendered "John," but "Tebaldus" remains "Tebaldus." Although some scholars writing in English refer to the tenth-century bishop and author of the *Praeloquia* as Rather of Verona, I have chosen to use the Latin form "Ratherius" in this case to avoid confusion with the common adverb "rather."

Names of ecclesiastical institutions and places in the Veronese diocese have been rendered in their modern Italian form. This has the advantage of allowing the reader to distinguish ecclesiastical institutions from their namesakes (e.g., San Zeno, the wealthy and powerful monastery, from Saint Zeno, the fourth-century bishop of Verona).

## Money

Verona was the site of a long-established mint (one of only four operating in northern Italy through the early twelfth century). Transactions were calculated in Veronese denarii (12 denarii = 1 solidus; 20 solidi = 1 libra, or pound). For rates of exchange between Veronese coin and that of other northern Italian cities, see Peter Spufford, *Handbook of Medieval Exchange* (London, 1986), pp. 40, 87, 103–4, 107.

## Dates

The year in early medieval Veronese documents was given in years from the incarnation; these years began on the feast of the Annunciation, 25 March. Notaries also gave the indiction—a cycle of fifteen years, originally used by the Romans to revise tax lists, employed by medieval notaries to confound forgers. Before the millennium they followed the Greek or Constantinopolitan style of beginning the year of the indiction on 1 September.

During the eleventh century there were changes in the reckoning of both the year and the indiction. Around the turn of the millennium notaries began to use the Roman indiction, which commenced on either 25 December or 1 January. Usage of the indiction was irregular, however, through most of the eleventh century. In the 1080s the Roman indiction became customary and, probably for convenience in reckoning, most notaries began to give the date in years from the nativity (which, like the indiction, began on 25 December). The calculation of years from the incarnation did not disappear entirely until the mid-twelfth century.

In the text and notes, I have changed the dates to the common style. For a more detailed analysis of Veronese chronological conventions, see Vittorio Fainelli, "La data nei documenti e nelle cronache di Verona," *Nuovo Archivio Veneto* n.s. 41 (1911): 128–76.

## Orthography

Editors of medieval Latin texts have followed many different orthographical conventions: some uniformly classicize medieval spelling, others reproduce their texts as exactly as possible, and yet others define a medium between these two extremes suitable to their particular authors and manuscripts. My policy has been to quote printed editions of medieval sources exactly as they have been published, attempting no standardization of orthography. There is one exception to this rule. The *Codice diplomatico veronese* indicates expansions of medieval abbreviations by enclosing them in parentheses (e.g., s(an)c(t)a). For ease in reading I have eliminated the parentheses, still retaining, however, the exact reading and spelling published by the editor. Brackets indicating hypothetical readings in difficult or damaged manuscripts have also been retained. In my own transcriptions of Veronese sources I have reproduced the medieval orthography of the documents, standardizing spelling according to the general norms of local notarial practice (as in *scola*, which in a few documents is spelled *schola* but is usually spelled without the "h" by Veronese notaries).

THE FORMATION OF
A MEDIEVAL CHURCH

# INTRODUCTION

**T**HIS book is about change: how we measure it, how we explain it, and how we use it to carve the past into periods. In the field of ecclesiastical history, more than in other areas of historical inquiry, change has posed difficulties. It has been burdened with an insufferable weight of moral significance, always characterized in relation to some concept of virtuous perfection. This value-laden approach to describing change yields cycles of "reform" and "decadence." Another tendency among ecclesiastical historians has been to minimize change or to limit its purview in order to protect or enhance the eternal quality of the Church. Unseemly origins and infelicitous lapses are smoothed over to create a narrative of steadfast persistence. Here, the morality of change will be left to the judgment of others and its occurrence will not impugn the aspirations of Christians past or present. For, in my view, the Church changed over the Middle Ages because it was an institution which, no matter how devoted to things eternal and otherworldly, struggled in a mutable world.

The most important period of change in the history of the medieval Church began in the mid-tenth century and ended in the mid-twelfth. This period was one of immense growth and creativity affecting all aspects of ecclesiastical life. Moreover, it resulted in a recognizably "medieval" Church: one with a hierarchical organization culminating in the pope, one devoted to pastoral care through local churches staffed by clerics under the supervision of the bishop, one enlivened by a multitude of diverse religious institutions, and one in which the pursuit of holiness was open to all Christians. These characteristics, if they existed at all before the mid-tenth century, existed only as ideals and not as institutional realities.[1]

1. The idea of papal primacy was formulated under Leo I (440–461), but this theory was only beginning to be translated into practice in the twelfth century. See Geoffrey Barraclough, *The Medieval Papacy* (London, 1968), p. 9; Walter Ullmann, *The Growth of Papal Government in the Middle*

What forces transformed ideals into realities? The causes of these many changes in the Church were numerous and their interactions complex. But two causes receive special emphasis here: demographic growth and economic development. The expansion of population and settlement which began in the late tenth century throughout western Europe provoked a crisis in pastoral care which profoundly altered the organization and mission of the medieval Church. The multiplication of souls commended to its care rapidly overtaxed the Church's institutions for the training of priests and laid bare its insufficiencies in organization and discipline. Demographic growth fueled an intense dissatisfaction with the clergy, which launched the reforms of the eleventh century and made clear the need for jurisdictional clarity that these reforms pursued. The crisis of pastoral care precipitated by population growth contributed not only to the Gregorian Reform and the investiture conflict but also, a century and a half later, to the pastoral orientation of the Fourth Lateran Council's agenda.

The Church's response to this crisis was influenced at every turn by economic change. Economic expansion and growing economic sophistication provided resources for both institutional and spiritual creativity. These resources supported the building of churches and the foundation of monasteries. They allowed groups of committed individuals to create new kinds of institutions, and this new diversity made religious life accessible to believers from nearly all social strata. Economic sophistication also further empowered the already powerful, as bishops borrowed money to litigate claims, to travel to Rome, to adorn their churches, to build themselves palaces, and to gain political influence.

---

*Ages,* 2d ed. (London, 1962), pp. v, 2–14 (on Leo's formulation), 262, 325–31, 373, 447–48 (on "the translation of abstract principles into concrete governmental actions"). The legislation of the Carolingian era set out an ideal system of pastoral care and episcopal supervision, but we have no convincing evidence of its effective implementation. The repetition of canons against the same abuses in council after council is hardly reassuring; Wallace-Hadrill describes the tone of legislation as "frustrated" in the early ninth century and as bordering on "panic" by the 840s. J. M. Wallace-Hadrill, *The Frankish Church* (Oxford, 1983), pp. 258–70, 278–92. Until the twelfth century, the dominant form of religious life in western Europe was monasticism (the pursuit of Christian perfection in special communities). Since an endowment was necessary to enter a monastery, this vocation was limited to individuals with substantial property, and early medieval monasteries were dominated by the nobility. Hubert Jedin, *Handbook of Church History* (New York, 1965–70) 3: 690–707 (on the role of monasticism in the early medieval Church); 4: 453–65 (on the emergence of different forms of religious life in the twelfth century). See C. H. Lawrence, *Medieval Monasticism* (London, 1984), pp. 110–11 on the social character of monastic recruitment.

The period I define and the causes of change I emphasize here both emerged from my attempt to measure change systematically. Basic to this attempt is the conviction that institutions offer us the surest measures of religious change in the Middle Ages. Medieval sources only rarely reveal personal religious experiences or thoughts, and these infrequent glimpses are difficult to compare across time. The most abundant and continuous documentation available was produced by ecclesiastical institutions[2] and illuminates not only their existence and ideals, but also their relations with the surrounding world. The development of ecclesiastical institutions across the Middle Ages reveals significant changes, both quantitative and qualitative. The period 950–1150 is notable not only for the number of new institutions but also for the new kinds of institutions founded. Demographic growth and economic development are behind the quantitative increase in institutions, and both strongly influenced the form and character of these institutions. They were also critical in the formation of the institution as a whole, the medieval Church.

These are the main arguments of this book, but there are several others. One could not discuss this period without touching on reform, and the evidence considered here suggests that reform occurred even in dioceses that remained loyal to the emperor.[3] Political allegiances during the inves-

2. Throughout this book, I will use the term "ecclesiastical institutions" as a general designation of all the institutions that constituted the Church. I include under this rubric churches, oratories, chapels, monasteries, canonries, and other religious houses. The term "religious institutions" will be used to designate only those institutions devoted to the religious life as defined in canon law. "Church" (capitalized) refers to the entire Catholic Christian community and its institutions; when used in the Veronese context ("the Veronese Church") it connotes all the institutions in the diocese. My aim is not to give special honor or distinction to the institution, but to help the reader distinguish between individual houses of worship (churches) and larger and more complex communities of belief with distinct juridical organizations.

3. Ecclesiastical authors in the eleventh and twelfth centuries used "reform" (reformatio) in both a personal and an institutional sense. The interior rekindling of spiritual ardor they urged is usually beyond the reach of our sources. But the institutional renewal and reorganization they advocated is discernible in medieval documentation. Chiefly the reformers tried to restore the vita apostolica through the adoption of institutional arrangements that they referred to as the communal life. Clerics "should live and sleep together, and hold in common what comes to them from churches . . . and should strive most greatly to achieve the apostolic, that is, the common life." They also urged the restoration of discipline, especially the bishop's authority over his clergy. In monastic life, the reformers sought strict adherence to the Benedictine Rule and the restoration of monastic property. Throughout this book, I have used the term "reform" to characterize actions or occurrences that medieval Veronese documents call reform, and developments that demonstrate or suggest implementation of the institutional arrangements

titure crisis are not reliable indicators of reform. The end of direct imperial investiture in 1122 also had some paradoxical results: it may have freed bishops from imperial control, but it also made them immediately more politically vulnerable, and often politically entangled, in their own communities.

Another set of findings concerns religious life, which took a variety of new forms in the eleventh and twelfth centuries. Although many historians have linked the emergence of new social groups in this period to the development of these new religious institutions, I argue in Chapter 4 that members of these new social groups were actually very conservative in their religious tastes. New religious movements succeeded because they appealed to all levels of medieval society. Their success, however, did not mean that traditional religious institutions declined. I contend in Chapter 3 that Benedictine monasticism remained vital well into the thirteenth century: it experienced no "crisis" when new religious institutions emerged. Finally, the new religious movements of the early twelfth century already, a century before Saint Francis, embraced poverty as a religious virtue and strove to ameliorate the sufferings of the poor.

All these arguments are based on an intensive study of one diocese, that of Verona, Italy. In choosing this approach, I have aimed to connect ecclesiastical institutions firmly to the society that created, sustained, and transformed them over the Middle Ages. In choosing Verona, an average diocese in many respects, I have intended to suggest a new view of the relationship between medieval society and ecclesiastical development. My analysis also seeks to reconcile two different traditions in the study of medieval Christianity.

A real divide separates the traditional Church history of the nineteenth and early twentieth centuries from recent approaches to the study of medieval Christianity. Before the Second World War, historians of medieval Christianity emphasized institutions and ideas. Essentially, they studied the medieval Church and its doctrinal development.[4] They focused special

---

contemporaries urged as reforms. For a discussion of the meaning of this word in the twelfth century, and for the quotation above, see Giles Constable, "Renewal and Reform in Religious Life," in *Renaissance and Renewal in the Twelfth Century*, ed. Robert L. Benson and Giles Constable with Carol D. Lanham (Cambridge, Mass., 1982), pp. 37–67. Constable's translation of the canon of the Roman Council of 1059 on the common life is on p. 54.

4. The very divisions Louis John Paetow adopted in the section on Church history in his *Guide to the Study of Medieval History*, rev. ed. (New York, 1931) reveal these interests. There are subsections on the Church in France, Germany, Italy, and Spain, on "Church and State in the Middle Ages,"

attention on the growth of "national" Churches,[5] as well as on the development of internal administrative structures and canon law.[6] This was most definitely history from the top down: it featured powerful popes, bishops, and abbots. This traditional Church history sometimes bore the imprint of confessional loyalties. In the most extreme accounts, the Middle Ages was either the Golden Age of Christianity or the period of darkness and corruption preceding and justifying the Protestant Reformation.[7]

These partisan tendencies as well as traditional Church history's focus on the empowered led to a rejection of its subjects and methods in the postwar era. Answering Lucien Febvre's call for a "new kind of history,"

---

on the medieval papacy, councils, dogma, and monasticism. This tradition of Church history has prospered longest in England and Germany; the work of David Knowles and Hubert Jedin demonstrates the continuing value of this school: David Knowles, *The Monastic Order in England* (Cambridge, 1940); *The Religious Orders in England*, 3 vols. (Cambridge, 1948–59); *The Evolution of Medieval Thought* (London, 1962); Hubert Jedin, *Geschichte des Konzils von Trent*, 4 vols. (Fribourg, 1949), trans. Ernest Graf, *A History of the Council of Trent*, 2 vols. (London, 1957–61); *Handbuch der Kirchengeschichte*, 7 vols. (Fribourg, 1962–79), trans. *Handbook of Church History*, 10 vols. (New York, 1965–70). Colin Morris's *The Papal Monarchy: The Western Church from 1050 to 1250* (Oxford, 1989) is an example of the continuation of this tradition. Although Morris includes a chapter on general social and economic changes in medieval Europe and asserts that changes in the Church are inexplicable without them, his chronology and causation are entirely determined by institutional, theological, and canon law developments.

5. The great monuments of such efforts are *Italia sacra*, ed. Ferdinando Ughelli, 2d ed., 9 vols. (Venice, 1717–22); the *Gallia christiana*, compiled by the Benedictines of St. Maur and continued by the Académie des inscriptions et belles-lettres, 16 vols. (Paris, 1744–); *España sagrada*, ed. H. Florez et al., 51 vols. (Madrid, 1747–1879); Albert Hauck, *Kirchengeschichte Deutschlands*, 5 vols. (Leipzig, 1887–1929).

6. Fine examples are R. L. Poole, *Lectures on the History of the Papal Chancery* (Cambridge, 1915); P. Fournier and G. Le Bras, *Histoire des collections canoniques en Occident*, 2 vols. (Paris, 1931–32); W. E. Lunt, *Papal Revenues in the Middle Ages*, 2 vols. (New York, 1934); Geoffrey Barraclough, *Papal Provisions* (Oxford, 1935); Stephan Kuttner, *Repertorium der Kanonistik* (1140–1234), Studi e Testi 71 (Vatican City, 1937).

7. Compare Fernand Mourret, *A History of the Catholic Church*, trans. Newton Thompson, 8 vols. (St. Louis, Mo., 1931–57) with any of H. C. Lea's works: *A Historical Sketch of Sacerdotal Celibacy in the Christian Church* (Philadelphia, 1867); *A History of the Inquisition in the Middle Ages*, 3 vols. (1888; rpt. New York, 1922); *A History of Auricular Confession and Indulgences in the Latin Church* (Philadelphia, 1896). Predictably, Mourret credits the popes of the twelfth and thirteenth century with bringing Christianity to its "fullest development" (4: 3) and charges that the sixteenth-century reformers "did but aggravate the evils for which they claimed to bring relief" (5: v). Lea, on the other hand, assures his readers that he presents "an impartial account," but characterizes the dominance of the Church in the twelfth and thirteenth centuries as "spiritual despotism" (Lea, *Inquisition*, preface and p. 1).

scholars interested in medieval Christianity sought to illuminate the faith of the common believer. This new religious history was strongly influenced by anthropological and sociological approaches to the study of religion. It focused on religious practice and its social context rather than on institutions.[8] Moreover, as its concentration on heresy indicates, it has been marked by a tendency to associate institutions with the repression of popular piety.[9]

The hostility of this generation of historians toward institutions, however, has severely limited the new religious history's ability to replace Church history. At present the fascinating and provocative work of this school exists more as an addendum to old-style Church history than as a real alternative to it. It is my aim here to offer a different approach, combining the strengths of both traditions. I share the interests of the new religious historians in the norms of religious belief and practice, as well as their awareness of social and economic influences. What were the broadly shared ideas and broadly felt changes that characterized Christianity in the central Middle Ages? How was the Church influenced by the world it sought to convert? I also adopt the institutional focus of traditional Church history. Ecclesiastical institutions were not necessarily repressive. Moreover, as expressions of belief and disseminators of religious ideas and practices, institutions offer us the surest measure of religious change in the Middle Ages. My intention, then, is to make some small contribution toward a new kind of Church history.

8. John Van Engen has recently published a fine historiographical essay on these trends: "The Christian Middle Ages as an Historiographical Problem," *The American Historical Review* 91 (1986): 519–52. The focus on the religion of the people is well illustrated by the work of French scholars: Jacques Toussaert, *Le sentiment religeaux en Flandre à la fin du moyen âge* (Paris, 1963); Etienne Delaruelle, *La piété populaire au moyen âge*, ed. Raoul Manselli and André Vauchez (Turin, 1975); Emmanuel Le Roy Ladurie, *Montaillou: The Promised Land of Error*, trans. Barbara Bray (New York, 1978); André Vauchez, *La sainteté en occident aux derniers siècles du moyen âge* (Rome and Paris, 1981); Jean Claude Schmitt, *The Holy Greyhound: Guinefort, Healer of Children since the Thirteenth Century*, trans. Martin Thom (Cambridge and Paris, 1983); and André Vauchez, *Les Laics au moyen âge: Pratiques et expériences religieuses* (Paris, 1987). On the influence of social science methodology on the development of this school, the classic work is Gabriel Le Bras, *Études de sociologie religeuse*, 2 vols. (Paris, 1955–56).
9. See Van Engen, "The Christian Middle Ages," p. 523, on the work of H. Grundmann, and pp. 535–36. This is particularly strong in Schmitt, *The Holy Greyhound*, and Le Roy Ladurie, *Montaillou*, as well as in the work of Raoul Manselli, *Studi sulle eresie del secolo XII*, 2d rev. ed. (Rome, 1975). For an overview of the voluminous new literature on heresy, see Malcolm Lambert, *Medieval Heresy* (New York, 1977) and Jeffrey Burton Russell and Carl T. Berkhout, *Medieval Heresies: A Bibliography, 1960–1979* (Toronto, 1981).

Why choose Verona? A survey of institutional change across the entire Middle Ages and close examination of institutions and their relations with economies and social groups required a limited scope. Obviously, it would be impossible to find one diocese representative of all of western Europe. But the diocese I have chosen, that of the northern Italian city of Verona, does share important characteristics with many others. Just as important, its ecclesiastical institutions are well documented. The State Archive in Verona, the city's Capitular Archive, and the Vatican Archive hold thousands of medieval charters from Veronese ecclesiastical institutions. These charters are even numerous for the period before 1000, allowing a secure comparison of the Veronese Church before and after the transformations of the eleventh and twelfth centuries. Mostly concerning land conveyances, these documents illuminate social and economic change as well as the internal development of ecclesiastical institutions and their relations with lay society.[10]

To what extent is Verona representative? Socially and economically it is quite broadly typical of medieval European cities. It was an urban center of average size, with about 20–25,000 inhabitants in the thirteenth century (probably peaking at 35–40,000 before the Black Death).[11] It experienced strong, but not exceptional, economic development beginning in the second half of the tenth century. Verona profited from its location on an important trade route linking Venice and the cities of south Germany, but it never became a major center of international trade or manufacture. Economic growth did give rise to a middle class of notarial, mercantile, and artisan families in the eleventh century, and these new families allied with the local nobility early in the following century to govern the city.

Verona's political history is also fairly representative of broad European patterns through the twelfth century.[12] Originally a Roman provincial

10. See Appendix A for a detailed description of all the sources used in this study.

11. David Herlihy, "The Population of Verona in the First Century of Venetian Rule," in *Renaissance Venice*, ed. J. R. Hale (London, 1974), p. 95. Exceptionally large cities in the Middle Ages were Paris (at least 210,000 inhabitants in 1328), Venice and Milan (each perhaps as large as 180,000), and Florence (about 120,000 inhabitants in 1338). Other large cities were Bruges (about 50,000 inhabitants) and London, Toulouse, Montpellier, Ghent, Liège, and Cologne (about 40,000 each). There were numerous cities in Italy that, like Verona, had populations of around 30,000: Bologna, Cremona, Ferrara, Lucca, Naples, Padua, Pisa, Siena. See David Herlihy, "Demography," in *Dictionary of the Middle Ages*, ed. Joseph R. Strayer, 12 vols. (New York, 1982–89) 4: 141.

12. After the twelfth century, Verona's political history can only be said to be typical of northern Italian cities. The free commune, weakened by factional infighting, fell under the sway of

town, Verona came under the domination of migrating Germanic tribes, first the Goths (489–568) and then the Lombards (568–774). It was incorporated into the Carolingian empire with Charlemagne's conquest of the Kingdom of Italy in 774, and enjoyed the cultural renaissance and rule by counts and missi for which the Carolingian era is famous. In the late ninth and early tenth centuries, as Carolingian rule disintegrated, Verona, like most other communities in western Europe, suffered repeated devastation at the hands of "pagani" and political instability as competing lords fought over the remains of the empire.[13]

As we move beyond the tenth century, however, the geographical extent of Verona's political typicality narrows. In the old west Frankish lands, competition among numerous strong territorial lords continued through the eleventh century. At the very earliest, there was a revival of royal power with the reign of Louis IV (1108–1137).[14] Verona's political experience, therefore, was not representative of France's in the eleventh and twelfth centuries. It was, however, fairly typical of a significant swath of Europe stretching from the North Sea to the Adriatic. In the old east Frankish lands, the violent period of political fragmentation had come to an end with the restoration of empire under Otto I. From his conquest of Italy in 961 through Frederick Barbarossa's reassertion of imperial rights in the second half of the twelfth century, Verona shared the political fortunes of the medieval German empire. Like many cities within the empire, it achieved significant latitude in self-government in the wake of the investiture conflict.[15]

The early history of Verona's Church follows a pattern of development common to the sees of continental Europe that received Christianity in the

despots (first Ezzelino da Romano in 1232, then members of the local Della Scala family in 1259). At the beginning of the fifteenth century, Verona was incorporated into the Venetian territorial state.

13. These particular "pagani" were Magyars. Verona's distress occurred during the later part of this age of invasions. As early as the late eighth century, northern Europe had begun to experience Viking raids, which then reached their peak in the mid-ninth century. Muslim raids into southern France and northwestern Italy follow a similar chronology. The Magyars entered northeastern Italy in 899, and annals record at least thirty-three raids from 899 to 955. They burned and pillaged the suburbs of Verona as late as 951. See Georges Duby, *The Early Growth of the European Economy*, trans. Howard B. Clarke (London, 1974), pp. 112–13, and Andrea Castagnetti, *Il veneto nell'alto medioevo* (Verona, 1990), pp. 72–74.

14. Jean Dunbabin, *France in the Making, 843–1180* (Oxford, 1985), pp. 132–40, 256–68.

15. Alfred Haverkamp, *Medieval Germany 1056–1273*, trans. Helga Braun and Richard Mortimer (Oxford, 1988), pp. 162–69.

centuries of Rome's imperial twilight. During the third and fourth centuries, churches emerged outside the city on ground sanctified by martyrs' blood. During the centuries of dominance by Germanic chieftains, the bishop and his community struggled to convert their rulers. By the eighth century, their efforts had met with success. When incorporated into the Carolingian empire, the Veronese Church participated in the educational reforms and liturgical vibrancy emanating from the imperial court in the ninth century. Monasticism flourished under imperial patronage, and the city's bishops participated in the renovatio imperii by acting as their sovereign's local representatives. When Carolingian rule crumbled, the Church suffered as well. Lay lords seized ecclesiastical lands, and religious life was disrupted by warfare and invasions.

The reform movement that developed in the eleventh century as Europe recovered from invasions and civil strife, and in particular the conflict over lay investiture which was the movement's most forceful expression, affected all of western Europe. Clearly, the effect of these developments varied with local conditions and political alliances. The story of their influence, however, is usually constructed from the experience of those sees allied with the papacy (most frequently, Milan).[16] Verona's experience was different; it remained allied with the emperors. This does not, however, make Verona grossly atypical. Three-quarters of the sees within the empire remained loyal to their Salian lords.[17] My choice of Verona was

16. General accounts usually focus on events in Rome and briefly mention the strong popular outcry for reform in Milan. Uta-Renate Blumenthal, The Investiture Controversy: Church and Monarchy from the Ninth to the Twelfth Century (Philadelphia, 1988), pp. 65–98, with mention of Milan on pp. 95–96. Friedrich Kempf's narrative of the reform in The Handbook of Church History similarly highlights events in Rome, but attempts to ascertain the progress of the movement throughout Europe by looking at relations between European rulers and the papacy and the occurrence of reform synods. The only more detailed discussion of reform on a local level is a description of events in Milan, and mention of married and concubinary priests being driven out of Cremona and of the deposition of Piacenza's simoniacal bishop. Jedin, Handbook 4: 351–66, 374–75 (pp. 364–66 for Milan, Cremona, Piacenza).

17. Herbert Zielinski, Der Reichsepiskopat in spätottonischer und salischer Zeit: Teil I (Stuttgart, 1984), p. 183; see also maps 12–15 on pp. 296–99, which give a good visual overview of disputed and undisputed sees.

The number of Italian sees remaining in the imperial camp has also been underestimated, since work on the conflict in Italy has focused on the regions controlled by Canossa. After a number of bishops gathered at the Council of Worms in January 1076 withdrew their obedience from Gregory VII, northern Italian bishops met at Piacenza and declared their support for the council's actions. The bishops gathered at Piacenza also withdrew their obedience from the pontiff. No list of these bishops survives, but when the pope called upon the Roman synod

motivated at least in part by the desire to illuminate this other side of the spectrum: Verona represents the experience of reform and the investiture conflict from the vantage point of an imperial see. The experience of most dioceses in western Europe probably lies somewhere between these extremes of strong papal or imperial allegiance. Veronese evidence suggests, in fact, that political alliances are poor indicators of reform.

The development of the Veronese Church after the twelfth century was also not unusual. Like other communities throughout Christendom in the late twelfth and thirteenth centuries, the Church in Verona was concerned about heresy at home and supportive of efforts against unbelievers abroad. Both mendicant orders flourished in the city. Saint Francis passed through in 1220; two centuries later Saint Bernardino of Siena preached to wildly enthusiastic crowds. One of Verona's native sons became an exemplary Dominican, so much so that he was martyred outside Milan in 1252 (and thus came to be called Saint Peter the Martyr). In the later Middle Ages confraternities of all sorts multiplied and flourished in the city.

Verona and its Church were touched by most of the major developments, both secular and religious, of the European Middle Ages. There are, of course, some limitations to its invocation as a model of ecclesiastical development. Its political experience within and allegiance to the empire in the eleventh and early twelfth centuries makes it most directly comparable to other imperial sees. Its social and economic profile, however, suggests the possibility that many aspects of Verona's ecclesiastical development may be more widely shared. Future studies will clarify how representative the development of Verona's Church may be. In the meantime, I have attempted to keep that development at the forefront of the narrative that follows and have thus usually incorporated comparative material on various questions into the notes.

My focus on the years 950–1150 emerged from a computer-assisted study of the development of all ecclesiastical institutions in the diocese of

of 1076 to excommunicate them, they were too numerous to name individually: the decree excommunicates "the bishops of Lombardy who with scorn for canonical and apostolic authority conspired against the office of blessed Peter prince of the apostles" ("Episcopos Longobardiae, qui spreta canonica & apostolica auctoritate contra beatum Petrum apostolarum principem sacramentum conspiraverunt . . ."). Ten Italian sees were also represented at the Council of Brixen, which declared Gregory deposed. Blumenthal, *Investiture Controversy*, p. 121; Mansi 20: 468; Michael Stoller, "Eight Anti-Gregorian Councils," *Annuarium historiae conciliorum* 17 (1985): 270–71.

Verona across the entire Middle Ages.[18] This study revealed several surprising patterns. Most important, the pattern produced throughout the medieval period by the foundation of these institutions bore no resemblance to standard chronologies of Church history. The most rapid and varied development came not in the thirteenth century—the period widely considered the heyday of the medieval Church—but from the late tenth to the mid-twelfth century. This disjuncture calls attention to the principles underpinning the usual chronology of Church history. The standard chronology evaluates and organizes ecclesiastical development according to the institutional power wielded by the Church and the quality of its spirituality: both are deemed to have peaked in the thirteenth century and then to have deteriorated precipitously in the fourteenth and fifteenth centuries. This "rise and fall" pattern has, understandably, captivated scholars; it often results in wonderful narrative history. It also, however, values certain kinds of spirituality over others and seems to assume that institutional power coincides with religious virtue. Celestine V thought otherwise.

The pattern revealed by a systematic study suggests a different chronology. This chronology is determined by the quantity and novelty of institutional development, therefore giving prominence to periods of rapid change. Instead of "rise and fall," it results in alternating periods of intense change and relative quiescence or the continuation of previously established patterns. The period 950–1150, this book will suggest, was a period of rapid and profound change in the Church, whereas the centuries following it, notably the thirteenth, elaborated and continued the trends established earlier.

Changes in various aspects of ecclesiastical life occurred not at one moment, but across the entire two-hundred-year arc our period encompasses. Church building quickened from the late tenth century and peaked in the mid-twelfth. The secular clergy formed new institutions beginning in the mid-tenth century, a development that continued across the following century and seemed to culminate in changes in mentality and ideals in the late eleventh and early twelfth centuries. New types of religious institutions appeared in the first decades of the twelfth century. Changes in patterns of lay support for ecclesiastical institutions began in the eleventh century and were well established by the mid-twelfth. The transformation

---

18. For a description of this database, see Appendix B.

of the diocese's organization followed a similar chronology, with rapid change in the episcopate in the 1130s and 1140s. Most of the changes the Veronese Church experienced occurred gradually, some beginning as early as the mid-tenth century, all prominent by the mid-twelfth. It is the confluence of change in all areas of ecclesiastical life that defines 950–1150 as a significant period.

The historiography for these two centuries reveals the same dichotomy of styles and concerns evident in the general study of medieval Christianity. These two centuries roughly coincide with the era traditional Church history calls the Age of Gregorian Reform.[19] As the use of Pope Gregory VII's name suggests, this periodization emphasizes the role of the papacy and its supporters and characterizes the reform of the Church in the eleventh century as a movement that succeeded only as a result of their efforts. Despite attempts by American, French, and Italian scholars, this characterization has been remarkably impervious to revision during the twentieth century.[20] Several studies have connected the religious discon-

19. Augustin Fliche began his classic account in the tenth century, but in contrast to the chronology put forward here, he included the struggles among lay lords to revive Carolingian patterns of governance (thus "usurping" ecclesiastical rights) in the early part of the century and emphasized them in his interpretation. Other scholars, like Blumenthal, begin their discussions of the Gregorian Reform in the late ninth century, giving prominence as well as causal weight to the role of monastic reforms at Cluny and Gorze. Still others, like Tellenbach, define the era more narrowly as beginning in the mid-eleventh century and concluding with the Concordat of Worms in 1122. This chronology obviously emphasizes the role of the papacy and its circle in Rome. Fliche, La réform 1: 5–23; Blumenthal, Investiture Controversy, pp. 1–22; Gerd Tellenbach, Church, State, and Christian Society at the Time of the Investiture Contest, trans. R. F. Bennett (Oxford, 1940; rpt. Atlantic Highlands, N.J., 1979) and Karl F. Morrison, "The Gregorian Reform," in Christian Spirituality: Origins to the Twelfth Century, ed. Bernard McGinn and John Meyendorff with Jean Leclercq (London, 1986), p. 177.

The best general study is Blumenthal's Investiture Controversy; it is not only a concise and judicious overview of the entire period but also a good account of and guide to its historiography over the last several decades. I. S. Robinson's "Pope Gregory VII (1073–1085)," Journal of Ecclesiastical History 36 (1985): 439–83 is a comprehensive bibliographical essay on the complex literature (1947–1984) devoted to this pontiff and the reform movement that bears his name.

20. The best critique of the traditional conceptualization is Ovidio Capitani, "Esiste un'«età gregoriana»?," Rivista di storia e letteratura religiosa 1 (1965): 454–81; another is John Gilchrist, "Was There a Gregorian Reform Movement in the Eleventh Century?" Canadian Catholic Historical Association; Study Sessions 37 (1970): 1–10. The criticisms of both, however, have gone unheeded. The most recent issue of Studi gregoriani, the proceedings of a conference on the Gregorian Reform and Europe, is more than ever tightly focused on the person of Gregory VII. Nearly all the articles rely largely on Gregory's letters. Antonio García y García evaluates the success of the reform movement in Spain using as indicators papal correspondence, the acceptance of papal

tent and renewal of the eleventh century to broad social and economic changes and have highlighted the roles of local communities in effecting reform.[21] Particularly significant in Italian scholarship has been the work of Cinzio Violante (on Lombardy and Tuscany) and Paolo Sambin (on the Veneto). Both, with the aid of their students, have concentrated on mapping out the basic structures (dioceses, parishes, collegiate chapters, monasteries) of ecclesiastical life, giving due weight to social, economic, and

---

legates and other emissaries, the adoption of canonical collections associated with Gregory's supporters, and the actions of local councils. Jean Gaudemet's contribution on France uses only Gregory's registers, and Giuseppe Fornasari's article on the "Regnum Italiae" relies heavily on the same source. Gregory's letters are also the mainstay of H. E. J. Cowdrey's contribution on Scandinavia and the Anglo-Norman lands, but Cowdrey at least tempers his assessment of reform in England with some local sources. Antonio García y García, "Reforma gregoriana e idea de la 'Militia sancti Petri' en los reinos ibéricos," Studi Gregoriani 13 (1989): 242; Jean Gaudemet, "Grégoire VII et la France," ibid., p. 213; Giuseppe Fornasari, "La riforma gregoriana nel «Regnum Italiae»," ibid., pp. 299–301, 312–14; H. E. J. Cowdrey, "The Gregorian Reform in the Anglo-Norman Lands and in Scandinavia," ibid., pp. 323, 341, 343–44. The volume culminates (pp. 399–416) in a report on a recent exhumation and reexamination of Pope Gregory's relics. See also Giorgio Picasso, "«Studi gregoriani» e storiografia gregoriana," Benedictina 33 (1986): 51–60. Giuseppe Fornasari and Jean Leclercq have lately called for a "new direction" in studies on Gregory VII, but what they desire is a renewed emphasis on his spirituality. Giuseppe Fornasari, "Coscienza ecclesiale e storia della spiritualità: Per una redefinizione della riforma di Gregorio VII," Benedictina 33 (1986): 25–50; Jean Leclercq, "Gregorio VII nel nostro secolo," ibid., pp. 122–23.

21. The work of Cinzio Violante has placed reform and religious renewal in a broad social, economic, and political context. See especially "I movimenti patarini e la riforma ecclesiastica," Annuario dell'Università Cattolica del Sacro Cuore (1955–56, 1956–57): 209–23. R. I. Moore's article "Family, Community and Cult on the Eve of the Gregorian Reform," Transactions of the Royal Historical Society, ser. 5, 30 (1980): 49–69, insightfully connects important social changes (expansion of settlement, division of families and communities) and religious discontent. The role of the nobility is highlighted in John Howe's article "The Nobility's Reform of the Medieval Church," American Historical Review 93 (1988): 317–39.

French scholarship has focused on local studies of reform: G. Devailly, "Une enquête en course: L'application de la réforme grégorienne en Bretagne," Annales de Bretagne 75 (1968): 293–316; several articles in Bulletin philologique et historique (jusqu'à 1610) du Comité des travaux historiques et scientifiques 2 (1968), notably J.-M. Bienvenu, "Les caractères originaux de la réforme grégorienne dans le diocèse d'Angers," pp. 545–60; J.-C. Tillier, "Les conciles provinciaux de la province ecclésiastique de Bordeaux au temps de la réforme grégorienne (1073–1100)," pp. 561–82; G. Devailly, "Les restitutions de paroisses au temps de la réforme grégorienne. Bretagne et Berry: Étude comparée," pp. 583–98; Elisabeth Magnou-Nortier, La société laïque et l'Église dans la province ecclésiastique de Narbonne (zone cispyrénéene) de la fin du VIIIe à la fin du XIe siècle (Toulouse, 1974). See also Bruce Lanier Venarde, "La réforme à Apt (Xe–XIIe siècles): Patrimoine, patronage et famille," Provence Historique 152 (1988): 131–47.

political factors.[22] Yet new syntheses continue to follow traditional descriptions and chronologies: Colin Morris's recent survey of the Church from 1050 to 1250 includes chapters on social and economic change and acknowledges the complexity and diversity of eleventh-century reform, but still equates the reformers with the papal party.[23]

In suggesting both a new chronology and a new constellation of causes behind the massive changes of these two centuries, I intend no denigration of those chief reformers who have captivated historians for so long. Gregory VII, Humbert of Silva Candida, Peter Damian, and their colleagues were immensely important. But so too were other individuals, many of whose names have gone unrecorded, as well as impersonal forces, which weighed heavily on those individuals no matter how elusive they may be in our sources. Profound changes occurred over these two centuries, even in rather ordinary places.

One such place, the city of Verona grew in a sharp bend of the Adige River where it begins to meander southward across the plain of the Po toward Venice and the Adriatic. During Roman times it was a prosperous provincial municipium.[24] Then, as during the entire Middle Ages, the river was its main source of wealth. It connected the Germanic lands north of the Alps with the Mediterranean world. The products and people of both frequently passed through Verona on the Adige's current.

The Adige has long been a source of great pleasure to the Veronese. Today it still draws them for quiet passeggiate along its tree-lined banks. In the fourth century, the city's bishop, Zeno, frequently sat fishing on a rock on the river's edge. Here the messengers of a pagan king found him and

22. Much of the work of Violante and his students has been presented and debated at the conferences of the Centro di studi sull'alto medioevo at Spoleto and those of the Centro di studi medioevali at Mendola (see Bibliography for complete references to the proceedings of these conferences). It continues under Violante's lively and congenial direction in the Dipartimento di Medievistica at Pisa. A good guide to the work of Sambin and his students is Robert Brentano, "Italian Ecclesiastical History: The Sambin Revolution," *Medievalia et Humanistica* n.s. 14 (1986): 189–97. Since the publication of Brentano's piece, two collections of excellent studies have appeared—*Pievi, parrocchie, e clero nel Veneto dal X al XV secolo*, ed. P. Sambin (Venice, 1987), and *La chiesa di Venezia nei secoli XI–XIII*, ed. Franco Tonon (Venice, 1988)—and a new book by Sambin's heir apparent, Antonio Rigon, *Clero e città: «Fratalea cappellanorum», parroci, cura d'anime in Padova dal XII al XV secolo* (Padua, 1988).

23. Morris, *Papal Monarchy*, pp. 79–108.

24. The best general history of Verona is *Verona e il suo territorio*, 7 vols. (Verona, 1960–1969), abbreviated throughout as *VerST*. Volume 2 covers our period.

begged him to free the king's daughter of a demon's tortures. The river figures prominently in all of Zeno's miracles. During another quiet afternoon of fishing, the bishop cast a demon out of a runaway ox about to plunge a poor man and his cart into the river. And once when he was preaching in his church, the river's waters rose up over their banks. His words, however, kept them at bay: his flock was amazed to see the water rise up beyond the church's roof but not enter it, as if a wall protected the basilica.[25]

Zeno is credited not only with these wonders, but with the city's conversion to Christianity. For this he was invoked as guardian by the many individuals—peasants, merchants, nobles, clerics, monks, and bishops—who populate this book, and he is still the patron saint of Verona. Two images of Saint Zeno are particularly evocative of his relationship with the city. The first is eminently pastoral: an early medieval statue of the bishop seated on a *cathedra* in his church. His grossly oversized right hand emphasizes the blessing he bestows upon his people, a fish dangles from his crosier, and there is a smile on his face. When the late afternoon sun glances into the side portico where he sits, this smile exudes not just contentment but real joviality. The authority of his enthroned posture is tempered by this happy expression, yielding a reassuring image of fatherly concern.

The second image of Saint Zeno greets every visitor to his church: in the lunette above the basilica's exquisite bronze doors the bishop presides over the union of the people and the nobility in defense of the city's communal government. The saint stands with the infantry on his right and mounted knights on his left, raising his hand in benediction. His looming figure seems the only thing impeding an imminent clash of the two groups of citizens, each lurching forward with weapons raised; only a saint could have united these disparate social elements for military action. An inscription informs us that he "gave the people a standard worthy of defense; Zeno bestows the flag with a serene heart."[26] The bishop, despite his serene heart, is not smiling. The protection of his people and his church is a serious matter.

Both roles—benevolent pastor and forceful protector—had to be taken

25. *Vita sancti Zenonis episcopi Veronensis auctore Coronato notario*, cap. 3–4, 9, *AASS* April 2: 70–71.
26. "+ DAT PRASUL SIGNUM POPULO MUNIME DIGNUM + VEXILLUM ZENO LARGITUR CORDE SERENO +" Luigi Simeoni, *La basilica di S. Zeno di Verona* (Verona, 1909), pp. 51–52.

Figure 1   Statue of S. Zeno (Basilica of S. Zeno, Verona). Photo: Alinari/Art Resource

seriously by Zeno's successors. The latter role, however, is noticeably more prominent in our early medieval sources. The only recorded invocation of God's judgment in an ordeal in medieval Verona, for example, concerned the extent of the bishop's responsibility for repairing the city's walls.[27] A more important defensive role for the bishop was the acquisition of *custodes sanctissimi*, the holy martyrs and saints whose relics truly fortified the city. Bishop Anno's success in arranging the return of the remains of two third-century Veronese martyrs, Firmus and Rusticus, is celebrated in an early ninth-century poem called the "Versus de Verona," or "Ritmo Veronese." Its joyful catalog of Verona's protectors takes us all around the city.[28]

The poem starts where a traveler from the north, having navigated the steep and craggy alpine passes,[29] would first encounter the city. From the road approaching the northwestern gate, one could look across the river to the cathedral, Santa Maria Matricolare, and the several churches and monasteries clustered around it. Guarding the gate and lending its name to it was the church of Santo Stefano. Here the martyr Stephen, the early Veronese bishops Florentius, Vindemalis, Maurus, Andronicus, and Probus, the confessor Mamas, and forty Diocletianic martyrs kept watch. Passing through the gate, one entered the most heavily fortified part of the city: the *castrum*, a steep hill that the Lombards had enclosed in walls. Crowning this fortified embankment was the church of San Pietro in Castello, protected by the apostles Peter, Paul, and James; just beyond the walls was an ancient church dedicated to John the Baptist (San Giovanni in Valle).

Exiting the Porta Organo, the weary traveler might find rest with the monks of Santa Maria in Organo. Its church and one nearby dedicated to Saints Nazarus and Celsus were guarded by a veritable army of holy Mila-

27. Two young clerics stood with their arms outstretched in the form of a cross to determine whether the bishop had to pay for one-third of the refortification costs. Pacificus, the cleric representing the bishop, stood all through the reading of the passion according to Matthew, and those present decided that God clearly thought the bishop should only pay one-quarter of the cost of rebuilding Verona's walls. CDV 1 no. 147.

28. The following description draws upon *Versus de Verona: Versum de Mediolano civitate*, ed. G. B. Pighi (Bologna, 1960), pp. 153–54, lines 58–87 and notes pp. 84–87. The topography of the early medieval city is well described in *VerST* 2: 32–43; for the communal era, see Gian Maria Varanini, "L'espansione urbana di Verona in età comunale: Dati e problemi," in *Spazio, società, potere nell'Italia dei comuni* (Naples, 1986), pp. 1–25.

29. Dante invoked the rugged terrain north of the city along the old Via Claudia Augusta when he described the descent into the seventh circle of hell: *Inferno* xii, 4–6.

# Figure 2   The city of Verona

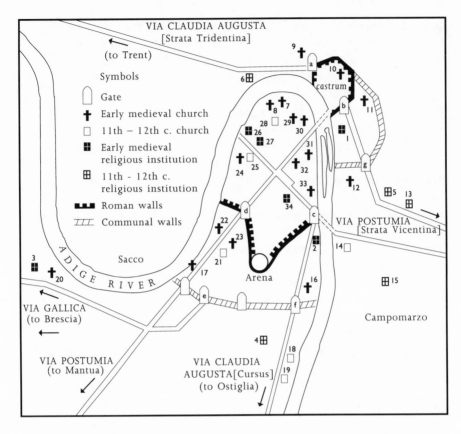

KEY

**Porte [Gates]**
a   Porta Santo Stefano
b   Porta Organo
c   Porta San Fermo
d   Porta San Zeno
e   Porta Orfani
f   Porta Rofioli
g   Porta Campomarzo

**Ecclesiastical Institutions**
1   Santa Maria in Organo
2   Santi Fermo e Rustico
3   San Zeno
4   Santissima Trinità
5   Santi Nazaro e Celso
6   San Giorgio in Braida
7   Santa Maria Matricolare
     (cathedral)

8   San Giorgio (cathedral chapter)
9   Santo Stefano
10   San Pietro in Castello
11   San Giovanni in Valle
12   San Vitale
13   San Sepolcro
14   San Paolo Apostolo
15   Santa Maria delle Virgini
16   San Pietro in Carnario
17   San Martino in Aquario
18   Santa Croce
19   San Jacopo e Lazaro della
     Tomba
20   San Procolo
21   Santa Maria della Fratta
22   San Lorenzo
23   Santi Apostoli
24   San Salvar da Forgnano
     (Vecchio)
25   San Fermo di Cortalta

26   Santa Maria in Solaro
27   San Pietro in Monastero
28   San Giusto
29   Santa Maria Consolatrice
30   Sant' Anastasia
31   Santa Margarita
32   Santa Maria Antica
33   San Salvar Corte Regia
34   San Tommaso Apostolo
     da Foro

*Other churches near cathedral not indi-*
*cated: Santa Felicita, San Jacopo alla*
*Pigna, Santa Maria alla Chiavica,*
*Santa Cecilia. Other churches in castrum*
*not indicated: San Bartolomeo, San*
*Siro, Santi Faustino e Giovita*

nese: Nazarus, Celsus, Victor, Ambrose, Gervase, and Protase. These were joined in the defense of the eastern approaches to the city by the Brescian martyrs Faustinus and Giovita and the saints Euplus and Calocerus, Vitalis and Agricola, in addition to the Blessed Virgin. To the south of these churches stretched one of the city's communal pastures, the Campomarzo. The horses and cows of citizens and religious houses grazed lazily here next to the Adige.

If you crossed the Pons Navium, or Bridge of the Ships, to enter the city, you passed the basilica of the newly returned martyrs Firmus and Rusticus (with their fellow martyrs Primus, Apollinaris, Mark, and Lazarus) and through the gate that also came to share their church's name. You immediately entered the neighborhood of the royal court, Corte Regia. The major road from the south, dotted with royal way stations and leading all the way to Rome, entered the city at the Porta San Fermo, where a royal entourage could be deposited conveniently at its lodgings. This was surely a neighborhood bristling with expectation and self-importance whenever kings or emperors were in the city, as they frequently were throughout the early Middle Ages and into the twelfth century.

Just beyond Corte Regia was the old Roman forum, or Piazza delle Erbe. It remains a market even today, as it was throughout the Middle Ages. As the commercial center of town, it was, not surprisingly, where the free commune that emerged in the twelfth century (1107) built its seat; after all, the earliest evidence of the commune's existence was a trade agreement with Venice. Close at hand too was the commune's early ally, the city's bishop, who controlled the market in the piazza. His cathedral, several clerical residences, and numerous small churches and monasteries were clustered in the northwest quarter of the city just beyond the market. The bells of the cathedral aurally underscored the dominance of the bishop and his clergy here.

The southwestern quarter of the city lodged another eminent personage, the count of Verona. Cortalta was his residence and administrative center in the city, although he, like the bishop, spent considerable time in the countryside surrounding Verona. The road running from Piazza delle Erbe along the edge of this neighborhood led out the Porta Borsari, or Porta San Zeno, to a suburban zone crossed with defensive ditches, or fratte. The churches of San Lorenzo and Santi Apostoli, with their relics of Sixtus, Laurence, Hippolytus, Apollinaris, and the Twelve Apostles, constituted this area's saintly line of defense. Further south and west, where Castelvecchio stands today, was the outpost of "the Great Confessor Martin," San Martino in Aquario. The aquatic reference here is not to the Adige but to a small stream that ran across the southern edge of the city. This "little Adige," or Adigetto, rejoined the river across from the Campomarzo; the new communal walls built in the mid-twelfth century followed its course. The area between the Adigetto and the older walls abutting the Roman arena probably had a distinct odor: the cattle market (Ferraboum) was here, and another communal pasture too.

If you followed along the river, past all of Saint Zeno's favorite fishing spots (and past the little church of San Zeno in Oratorio, which claims to have the rock that Zeno sat on most frequently), you would arrive in the patron's neighborhood. For our entire period, it constituted a separate vicus or villa under the authority of the abbot of the monastery of San Zeno. At its center was the immense basilica of the patron; it is bigger than the cathedral. Its size owes as much to imperial patronage as it does to Saint Zeno's popularity. Charlemagne's son Pippin richly rebuilt and reendowed San Zeno, "which at that time had been burned by faithless men, and nearly deprived of all the possessions which had been contributed to it up to that time."[30] It made sense for the city's Carolingian conquerors to appear as the friends of Saint Zeno, and their Ottonian and Salian successors thought so too. Emperors encamped their armies in the vicus sancti zenonis and tended to issue their diplomas at the basilica. Within the monastery's bell tower there is even a fresco depicting homage to a sovereign: a number of men in varied attire and with awestruck expressions face the king, some raising their clasped hands to offer their submission.[31]

San Zeno's neighborhood was far enough from the city's walls to lessen friction between townspeople and the soldiers often camped there. It is also just far enough removed from the densely settled old quarter to give one a sense of the city's setting. As with most medieval cities, a geographical transition marks its site. Verona rests just at the foot of the mountains and on the edge of the plain, by turns part of each: the plain claims it with its dense winter fogs, but in the clear sunlight it is the mountains that define the city in their foreground. Saint Zeno's successors, when they

---

30. ". . . quod olim ab infidelibus hominibus exustum fuisset et ab omnibus rebus sibi olim collatis pene priuatum." CDV 1 no. 117. Pippin needed to placate Saint Zeno. The unnamed "faithless men" were, in fact, the Frankish forces led by Count Vulvino that finally ended the Lombard domination of the city. VerST 2: 30–31, 69. The saint's church and monastery were, however, richly reendowed: CDV 1 nos. 143, 190, 273.

31. VerST 2: 764.

remembered that smiling pastoral image of their patron, traveled frequently over both mountains and plain. Most of the churches that comprised their diocese lay out there in the countryside surrounding the city,
and that too is where we must begin.

# 1  GROWTH

**T**HE most basic change in the Veronese Church from the millennium to the mid-twelfth century was the remarkable multiplication of churches and religious institutions that constituted its diocese.[1] In 1150 the Veronese Church comprised roughly twice as many ecclesiastical institutions as it had had in the year 1000 (see Table 1 and Figure 3). Not only were there more churches in the diocese, but there were churches in new areas. The Church at the millennium had clung to the shores of Lake Garda, the banks of the Adige River, and the paths of ancient roads. By 1150 it had conquered the plain and the mountains. What explains this prodigious growth and expansion? What forces and circumstances made possible the building of so many new churches in so many new places? Lastly, what does this growth mean?

At the millennium, roughly half of Verona's churches and monasteries were located within the walls of the city or just beyond them. To a tenth-century illuminator depicting the city, these churches were the main structures of note: in a drawing of that date known as the Iconografia Rateriana they filled the city's walls and overflowed out its gates.[2] The other

1. This conclusion derives from the special database I have compiled on Veronese ecclesiastical institutions. For a description of the sources and definitions used in compiling this database, see Appendix B, section II. Figure 3 and Table 1 illustrate the multiplication of ecclesiastical institutions in the diocese over the Middle Ages.

2. This drawing of the medieval city existed in a manuscript of Lobbes attributed to Ratherius, containing some of this bishop's works as well as materials predating him (such as a copy of the *Versus de Verona*). The Lobbes manuscript was destroyed by fire in 1793, but a copy of the Iconografia had been secured by Scipione Maffei following a visit to the library of the monastery in 1739. This copy is now in Cod. CXIV 106 in the Biblioteca Capitulare in Verona. A copy procured in the same period by another Veronese antiquarian, G. B. Biancolini, no longer

Figure 3   Number of ecclesiastical institutions in the
Diocese of Verona, c. 750– c.1500

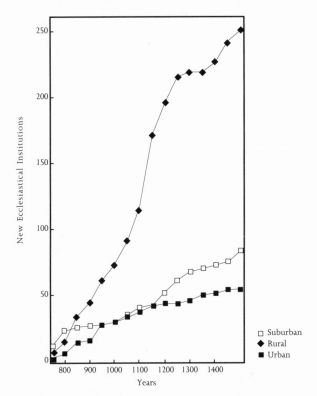

half of the diocese's institutions were in the countryside. It was here that
the most phenomenal growth occurred over the eleventh and twelfth
centuries,[3] and it is here that we shall focus our attention in this chapter.

Only some parts of the countryside surrounding Verona, however, merited the bishop's attention on the visitations of rural churches repeatedly
demanded by early medieval councils. Ecclesiastical institutions were not

exists. For a detailed discussion of the Iconografia and its dating, see C. Cipolla, "L'antichissima
iconografia di Verona secondo una copia inedita," *Memorie della R. Accademia dei Lincei*, ser. 5,
Classe di scienze morali, storiche e filologiche 8 (1900): 49–60.
3. Rural foundations constituted 56.4% of the diocese's institutions at the millennium; they
comprised 67% by 1150.

Table 1  Number of ecclesiastical institutions in the Diocese of Verona, c. 750–c. 1500

| Year | Urban | Suburban | Rural | Total |
|------|-------|----------|-------|-------|
| 750  | 2     | 11       | 5     | 18    |
| 800  | 5     | 22       | 14    | 41    |
| 850  | 14    | 25       | 33    | 72    |
| 900  | 15    | 26       | 43    | 84    |
| 950  | 27    | 27       | 60    | 114   |
| 1000 | 29    | 29       | 72    | 130   |
| 1050 | 33    | 34       | 90    | 157   |
| 1100 | 37    | 40       | 114   | 191   |
| 1150 | 41    | 42       | 171   | 254   |
| 1200 | 43    | 51       | 196   | 290   |
| 1250 | 43    | 61       | 215   | 319   |
| 1300 | 45    | 67       | 218   | 330   |
| 1350 | 49    | 69       | 223   | 341   |
| 1400 | 51    | 72       | 226   | 349   |
| 1450 | 53    | 75       | 242   | 370   |
| 1500 | 54    | 83       | 251   | 388   |

evenly distributed within the diocese. Figure 4 suggests that three factors influenced where churches were built before the millennium: water, land, and roads.

Of these, the Adige River is the most obvious geographical feature. Navigable into the Alps during the Middle Ages, the river linked northern Europe to the lagoons of Venice and to the Mediterranean world beyond.[4] Along the Adige south of the city there were settlements and churches at Zevio, Ronco, Porcile (Belfiore d'Adige), Nono, Tombazosana, Roverchiara, Angiari, and Porto Legnago.[5] North of the city by the year 1000 there were churches on the Adige at Parona, Bussolengo, and Caprino.[6]

4. Giulio Sancassani, "La legislazione fluviale a Verona dal libero Comune all'epoca veneta (secoli XIII–XVIII)" in *Una città e il suo fiume: Verona e l'Adige*, ed. Giorgio Borelli, 2 vols. (Verona, 1977) 1: 402.

5. Zevio, CDV 2 nos. 21, 59; Bionde, ACV, III–5–1v (AC 11 m9 n15); Ronco, CDV 2 no. 205; Porcile, Luigi Simeoni, *Verona: Guida storico-artistica della città e provincia* (Verona, 1953), pp. 276–77; Nono, CDV 1 no. 217 and CDV 2 no. 263; Tombazosana, Ratherius, "Urkunden," p. 28; Roverchiara, ibid.; Angiari, Vincenzo Faccioli, *La chiesa di S. Michele Arcangelo in Angiari* (Verona, 1972), pp. 72–74; Porto Legnago, ACV, III–5–4r (AC 45 m4 n13).

6. Parona (Santa Cristina), CDV 1 no. 159; Bussolengo, CDV 1 no. 203; Caprino, CDV 1 no. 125.

Figure 4  Distribution of rural ecclesiastical institutions in the Diocese of Verona, c. 1000

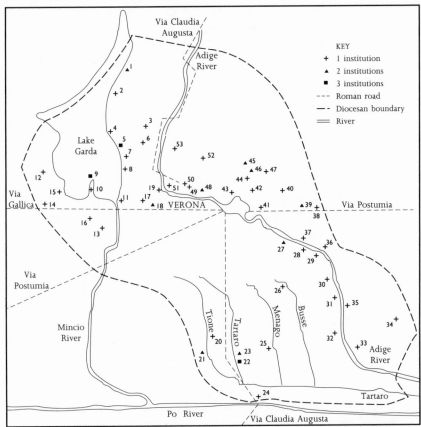

KEY

- + 1 institution
- ▲ 2 institutions
- ■ 3 institutions
- --- Roman road
- -·- Diocesan boundary
- === River

KEY

1 Malcesine (S. Zeno, S. Stefano)
2 Brenzone (SS. Vito e Modesto)
3 Caprino (S. Maria Maggiore)
4 Garda (S. Maria)
5 Bardolino (S. Zeno, S. Columbano, S. Severo)
6 Incaffi (S. Andrea)
7 Cisano (S. Giuliano)
8 Lazise (S. Martino)
9 Sirmione (S. Martino, S. Vito, S. Salvatore)
10 Mavina (S. Pietro in Mavina)
11 Peschiera (S. Martino)
12 Maguzzano (monastery)
13 Casale [Alto] (S. Ambrogio)
14 Lonato (S. Zeno)
15 Desenzano (S. Maria Maddalena)
16 Badia (S. Vigilio)
17 Sandrà (S. Andrea)
18 Palazzolo (plebs, S. Giustina)
19 Bussolengo (S. Maria)
20 Sorgà (S. Maria)
21 Moratica (S. Pietro, SS. Fermo e Rustico)
22 Gazzo (S. Maria, S. Prosdocimo, S. Vito)
23 Nogara (S. Pietro Apostolo, S. Zeno)
24 Ostiglia (S. Lorenzo)
25 Cerea (S. Zeno)
26 Oppeano (S. Giovanni Battista)
27 Zevio (S. Martino, S. Pietro)
28 Nono (S. Fermo)
29 Ronco (S. Maria)
30 Tombazosana (S. Ambrogio)
31 Roverchiara (S. Zeno)
32 Angiari (S. Michele)
33 Porto Legnago (S. Pietro)
34 Tellido (S. Pietro)
35 Bonavigo (S. Martino)
36 Zerpa (S. Salvatore)
37 Porcile (S. Michele)
38 Villanova (S. Pietro)
39 Soave (S. Giorgio, S. Martino)
40 Illasi (S. Giorgio)
41 S. Michele in Campagna (S. Michele in Campagna)
42 Poiano (chapel)
43 Quinzano (S. Giovanni Battista)
44 Marzana (church)
45 Grezzana (S. Martino, S. Maria in Stellis)
46 Sezano (S. Sofla, S. Lorenzo)
47 Maroni (S. Donato)
48 Parona (S. Cristina, SS. Filippo e Jacopo)
49 Castelrotto (S. Maria)
50 Negarine (S. Giusto)
51 Pescantina (church)
52 S. Floriano di Valpolicella (S. Floriano)
53 S. Giorgio di Valpolicella (S. Giorgio)

Ancient churches also ornamented the shores of Lake Garda. Lombard rulers and nobles had founded monasteries and chapels on the peninsula of Sirmione (so beloved of the Roman poet Catullus) and on the northeastern shore of the lake at Malcesine.[7] Carolingian diplomata reveal more churches: a chapel at Bardolino and a church at Desenzano donated to San Zeno, and a *plebs* (baptismal church) at Peschiera, where an abbot solicited a confirmation of his monastery's property.[8] Cisano, Garda, and Brenzone were also the sites of early medieval chapels and *plebes*.[9]

Many churches were located just north of the city in the rolling terrain that is a gentle prelude to the formidable mountains beyond. The very language of Veronese charters captures the area's appeal. For Veronese notaries (and most likely for those whose lands they described) this region was one of valleys. The verdant swath created by the Adige northwest of the city was called the vallis Provinianensis; just to its east lay the vallis Veriacus. By the late twelfth century the ridge separating these two seemed less obtrusive to notaries and landowners, and both valleys came to be called indiscriminately the vallis Pulicella (Valpolicella).[10] Two of the diocese's oldest and most beautiful churches lie here. The elaborately carved stone ciborium of San Giorgio bears an inscription from the reign of King Liutprand (712–744).[11] And it was beside the church of San Floriano that Emperor Berengar rested on his journey south toward the city in 905. In the shade of the ancient church he issued a diploma rewarding a faithful supporter.[12]

The next valley to the east, the vallis Paltenate (Valpantena), extended directly northward from the city. It too was dotted with ancient churches.

7. The monastery of San Salvatore at Sirmione was founded by Queen Ansa, wife of the Lombard king Desiderius (757–774), *CDV* 1 no. 53. By this time there were also three other churches in Sirmione: San Pietro in Mavina, San Martino, and San Vito, *CDV* 1 no. 46. For the *oraculum* of San Zeno in Malcesine, see Biancolini, *Chiese* 2: 473–75.

8. San Zeno in Bardolino donated to the monastery of San Zeno in Verona by Charlemagne, *CDV* 1 no. 84; Santa Maria Maddalena in Desenzano donated to the same monastery by Carloman (son of Louis the German) in 878, *CDV* 1 no. 266; the same king issued a diploma to the Abbot of Nonantola "in Peschiera, in a *plebs* of the Veronese Church" ("ad Piscariam, in plebe ueronensis Ecclesie") (San Martino in Peschiera) in 877, *CDV* 1 no. 262.

9. San Giuliano in Cisano, *CDV* 2 no. 136; Santa Maria in Garda, *CDV* 2 no. 63; San Vito in Brenzone, restored by Archdeacon Pacificus in the late eighth century, according to an epitaph in the cathedral, Pier Paolo Brugnoli, *La cattedrale* (Verona, 1955), p. 66.

10. Andrea Castagnetti, *La Valpolicella dall'alto medioevo all'età comunale* (Verona, 1984), p. 16.

11. Castagnetti, *La Valpolicella*, pp. 57–59.

12. *CDV* 2 no. 67.

Santa Maria in Stellis, the baptismal church of Grezzana, was built on the site of a Roman *nymphaeum*; first documented in 839, this church is thought by some to have existed from the fifth or sixth century.[13] Several early churches in the Valpantena were built and administered by the monks of the suburban monastery of Santa Maria in Organo. Abbot Audibert's (831–845) improvements to the churches of Santa Sofia and San Donato are recorded in cruciform inscriptions.[14] Another of the monastery's dependent churches, San Lorenzo in Sezano, was the site of a sizable community of clerics from at least 855.[15]

Still further to the east were the vallis Pretoriensis, the vallis Fontensis, and the vallis Longazeria. Few churches were found here in the early Middle Ages; we have evidence of only two chapels in Soave and a church in Illasi.[16] All three were in the southernmost part of the vallis Longazeria near the Via Postumia.

Other churches in the diocese arose along the routes of the old Roman roads still traversed by emperors and their armies.[17] To the east of the city along the Via Gallica there were churches at Sandrà, Palazzolo, and Lonato.[18] The monastery of Santa Maria in Gazzo and the churches of Nogara were on the Via Claudia Augusta, and where this important road crossed

13. VerST 2: 55.

14. "Abbot Audibertus built the altar and crypt of Santa Sofia" ("sancte suffie altario et cuba audibertus abbas edificabit"), Castagnetti, *La Valpolicella*, p. 63; Luigi Simeoni, "Iscrizioni medievali di monumenti veronesi," *AMAV* 85 (1908–9): 69–73.

15. CDV 1 nos. 194, 196, 197, 200, 201, 219, 229; CDV 2 nos. 210, 220, 223, 234, 239, 252, 253, 257, 262.

16. The chapels of San Giorgio and San Martino in Soave, VerST 2: 57–58, and the church of San Giorgio in Illasi, CDV 2 no. 163.

17. The Via Claudia Augusta was the north-south axis through the diocese. It crossed the Po at Ostiglia and continued across the plain to Verona, following the Tartaro River for a portion of the way. North of the city it followed the Adige up into the mountain passes that were so important to imperial control. The major east-west axis was, to the east of the city the Via Postumia (which exited the Porta Organo and skirted the foothills to Vicenza) and to the west the Via Gallica (which ran just south of Lake Garda toward Brescia). Egidio Rossini, "Insediamenti, chiese, e monasteri nel territorio di Verona," *Chiese-Ver.*, p. 52; Agostino Zarpellon, *Verona e l'agro veronese in età romana* (Verona, 1954), pp. 90–96. On the development of churches along Roman roads in another region, see Aldo A. Settia, "Strade romane e antiche pievi fra Tanaro e Po," *Bollettino storico-bibliografico subalpino* 68 (1970): 5–108.

18. Sant'Andrea in Sandrà, CDV 1 no. 203; a *plebs* in Palazzola, Simeoni, *Guida*, p. 243; San Zeno e San Giovanni Battista in Lonato, CDV 2 no. 89 and *Storia di Brescia*, ed. Giovanni Treccani degli Alfieri, 5 vols. (Brescia, 1963–64) 1: 504.

the Po there was a church at Ostiglia.[19] Many of the ecclesiastical institutions along these major roads were on the royal manors (*curtes*) that provided for emperors in their constant perambulations of the realm. The chapels of San Zeno and San Pietro at Nogara were on the royal *curtes* called Duos Robores and Roversella, both ceded to Count Anselm of Verona by Emperor Berengar.[20] Santa Maria in Gazzo was founded on lands provided by the Lombard kings Liutprand (712–744) and Hildeprand (735–744).[21] The very name of Palazzolo, derived from *palatium*, suggests an imperial way station on the Via Gallica.

Where were there no churches before the year 1000? Mainly where the land was inhospitable. The northernmost reaches of the diocese, Monte Baldo west of the Adige and the mountainous area called the Lessinia to its east, offered pasture lands but little else. These areas were only sparsely populated throughout the Middle Ages.[22] Immediately to the south and east of the city, on the plain of the Adige, were two expanses of land (the *campanea maior* and *campanea minor*) that were not particularly fertile in the Middle Ages and were unpopulated before the eleventh century. Even in the early twelfth century the hermit Gualfardus was able to escape there and live in undisturbed solitude for twenty years.[23] Part

19. Santa Maria in Gazzo, *CDV* 1 no. 30 and Alessandro Da Lisca, "La chiesa di S. Maria Maggiore al Gazzo Veronese," *AMAV* 119 (1940–41): 144–46; the churches of San Prosdocimo in Pradelle di Gazzo and San Vito were also in this area, *CDV* 1 nos. 217, 227. At Nogara before the millennium there were two chapels, San Pietro and San Zeno, *CDV* 2 nos. 66, 94, 95, 98, 154. On Nogara and its churches, see also Gabriella Rossetti, "Formazione e carattere delle signorie di castello e dei poteri territoriali dei vescovi sulle città nella langobardia del secolo X," *Aevum* 49 (1975): 272–74. San Lorenzo in Ostiglia, *CDV* 1 no. 75.

20. *CDV* 2 nos. 66, 98. San Lorenzo in Ostiglia was also on lands Count Anselm donated to the monastery of San Zeno, *CDV* 1 nos. 75, 117.

21. *CDV* 1 no. 30.

22. Rossini, "Insediamenti," pp. 46–48.

23. "His soul filled with longing, he went without anyone's knowledge into the forest called Saltuccius to live there. The forest was not far from the city of Verona, along the Adige. How strict, good, and holy a life he had led in that same forest for nearly twenty years nobody was able to know" (". . . nemus quod appellatur Saltuccius, inhabitandi causa, desideranti animo, nullo sciente, introivit: quod nemus non longe a civitate Veronae juxta Athesim fluvium distabat. In eodem vero nemore beatissimus vir Dei Gualfardus per viginti fere annos [quam] strictissimam, & quam bonam vitam & quam perutilem ibi duxisset, nullus hominum scire valebat"). When God sent some sailors to bring the holy man to the city, seeing him on the

forest, part pasture, and part swamp, these lands became property of the commune, and in 1178 their bounds were formally established. The *campanea* was slowly brought under cultivation from the twelfth century on. In 1185 the commune sponsored the foundation of a new settlement there called Villafranca, offering tax concessions and attractive leases to encourage its development.[24]

Another sparsely populated area with few churches before the millennium stretched further south and southeast of the *campanea* from the Mincio to the southeastern border of the diocese. In the Roman era, this plain had been well settled.[25] Even the smallest *paesi* here have an inscription or pieces of some Roman villa that reassure the present inhabitants of the long and fruitful cultivation of their soil.[26] Local beliefs aside, this tradition of settlement was in fact significantly disrupted in the early Middle Ages. Probably already depopulated by the rhythm of war and invasion that rocked northern Italy after the demise of Emperor Theodosius (395), the land here changed character dramatically when the course of the Adige shifted in the late sixth century (Figure 5). The great flood of 589 described by Paul the Deacon may have been what moved the course of the river westward; rather than continuing about ten kilometers further southeast to Cologna Veneta, the Adige turned south at Ronco (assuming its present course).[27] The result is indicated clearly by the place names that appear on

banks of the river, they thought him a "wild or forest man" ("qui ferum aut silvestrem hominem illum fore cogitantes"). *AASS* April 3: 828.

24. The *campanea maior*, the expanse south and west of the Adige, extended all the way to the Mincio, and the *campanea minor* included a smaller amount of land on the other side of the Adige, from the suburbs of the city to San Martino Buonalbergo. The bounds of the *campanea maior* were set on 13 and 14 July and 10 September 1178 and those of the *campanea minor* on 10 December 1178 by men from the area, under oath, in the presence of the podestà of the commune and many witnesses. Gianino Ferrari, "La campagna di Verona dal sec. XII alla venuta dei Veneziani (1405)," *Atti del Reale istituto veneto di scienze, lettere, ed arti* 74 (1914–15): 41–103; Andrea Castagnetti, "Primi aspetti di politica annonaria nell'Italia comunale: La bonifica della «palus comunis Verone» (1194–1199)," *Studi Medievali*, ser. 3, 15/1 (1974): 365–66.

25. Rossini, "Insediamenti," pp. 50–53.

26. This evidence has also been used by scholars to argue that there was great continuity between Roman and early medieval population centers. See Settia's notes on this literature in "Strade romane," pp. 14–15.

27. Andrea Castagnetti, *La pieve rurale nell'Italia padana* (Rome, 1976), pp. 34–36; Andrea Castagnetti, "La pianura veronese nel medioevo: La conquista del suolo e la regolamentazione delle acque," in *Una città*, 1: 38, 44–50.

Figure 5    The shift in the course of the Adige River

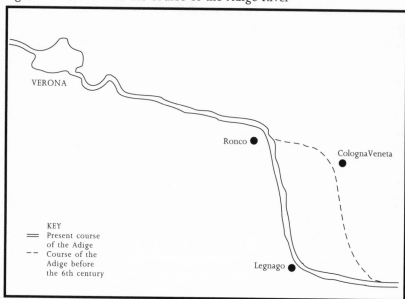

VERONA

Ronco ●

ColognaVeneta ●

KEY
═ Present course
    of the Adige
-- Course of the
    Adige before
    the 6th century

Legnago ●

the plain: they recall not long-cultivated fields, but swamps. Charters mention the "Palus Mala," "Palus Zevedana," and several nondescript boggy places called simply *palus* (swamp).[28] More numerous are place names revealing the limited high and dry lands on the plain and the arduous labor necessary to keep them habitable. Many locations are called "islands": "Insula Pagana," "Insula Porcharitia," "Insula Cenensis," "Insula Carpi."[29] Even more derive from *fossa* and *rupta* (drainage canals), often recalling their builders: "Rupta Adelmi," "Fossa Iohannis presbyteri," "Fossa Victoris."[30] Other place names conjure up the sandy remains of scoured land ("Sabbion," "Sablone," from *sabulo*, sand or gravel)[31] and the thickets of

28. *CDV* 1 no. 181; *CDV* 2 no. 169; *ASV*, Fondo Veneto, nos. 6755, 6767.

29. *CDV* 2 no. 263; Pighi, "Cenni," p. 154; *ASVR*, Ospitale Civico, no. 23; *CDV* 2 no. 266. Also "Insula Levanensis," *CDV* 1 no. 181; "Insula Nonensis," *CDV* 2 no. 263; "Insula Brexiana," *ACV*, III–5–2r (AC 48 m4 n13); "Insula Markaria," *ASV*, Fondo Veneto, no. 6755; and an "Insula" near Vigasio, *ASVR*, Ospitale Civico, no. 31.

30. *CDV* 1 no. 71; *ASVR*, SS. Nazaro e Celso, no. 439; *ACV*, I–5–2r (BC 39 m3 n3). There are also several places called "Fossa Alta": *MGH DD* 4: 135 (no. 96); *ASV*, Fondo Veneto, no. 6947; *ASVR*, Ospitale Civico, no. 78.

31. *Inventari altomedievali di terre, coloni, e redditi*, ed. Andrea Castagnetti et al. (Rome, 1979), p. 108; *ASV*, Fondo Veneto, no. 6947; *ASVR*, Scalzi, no. 2.

willow that thrived on the numerous streams and rivers marbling the plain ("Salecto," "Saleto," "Salesis de Peza Mala," from *salictum*, willow).[32]

As tenth- and eleventh-century documents map this broad expanse, however, they reveal renewed efforts to cultivate the plain. More than a dozen place names here derive from *roncare*, to clear land, and *bonificare*, to reclaim land by drainage: "Bonificus Anculfi," "Bonefisio," "Ronco," "Runkelolo," "Roncalia," "Runco Iohannis Cauci [Caeci?]."[33] Settlements tended to reappear first along rivers; from there the forests and marshes were pushed back.

This expansion of settlement was most impressive on the plain, but also affected other parts of the diocese. Settlements appear in the valleys east of the city: the vallis Pretoriensis, the vallis Fontensis, and the vallis Longazeria.[34] Even in long-settled areas like the Gardesana and the Valpantena, the appearance of new communities intensified. The designations used by notaries to locate a piece of land became more precise. In the tenth century it was often enough simply to give the place name, the *locus ubi dicitur*; in the twelfth century, notaries routinely used three or more elements to locate a piece of land. A vineyard was "in the Valpantena, in the place called Novalia, near the place called Carpenedo, where it is called Lavello Rubto"; another was "in the vallis Veriacus, in the village of San Vito, [at the place] called the field of Saint Paul."[35] More scribal effort was required to distinguish a field from a neighbor's. This increase in the prose of location suggests a terrain far more cluttered with human claims, more crowded with cultivators.

A crowded and more settled appearance suggests in turn a real demographic expansion. Indeed, throughout western Europe population was growing from the tenth century, and Verona seems no exception to the general trend.[36] This demographic increase and expansion of settlement

32. CDV 2 no. 263; ASV, Fondo Veneto, nos. 6783, 6946.

33. ASVR, Ospitale Civico, no. 78; ASVR, S. Maria in Organo, no. 46; CDV 1 no. 117; ACV, I–8–6v ("meta sec. XII"); ASV, Fondo Veneto, no. 6763; ASVR, Ospitale Civico, no. 23; also, "Ronco Pruvedru" CDV 2 no. 263; "Runco Boniacum" CDV 2 no. 65; "Ronco Saurello" and another "Ronco" near Moratica, MGH DD 5: 486 (no. 357); and "Runki" in Bionde ACV, III–7–7v (AC 70 m4 n12).

34. These observations are derived from a database of place names appearing in Veronese documents. See Appendix B, section III for a description of this database.

35. ASV, Fondo Veneto, no. 6539 [5 July 1051]: ". . . in valle paltenate in loco qui vocatur novalia prope loco qui dicitur carpenedo ubi dicitur lavello rubto"; ASVR, Ospitale Civico, no. 54 [19 January 1072]: ". . . in valle veriacus in vico sancti viti ubi dicitur campo sancti pauli."

36. David Herlihy, "The Agrarian Revolution in Southern France and Italy, 801–1150," *Speculum*

are key factors explaining the tremendous multiplication of ecclesiastical institutions in the Veronese diocese.

Scholars have long studied the relationship between settlement patterns and the development of ecclesiastical institutions.[37] From the late nineteenth century, they were most interested in the passage from the late Roman world to that of the early Middle Ages, and they stressed continuity (in particular, between the Roman *pagus* and the early medieval *plebs*).[38] Since the late 1950s, the focus of inquiry has shifted to the tenth and eleventh centuries (the late Carolingian and precommunal periods).[39] Change, rather than continuity, has dominated discussion. The disappearance of old villages,[40] the foundation of new communities,[41] and the building of fortifications[42] have come to be seen as important influences on the development of ecclesiastical institutions.

The impact of these changes, however, has been perceived mainly as influencing the location and status of churches. Encastlement, for example, sometimes changed the location of a community's church. This occurred at Malcesine, where an ancient church was simply abandoned and

33 (1958): 30; David Herlihy, "Demography," in *Dictionary of the Middle Ages*, ed. Joseph R. Strayer, 12 vols. (New York, 1982–89) 4: 139–40.

37. See the still-fundamental work of Pierre Imbart de la Tour, *Les origines religieuses de la France: Les paroisses rurales du 4e au 11e siècle* (Paris, 1900; rpt. Paris, 1979), pp. 7–58; and, more recently, Jean Gaudemet, "La paroisse au moyen âge: État des questions," *Revue d'histoire de l'Église de France* 59 (1973): 5–21. Catherine E. Boyd's *Tithes and Parishes in Medieval Italy* (Ithaca, N.Y., 1952), pp. 47–74, provides a good overview of ecclesiastical development in early medieval Italy.

38. Discussions of this literature and references may be found in Castagnetti, *La pieve*, pp. 4–8; Settia, "Strade romane," pp. 14–15; and Giuseppe Forchielli, *La pieve rurale* (Bologna, 1938), pp. 38–42; Andrea Castagnetti, *L'organizzazione del territorio rurale nel medioevo* (Turin, 1979), pp. 7–9 [2d ed., Bologna, 1982, pp. 21–26].

39. Cinzio Violante, "Il monachesimo cluniacense di fronte al mondo politico ed ecclesiastico (secoli X e XI)," in *Spiritualità cluniacense* (Todi, 1960), pp. 153–242; rpt. in Cinzio Violante, *Studi sulla cristianità medievale* (Milan, 1972), pp. 3–67. See also Castagnetti, *L'organizzazione*, pp. 1–3, 255–61 [2d ed., pp. 15–18, 337–46].

40. Castagnetti, *La pieve*, pp. 18–50, especially pp. 37–39; Aldo Settia, *Castelli e villaggi nell'Italia padana* (Naples, 1984), pp. 132–35, 263–66.

41. Colin Morris, *The Papal Monarchy* (Oxford, 1989), pp. 34–39; Georges Duby, *The Early Growth of the European Economy*, trans. Howard B. Clarke (London, 1974), pp. 158–61, pp. 181–210; R. W. Southern, *Western Society and the Church in the Middle Ages* (Harmondsworth, 1970), pp. 34–36.

42. Pierre Toubert, *Les structures du Latium médiéval*, 2 vols. (Rome, 1973) 1: 303–368; 2: 789–933; Rossetti, "Formazione e carattere," pp. 241–308, especially pp. 282–83.

its title transferred to a new church built within the castle.[43] In other cases, although older churches remained in use, a new church built within the castle came to exercise jurisdiction over them. At Soave, for example, there were two Lombard-era churches, and yet another church, San Lorenzo, was built within the castle. By 1145 this new church had become the *plebs*.[44]

Such modifications of location and status, however, seem minor when compared with the overall increase in the number of churches. This increase seems to me the most significant result of changes in settlement. Let us return briefly to the example of encastlement. In addition to causing changes in the location and status of churches, encastlement often led to the construction of a church where one had not previously existed. The place name Arbizzano, for example, first appears in 844. By 947 the settlement had a castle, and in 1056 there was a church within the fortress.[45] The building of a castle often led to increased settlement around it that subsequently gave rise to a church.[46]

Most of the new churches which appear after the millennium, in fact,

43. Rossini, "Insediamenti," p. 86.

44. The castle at Soave is first documented in 1001 when "William, an inhabitant of the high castle at Soave" ("Wilielmo abitator in castro alto soave") and his wife, Emeltruda, sold a piece of land to Vivaro "of the castle Bionde" ("de castro biunde"), *ACV*, II–5–1r (AC 53 m3 n5). San Lorenzo appears in 1142 and is identified as the *plebs* in Pope Eugene III's bull to Bishop Tebaldus, *ASVR*, SS. Nazaro e Celso, no. 1213b; Pighi, "Cenni," p. 154; see also *VerST* 2: 57–58.

These effects of encastlement, however, should not be overestimated. In the Veronese diocese, the number of instances where castle building did not affect location and status equals those in which it did. In Grezzana and Cerea, for example, the churches that were later identified as the *plebes* were in existence before the castle, and the building of a fortification did not lead to the construction of another church. Neither the church predating the castle of Illasi nor one built later was located in the fortress. For Grezzana see *CDV* 1 no. 153; G. G. Dionisi, *De duobus episcopis Aldone et Notingo* (Verona, 1758), pp. 179–81; and *ASVR*, S. Maria in Organo, no. 44 app*. On Cerea, *CDV* 2 no. 187; Ratherius, "Urkunden," p. 28; and Bruno Bresciani, *Castelli veronesi* (Verona, 1962), pp. 47–50. The castle of Illasi appears first in *ASV*, Fondo Veneto, no. 6748; the later church of Santa Giustina appears in a document now preserved only in an eighteenth-century copy, *BC*, Mss. Lodovico Perini, busta 22, "Padri Dominicani."

Generally, the uniform development suggested by Pierre Toubert's study of Lazio is not to be found in the Veneto. Aldo Settia's incisive reevaluation of encastlement in *Castelli e villaggi* captures the variety of developments and effects evident in Veronese documentation. For Verona specifically see Castagnetti, *La Valpolicella*, pp. 32–42; "La pianura," pp. 50–54; and *«Ut nullus incipiat hedificare forticiam»: Comune veronese e signorie rurali nell'età di Federico I* (Verona, 1984).

45. "Albutiano," *CDV* 1 no. 176; *castrum*, *CDV* 2 no. 236; "Silvester, priest of the baptismal church of Saint Peter within the castle of Arbizzano" ("Silvester presbyter de plebe sancti Petri sita infra castro Albuciano"), G. G. Dionisi, *Dell'origine e dei progressi della zecca di Verona* (Verona, 1776), p. 70.

46. Settia, *Castelli e villaggi*, pp. 247–86.

were located in new areas of settlement. Vigasio, located south of Verona on the upper reaches of the Tartaro River, first appears in a document of 926.[47] A church, San Zeno, was built here by 1004, and by the next century this *plebs* had two dependent chapels (San Michele and San Martino).[48] Another settlement on the plain, Pontepossero, is first documented in 981 and has a church by 1036.[49] Montorio appears in the vallis Fontensis in 922; by 1060 we know of a baptismal church (Santa Maria) there as well as a chapel.[50]

The sum effect of demographic expansion and the growth of new settlements on the development of new ecclesiastical institutions is evident in Figure 6. In 1150 there were churches where before the millennium there were none. By the mid-twelfth century there were churches throughout the plain and even in the mountainous areas in the north of the diocese. There were also more churches in previously developed areas: along the Adige, on the shores of Garda, and near the Po. By 1150 many rural communities had two churches, some even more. There were three churches at Lavagno, and four at Colognola, Soave, and Bardolino.

The kinds of ecclesiastical institutions being founded also indicate that it was the religious needs of an expanding flock that fueled this growth. Of the rural churches founded from 1000 to 1150, 38 percent were *plebes*. Another 27 percent of these new foundations were the only churches in their communities (and, therefore, probably built to provide basic religious services). Among the urban and suburban churches built from 1000 to 1150, more than half were eventually designated as parishes.[51] Several institutions founded in this period also responded to the new social problems of an expanding population. The hospitals of San Sepolcro, San Jacopo e Lazaro della Tomba, and Santa Croce were founded on the outskirts of the city to minister to the growing population of urban poor.[52]

---

47. *CDV* 2 no. 197: "Vico Aderis".

48. *ASV*, Fondo Veneto, nos. 6910, 6905.

49. *ACV*, II–4–6r (BC 45 mp n10) and Dionisi, *De duobus episcopis*, pp. 161–64; *ACV*, I–5–2v (BC 33 m5 n11).

50. *CDV* 2 no. 186; *ASVR*, Ospitale Civico, no. 53; *ASVR*, S. Maria in Organo, no. 22.

51. Of 88 churches (institutions for the religious life here excluded) appearing from 1000 to 1150, 33 were baptismal churches. Twenty-four churches built in this period were the only churches in their communities. Of the 15 new churches in the city and suburbs, 9 became parishes. The emergence of new *plebes* in the diocese of Pistoia also followed the expansion of settlement. See Natale Rauty, *Storia di Pistoia I* (Florence, 1988), pp. 355–59.

52. The number of foundations of this type of institution increased dramatically as emigration

Changes in the structures of churches also give evidence of the need to accommodate more Christians. Older churches were being enlarged and new churches built on a larger scale. In the eleventh century, the nave of San Giorgio in Valpolicella was extended.[53] At Santa Maria in Gazzo a new, larger church was built to accommmodate greater numbers.[54] Beginning in the 1130s, the cathedral church of Santa Maria Matricolare was entirely rebuilt and greatly enlarged. So too were San Zeno and San Lorenzo.[55]

These massive building projects bring to the fore another contributing factor. Although an expanding population created the need for bigger churches, an expanding economy made it possible to meet these needs with magnificent structures. The great boom in church building during the eleventh and twelfth centuries indicates significant resources in materials and both skilled and unskilled labor. Not only were numerous new churches built, but after a severe earthquake in 1117, many older churches were also rebuilt.[56] Often the rebuilding was not only on a larger, but also on a more grandiose and sumptuous scale: the sculpted portals of both the cathedral and San Zeno attest to the rich decorative ornamentation of the Romanesque churches of this period.[57]

Verona was a wealthy city by the twelfth century; trade had made it so. In 1107 a group of forty-two Veronese negotiated a pact with Venice granting Verona's merchants reduced tolls in Venice in return for military aid against their common enemies the Paduans and Trevisans.[58] The charters of the eleventh and twelfth centuries reveal merchants (*negocientes*) and money

---

from the countryside to the city rose in the early thirteenth century. See Giuseppina de Sandre Gasparini, "L'assistenza ai lebbrosi nel movimento religioso dei primi decenni del duocento veronese: Uomini e fatti," in *Viridarium Floridum* (Padua, 1984), pp. 25–59.

53. Castagnetti, *La Valpolicella*, p. 143.

54. Da Lisca, "La Chiesa di Santa Maria," p. 148.

55. Edoardo [Wart] Arslan, *L'architettura romanica veronese* (Verona, 1939), pp. 183–203. Good archaeological data are available for the cathedral and its cloister: Cinzia Fiorio Tedone, "Tombe dipinte altomedievali rinvenute a Verona," *Archeologia veneta* 8 (1985):270–71.

56. "In this year many towers and countless buildings fell down as a result of the earthquake throughout Lombardy and other lands" ("Hoc anno multe turres et innumerabilia edificia propter terre motum per Longobardiam et alia terras corruerunt"). *Annales Sanctae Trinitatis*, MGH SS 19: 2.

57. Edoardo Arslan, *La pittura e la scultura veronese dal secolo VIII al secolo XIII* (Milan, 1943), pp. 86–114.

58. Luigi Simeoni, "Le origini del comune di Verona," *Studi storici veronese* 8–9 (1957–58): 141–42; the text of this important document may be found in Andrea Castagnetti, *La società veronese nel medioevo I: La rappresentanza veronese nel trattato del 1107 con Venezia* (Verona, 1983), pp. 30–37.

Figure 6   Distribution of rural ecclesiastical institutions
in the Diocese of Verona, c. 1150

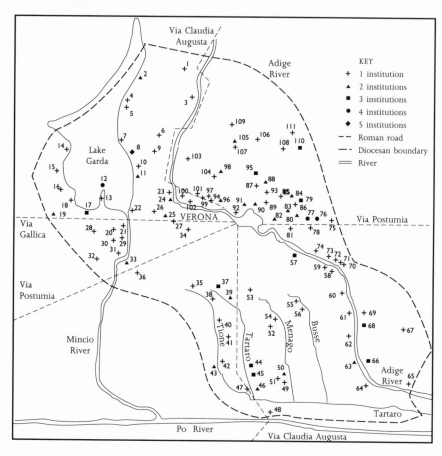

KEY

(The names of churches
founded after 1000 are
italicized.)

1   Brentonico (*plebs*)
2   Malcesine (S. Zeno, S.
    Stefano)
3   Avio (*S. Maria*)
4   Brenzone (SS. Vito e
    Modesto)
5   Castelletto di Brenzone (*S.
    Zeno*)
6   Caprino (S. Maria Maggiore)
7   Garda (S. Maria)
8   Bardolino (S. Severo, S.

    Zeno, S. Columbano, S.
    *Maria Ausiliatrice*, *S. Cristina*)
9   Incaffi (S. Andrea)
10  Cisano (S. Giuliano)
11  Lazise (S. Martino, *S. Cri-
    tina*)
12  Sirmione (S. Salvatore, S.
    Martino, S. Vito, *S. Maria*)
13  Mavina (S. Pietro in
    Mavina)
14  Manerba (*S. Maria*)
15  Padenghe (*S. Maria e S.
    Emilio*)
16  Maguzzano (monastery)
17  Rivoltella (*plebs* + *chapels*)
18  Desenzano (S. Maria)
19  Lonato (S. Zeno, *S. Cipriano*)

20  Pozzolengo (*S. Lorenzo*)
21  Ponti (*S. Antonio*)
22  Peschiera (S. Martino)
23  Pastrengo (*S. Zeno*)
24  Bussolengo (S. Maria, *S.
    Salvatore*)
25  Palazzolo (plebs, *S.
    Giustina*)
26  Sandrà (S. Andrea)
27  Sona (*S. Salvatore*)
28  Badia (S. Vigilio)
29  S. Lazaro (church)
30  Casale [Alta] (S. Ambrogio)
31  Monzambano (*S. Maria*)
32  Castellar Lagusello (*S.
    Nicolò*)
33  Valeggio (*S. Maria, S. Pietro*)

changers (*monetarii*), as well as many artisans.[59] Ecclesiastical institutions shared in the profits of this more active and diverse local economy. The bishop controlled the tolls on all bulky goods disembarked at the Sabbionara, the river wharf just below the cathedral. The city's annual market fairs were held at San Zeno and San Michele in Campagna.[60]

59. A few examples from the eleventh century: *negocientes* ASVR, S. Michele in Campagna, no. 3 (1037); Ospitale Civico, no. 37 (1041); S. Michele in Campagna, no. 11 (1070) and nos. 18–22 (1085–1086), all references to "Mazeli, merchant (*negociens*) of the city of Verona"; S. Anastasia, no. 9 (1095). *Monetarii* are mentioned in ACV, II–5–7r (AC 59 mp n2) (1099) and in ASV, Fondo Veneto, no. 6790 (1045). The neighborhood around Santo Stefano, where the Via Claudia Augusta entered Verona, had many blacksmiths: ASVR, S. Stefano, nos. 8, 11, 14; ACV, S. Stefano cart. 1, iv; III–6–1r (AC 38 m4 n6); III–6–3r (AC 60 m4 n12); ASV, Fondo Veneto, no. 6754 doc. 2.

60. VerST 2: 131, 127–28. On the various tolls controlled by the bishop, the canons, and several other ecclesiastical institutions, see Luigi Simeoni, "Dazii e tolonei medievali di diritto privato a Verona," *Studi storici veronesi* 8–9 (1957–58): 191–248.

| | | | | | |
|---|---|---|---|---|---|
| 34 | Sommacampagna (S. Andrea) | 61 | Roverchiara (S. Zeno) | 86 | Marcelise (S. Maria) |
| 35 | Grezzano (plebs) | 62 | Angiari (S. Michele) | 87 | Marzana (church) |
| 36 | [Bonefisio] (S. Lorenzo) | 63 | Legnago (S. Salvatore, S. Martino) | 88 | Sezano (S. Lorenzo, S. Sofia) |
| 37 | Vigasio (S. Zeno, S. Martino, S. Michele) | 64 | Villa [d'Adige] (church) | 89 | Poiano (chapel) |
| 38 | Trevenzuolo (S. Maria Maddalena) | 65 | Terrazzo (church) | 90 | Avesa (S. Maria, S. Martino) |
| 39 | Isola della Scala (S. Stefano, Bastia) | 66 | Porto Legnago (S. Pietro, S. Maria, S. Vito) | 91 | Quinzano (S. Giovanni Battista, S. Alessandro) |
| 40 | Pontepossero (S. Zeno) | 67 | Minerbe (S. Zeno) | 92 | Monte Donico (S.Leonardo in Monte Donico) |
| 41 | Sorgà (S. Maria) | 68 | Bonavigo (S. Martino, S. Maria, S. Stefano) | 93 | Vendri (S. Zeno) |
| 42 | Bonferraro (church) | 69 | Coriano (S. Tommaso Apostolo) | 94 | Corrubbio (S. Martino) |
| 43 | Moratica (S. Pietro, SS. Fermo e Rustico) | 70 | Albaredo (S. Maria) | 95 | Grezzana (S. Martino, S. Maria in Stellis, S. Cristina) |
| 44 | Nogara (S. Pietro, S. Zeno, S. Silvestro) | 71 | Cavalpone (S. Apollinare) | | |
| 45 | Gazzo (S. Maria, S. Vito, S. Prosdocimo) | 72 | Zerpa (S. Salvatore) | 96 | Parona (S. Cristina, SS. Filippo e Jacopo) |
| | | 73 | Bionde (S. Maria) | 97 | Arbizzano (S. Pietro) |
| 46 | Redondesco (S. Zeno, S. Michele "iuxta Tartaro") | 74 | Porcile (S. Michele) | 98 | Negrar (S. Martino, S. Pietro) |
| | | 75 | Villanova (S. Pietro) | | |
| 47 | S. Pietro in Valle (S. Pietro in Monastero) | 76 | Soave (S. Giorgio, S. Martino, S. Maria, S. Lorenzo) | 99 | Castelrotto (S. Maria) |
| | | | | 100 | Arcè (S. Michele) |
| 48 | Ostiglia (S. Lorenzo) | 77 | Colognola (S. Giustino, S. Vittore, SS. Fermo e Rustico, S. Nicolò) | 101 | Negarine (S. Giusto) |
| 49 | Casaleone (church) | | | 102 | Pescantina (church) |
| 50 | Cerea (S. Zeno, S. Maria) | 78 | Caldiero (S. Pietro) | 103 | S. Giorgio di Valpolicella (S. Giorgio) |
| 51 | Ravagnana (church) | 79 | Illasi (S. Giorgio, S. Giustina, S. Maria in Figarole?) | | |
| 52 | Salizzole (church) | | | 104 | S. Floriano di Valpolicella (S. Floriano) |
| 53 | Mazagata (S. Maria e S. Zeno) | 80 | Lavagno (S. Briccio, S. Martino) | | |
| 54 | Bovolone (S. Fermo) | | | 105 | Prun (S. Martino, S. Paolo) |
| 55 | Oppeano (S. Giovanni) | 81 | S. Martino Buonalbergo (monastery) | 106 | Arzere (S. Felice) |
| 56 | Isola Rizza (plebs) | 82 | S. Michele in Campagna (S. Michele in Campagna, S. Pancrazio) | 107 | [Vallio?] (S. Stefano) |
| 57 | Zevio (S. Pietro, S. Martino, "ecclesia curtis regie?") | | | 108 | Saline (S. Mauro in Saline) |
| | | | | 109 | Mondragone (S. Faustino) |
| 58 | Ronco (S. Maria) | 83 | Montorio (S. Anna, S. Maria) | 110 | Calavena (S. Maria, SS. Pietro e Vito, S. Martino) |
| 59 | Scardevara (church) | 84 | Mezzane (S. Cassiano, S. Maria) | | |
| 60 | Tombazosana (S. Ambrogio) | 85 | Mizzole (S. Michele) | 111 | S. Andrea (S. Andrea) |

While the prosperity of the city in the eleventh and twelfth centuries not surprisingly supported a tremendous amount of church building, the size and beauty of rural churches also attest to significant resources in smaller centers of population. The church of San Floriano in Negrar was rebuilt in the twelfth century with sculpted capitals and arches that rivaled contemporary work in the city. The churches of San Pietro in Caldiero and Santa Maria in Bonavigo were decorated with beautiful frescos in a Byzantine style. Several pieces of sculpture from the school of the master Niccolò survive in even small churches in the *basse*, the lower plain.[61]

This period of rapid expansion of the Church slowed in the late twelfth century. Several factors combined to put the brakes on new foundations. The most important factor was a slowdown in new settlements sufficiently distant from older centers to require new churches. The expanding population of the eleventh and early twelfth centuries had moved into the easily reclaimable lands. Settlements had been established on the "easy" frontiers, and the populations of these centers continued to expand. New settlements were founded in the late twelfth and thirteenth centuries, but they were fewer and usually required communal backing. While the lands reduced to arable just after the millennium were usually regained from the forest or shallow marsh lands, those reclaimed after the mid-twelfth century were regained from swamps and required dike building and drainage, projects requiring greater resources and concerted community effort.[62] The slowed pace of new settlement slowed the demand for new churches.

A restructuring of both civil and ecclesiastical authority also contributed to the decreased rate of new foundations after the mid-twelfth-century peak. A free commune emerged in Verona in 1135. After it established control of the city and had survived its first military challenges in the middle of the century, the new government began bringing the countryside under its authority in the late twelfth century. But the same vacuum of authority and the same "power and imagination"[63] that led to the development of the urban commune had also led to the development of

61. Castagnetti, *La Valpolicella*, pp. 133–37; Arslan, *La pittura*, pp. 122–27, 104–6. The master sculptor Niccolò is credited not only with the sculpted entries of the Veronese cathedral and San Zeno, but also that of the cathedral at Ferrara.

62. The foundation of Villafranca in 1185 and the drainage of Palù are good examples, both illumined by the work of Andrea Castagnetti, "La pianura," pp. 76–82, and "Primi aspetti," pp. 363–413.

63. An apt description of the forces behind the Italian communal movement coined by Lauro Martines, *Power and Imagination* (New York, 1979).

rural communes and rural lordships. In the late twelfth century and the early thirteenth, these groups were slowly coming to terms with the authority of the urban commune.[64]

Parallel and contemporary with the slow establishment of a new civil order was the emergence of a new ecclesiastical order. A particular litigiousness marked relations among ecclesiastical institutions from the mid-twelfth century. The phenomenal growth of the eleventh and early twelfth centuries was put in order during the second half of the twelfth century. Both the bishop and the various religious houses in the city sought to establish or clarify their rights to smaller institutions. All sides sought papal bulls confirming their possessions, and Pope Lucius III's sojourn in Verona from July 1184 until his death in November 1185 seemed largely spent confirming or settling the claims of various ecclesiastical institutions.

This scramble for bulls was a scramble to protect economic resources. Particularly in dispute were tithes, and attempts to protect or gain the control of tithes restricted the foundation of new churches. *Plebes* accustomed to receiving the tithes of an entire jurisdiction were reluctant to allow the emergence of a new church that might take part of their tithe income away. The construction of San Paolo in Campomarzio, for example, led to a long controversy with the older church of San Vitale. Peace was restored only in 1186 when Pope Urban III sent two cardinals to assign parishes to the two churches and to define their boundaries.[65] Pope Lucius III in 1184 had not only taken the *plebs* of San Zeno in Lonato under apostolic protection and confirmed its possessions but also decreed that no one should presume to build a church or oratory "within the territory of a parish" (*in fine parochiae*) without the permission of the apostolic see or the local bishop.[66] Four years later, Pope Clement III granted the bishop of

64. Andrea Castagnetti, *La Marca Veronese-Trevigiana* (Turin, 1986), pp. 66–67, and «Ut nullus».

65. Kehr, IP 7.1: 240–42. For similar cases in Tuscany, see Luigi Nanni, *La parrocchia studiata sui documenti lucchesi dei secoli VIII–XIII* (Rome, 1948), pp. 145–58; Duane J. Osheim, *A Tuscan Monastery and Its Social World* (Rome, 1989), pp. 122–25. Litigation over parochial boundaries follows the same chronology in Venice and in Pisa as well; see Daniela Rando, "Aspetti dell'organizzazione della cura d'anime a Venezia nei secoli XI–XII," *La Chiesa di Venezia nei secoli XI–XII*, ed. Franco Tonon (Venice, 1988), pp. 56–57, 61–62 and Mauro Ronzani, "L'organizzazione della cura d'anime nella città di Pisa (secoli XII–XIII)," *Istituzioni ecclesiastiche della Toscana medioevale* (Galatina, 1980), p. 59.

66. ". . . inhibet, ne ullus in fine parochiae ecclesiam vel oratorium sine assensu eius et dioecesani episcopi aedificare praesumat." Kehr, IP 7.1: 300. Alexander III issued a similar decree (1160–1176) protecting the territory of a church subject to a Pisan monastery: Ronzani, "L'organizzazione," p. 50.

Verona a privilege ceding him control over church building throughout the diocese. The pontiff forbade "anyone to undertake to build a new chapel or oratory in the Veronese diocese without his [the bishop's] approval."[67]

From the late twelfth century, then, greater control was exerted over the increase in the number of new ecclesiastical foundations. The growth of the Veronese Church proceeded at a much more moderate rate over the high and late Middle Ages than it did between 950 and 1150. The phenomenal increase in the number of ecclesiastical institutions in the city and its diocese over the eleventh and early twelfth centuries was truly a singular development, the result of unique circumstances. Rapid population growth and strong economic expansion in a period of political transition and innovation resulted in the astonishing increase in foundations during this period.

That is not to say that religious belief or practice had nothing to do with these foundations. The building of every church and monastery was certainly motivated by faith. But religious belief can be expressed in many ways: in prayer, in almsgiving, in pilgrimage, in feeding the poor, in donations to established institutions. It need not always result in the foundation of a new church. That it often did during the eleventh and early twelfth centuries reflects new needs: the need of newly founded communities for a house of worship, the need of rapidly growing communities to have churches large enough for all to hear the gospel, the need of villages constantly beset by invaders to have a safe place in which to beseech God's mercy. That these new needs were met with the construction of churches, rather than with other solutions, was made possible by certain circumstances: the resources, both human and material, to build and endow new structures; and the latitude or autonomy enjoyed by communities to devote these resources to found institutions. The boom in institutional growth in the Veronese Church certainly indicates great religiosity. But the expression of that faith was shaped by the social, economic, and political conditions of the eleventh and twelfth centuries.

67. "... prohibet, ne aliquis in Veronen'. dioecesi cappellam seu oratorium sine eius assensu de novo aedificare praesumat." Kehr, IP 7.1: 228. A similar prohibition had been issued earlier to Lucca by Pope Calixtus II. Duane J. Osheim, *An Italian Lordship* (Berkeley and Los Angeles, 1977), pp. 21–22.

# 2 THE SECULAR CLERGY

**T**HE rapid growth of the Veronese diocese in the eleventh and early twelfth centuries, as we have seen, reflects in large part an expansion of pastoral care. How did this rapid expansion affect those responsible for the care of souls, the secular clergy? In the early Middle Ages the cathedral chapter was the dominant institution of the secular clergy in the Veronese diocese. Over the eleventh and early twelfth centuries, as the number of churches and clerics multiplied, the cathedral chapter lost its commanding preeminence, as new institutions for the secular clergy emerged. More than just institutional change occurred, however. The ideals enunciated by eleventh-century reformers slowly transformed the lifestyle and mentality of the secular clergy in Verona. By the mid-twelfth century, the secular clergy had become more distinctly set apart from the laity and enjoyed greater esteem and authority within the Veronese Church.[1]

1. There is no well-developed general literature on the secular clergy (status, institutions, and daily life) in the early and central Middle Ages. What has been written reflects both the fragmented nature of the documentary evidence and historians' preoccupation with Gregorian Reform.

The only sizable bodies of documents in archival collections concerning the secular clergy for our period are those generated by cathedral chapters and clerical congregations. Thus, these institutions of the secular clergy are the ones to have received attention: Hagen Keller, "Origine sociale e formazione del clero cattedrale dei secoli XI e XII nella Germania e nell'Italia settentrionale," pp. 136–86 in *Le istituzioni ecclesiastiche della «societas christiana» dei secoli XI–XII: Diocesi, pievi, e parrocchie* (Milan, 1977); M. Giusti, "Le canoniche della città e diocesi di Lucca al tempo della riforma gregoriana," *Studi gregoriani* 3 (1948): 321–67; Yoram Milo, "From Imperial Hegemony to the Commune: Reform in Pistoia's Cathedral Chapter and Its Political Impact," in *Istituzioni ecclesiastiche della Toscana medioevale* (Galatina, 1980), pp. 87–107; Antonio Rigon, *Clero e città: «Fratalea cappellanorum,» parroci, cura d'anime in Padova dal XII al XV secolo* (Padua, 1988); Bianca Betto, *Le nove congregazioni del clero di Venezia (sec. XI–XV): Ricerche storiche, matricole, e documenti vari,*

In the early Middle Ages, the cathedral chapter was the central and dominant institution of the secular clergy in the Veronese diocese. Although there were clerics attached to the cathedral before the ninth century, it was Bishop Ratoldus who endowed and organized their chapter, on 24 June 813.[2] He expressed two motives. The first was to provide pastoral care for his people, since he alone could not feed his entire flock.[3] The second was to establish secure financial support for his clergy: "We want to arrange their stipends so that they having [support] will be able to pursue His righteousness in the holy church of God."[4] To this end, Bishop Ratoldus gave his clergy several houses near the cathedral and further specified, "we wish that there may be a *scola* of priests [*scola sacerdotum*] in these houses and in this place."[5]

What did Bishop Ratoldus mean by a "*scola sacerdotum*"? Several meanings are possible. In general, a *scola* (or *schola*) in classical and medieval usage was

---

(Padua, 1984). Two excellent studies of the evolution of pastoral care in urban centers are Paolo Sambin, *L'ordinamento parrochiale di Padova nel medioevo* (Padua, 1941) and Mauro Ronzani, "L'organizzazione della cura d'anime nella città di Pisa (secoli XII–XIII)," in *Istituzioni ecclesiastiche della Toscana medioevale*, pp. 35–85. Documents concerning rural churches tend to be scattered among many collections, and as a result, the clergy of these important institutions have not been studied as a group. A large literature does exist on rural *plebes*, but has been focused on juridical issues (see discussion above, pp. 32–33 and notes).

Allegations about the failings of the clergy in the writings of the great reformers (Peter Damian, Cardinal Humbert of Silva Candida, Pope Gregory VII) and in the conciliar legislation of the eleventh century have largely determined which aspects of clerical life have received the most attention from historians. Good work, therefore, has been done on simony, celibacy and the communal life, and clerical education. Joseph H. Lynch, *Simoniacal Entry into Religious Life from 1000 to 1260* (Columbus, Ohio, 1976); *La vita comune del clero nei secoli XI e XII*, 2 vols. (Milan, 1962); Giuseppe Forchielli, "Collegialità di chierici nel veronese dall'VIII secolo all'età comunale," *Archivio veneto*, ser. 5, 3 (1928): 1–117; *La scuola nell'occidente latino dall'alto medioevo*, 2 vols. (Spoleto, 1972); Pierre Riché, *Education and Culture in the Barbarian West From the Sixth through the Eighth Century*, trans. John J. Contreni (Paris, 1962; Columbia, 1976).

2. The institutional independence of the Veronese cathedral chapter is precocious. Most northern Italian chapters did not have patrimonies clearly distinct from the bishop's until the tenth century. *La vita comune* 2: 139, 151, 163–64, 184–86, 193, 239; Sabatino Ferrali, "Le temporalità del vescovado nei rapporti col comune a Pistoia nei secoli XII e XIII," in *Vescovi e diocesi in Italia nel medioevo (sec. IX–XIII)* (Padua, 1964), p. 366; Duane J. Osheim, *An Italian Lordship* (Berkeley, 1977), p. 15.

3. ". . . adiuuante ipso qui nos pastores esse uoluit et pascere suas oues potius quam nosmet ipsos mandauit . . ." *CDV* 1 no. 101.

4. ". . . disponere de eorum stipendia uolumus quatenus suam habentes iusticiam securi possint in sancta Dei ecclesia militare." Ibid.

5. "In has enim casas et in hoc loco uolumus ut sit scola sacerd[otum] . . ." Ibid.

a corporation.[6] The debate over what kind of corporation a *scola sacerdotum* might have been centered around two possibilities: a place of instruction for clerics, or simply a clerical confraternity. Giuseppe Forchielli, in his exhaustive study of the spread of collegiality among the Veronese clergy, devoted considerable attention to this question and decided that what Ratoldus constituted was definitely a place of instruction and clerical formation.[7] The evidence is, in fact, quite clear. Ratoldus's arrangements for the endowment of the *scola* indicate a pedagogic purpose. He specifically designated the tithes from the neighborhood just beyond the Porta San Fermo for the support of one canon, who was to oversee the studies of subdeacons and acolytes.[8] An imperial diploma of 820 confirmed Ratoldus's foundation "so that the clerics, who at present or in the future may be there, may be instructed [*erudiantur*] without concern for sustenance and clothing, being provided for from the goods of their church."[9]

Ratoldus's endowment created both a patrimony and physical seat for the city's secular clergy. No contemporary evidence suggests, however, that the clergy of this new *scola* lived under one roof. What Ratoldus gave were five houses (*casas*) near the cathedral (two had been the property of clerics), several smaller houses (*casellas*), and a garden near them. He directed that the *scola* be established in these houses (plural).[10] He did not

6. Pierre Riché notes that *schola* can denote groups of lectors, cantors, notaries, and scribes (as well as clerics). Riché, *Education and Culture*, p. 407.

7. Forchielli devoted the whole first chapter (pp. 1–42) of his study to a detailed examination of the various possible usages of the term *scola*. He showed that the argument for the confraternal interpretation arose from confusion between the later clerical Congregations and the cathedral chapters. On the instructional character of the *scole* see Forchielli, "Collegialità," pp. 23–27, and p. 93 et seq. *Scola* is not among the many terms Gilles Gerard Meersseman considered to connote confraternal groups generally: *Ordo fraternitatis*, 3 vols. (Rome: Herder, 1977) 1: 3–7. Nor does he include *scole* in his more specific study of clerical confraternities: "Die Klerikervereine von Karl dem Grossen bis Innocenz III," *Zeitschrift für Schweizerische Kirchengeschichte* 46 (1952): 1–42, 81–112.

8. "Next, we bestow upon that canon, who should be in charge of the subdeacons' and acolytes' studies, all the tithes offered by the men living in the village near the San Fermo gate" ("Deinde omnes decimaciones que dantur ab hominibus habitantibus in uilla que stat iuxta portam sancti Firmi largimus illi canonico qui subdiaconibus atque acolitis de secretario preesse debet studio"). *CDV* 1 no. 101.

9. "Atque ut clerici, qui in ea praesentibus futurisque temporibus fuerint, postposita alimoniae et vestimentorum occasione erudiantur de rebus Ecclesiae suae in eorum usus aliqua condonasset." *CDV* 1 no. 122. This is in keeping with canon 135 of the Council of Aachen in 816. *MGH Concilia* 2/1: 413.

10. "First, we give and concede to the clergy of our church of Santa Maria that house which

enjoin the clergy to live the *vita comunis*. The imperial diploma confirming Ratoldus's grant asserts that he established the *scola* "according to canonical custom" (*iuxta canonicam institutionem*),[11] but it seems precipitous to leap from this to the assertion that the Veronese canons were living according to the Rule of Chrodegang of Metz.[12] Some form of the common life may have been established in the buildings Ratoldus ceded. But into the early eleventh century, all we know positively is that the canons and their young charges lived in several houses clustered around the cathedral.[13]

Whatever their living arrangements, the cathedral canons enjoyed im-

---

once belonged to the cleric Anspertus, with its entire garden and yard, just as it came to us in an exchange with Abbot Teudoaldus. Similarly, we also give those houses that once belonged to the priest and *vicedominus* Ursacius with all things pertaining to it, and the house that belonged to Zenarius and the house that belonged to Gaiolus, both of which came to us through an exchange, and also other little houses in the same place, and a little garden that is behind the aforesaid houses of Anspertus and Ursonus [*sic*]. For in these houses and in this place we want there to be a *scola* of priests where they may be able to have their subsistence." ("Primo quidem damus atque condedimus clericis sancte Marie domus nostre . . . casam illam que fuit quondam Ansperti clerici una cum ortis et curte in integro sicut nobis a Teudoaldo abbate in comutacione aduenit. Similiter et damus casas illas que fuerunt quondam Ursacio presbitero uicedomino cum omni integ[rita]te sua, seu casa que fuit Zenario et casa que fuit Gaiolo, que case nobis per commutacionem ab ipsis [aduenit] seu et alias casel[las nostras] que ibidem sunt atque orticellum qui est post casas iamdictorum Ansperti et Ursoni. In has enim casas et in hoc loco uolumus ut sit scola sacerd[otum u]bi sua stipendia possint habere . . ."). *CDV* I no. 101.

11. *CDV* I no. 122. This confirmation was issued in 820, after the Council of Aachen's *De institutione canonicorum* of 816. This imperial promulgation incorporated much of the rule for canons written by Bishop Chrodegang of Metz in the late eighth century; the *De institutione* disseminated Chrodegang's ideas throughout Europe. This collection of guidelines for "canonical" living directed that clerics live within a cloister surrounded by walls, having only one entrance, and containing a refectory, dormitory, and a storeroom. *MGH Concilia* 2/1: 398 (Concilium Aquisgranense 816, can. 117). There is no evidence, however, of such a structure existing in Verona before the late eleventh century. The canons may have shared a common table or slept in the same place for all or part of the year in the houses Ratoldus donated. But the diploma's assertion in 820 that Ratoldus instituted the *scola* "according to canonical custom" (*iuxta canonicam institutionem*) should not be interpreted as overwhelming evidence that Chrodegang's vision of the *vita comunis* reigned in Verona.

12. As in *VerST* 2: 83. The rule of Chrodegang of Metz insisted upon a refectory, where the canons would eat together, and a dormitory, where they would sleep. We have evidence for neither in Verona before the late eleventh century, when a cloister was built for the chapter. Chrodegang of Metz, *Regula canonicorum*, ed. Wilhelm Schmitz (Hannover, 1889), chaps. 3 and 21, pp. 4–5, 14.

13. This arrangement may also be found in other dioceses before the eleventh century. Before their bishop ordered them to live a communal life and built them a cloister, the canons of Reims lived "in their own lodgings" (*in propriis hospiciis*). Richer, *Histoire de France*, ed. and trans. Robert Latouche, 2 vols. (Paris, 1937) 2: 30–32.

mense esteem and great authority in the diocese. Since Verona's bishops from the early ninth to the early twelfth century were foreigners, the chapter was the guardian of local ecclesiastical traditions.[14] By the tenth century, it clearly controlled the Veronese secular clergy. While the bishop formally invested priests with their churches, the cathedral chapter seems to have provided, perhaps nominated, the candidates. As the clergy of the city's baptismal church,[15] the canons certainly exercised care of souls within the city walls. Some evidence also suggests that they exercised pastoral care in the immediate suburbs of the city. The tenth-century will, for example, of the chapter's archdeacon Dagibert left a part of his goods to provide Lenten meals for "priests and deacons and all the suburban priests of the city." This suggests that the chapter either sent one of its own members or assigned another cleric to offer masses in the various churches of the city and suburbs.[16] To whom did they assign these churches? Not all the young men trained by the cathedral *scola* became canons. The complaints of Bishop Ratherius in the tenth century suggest that those who did not become canons attached to the cathedral were appointed to other churches.[17] An early tenth-century liturgical manuscript, copied in the chapter scriptorium but used in San Giorgio in Valpolicella, suggests that the chapter also provided clerics for rural churches.[18] The chapter's func-

14. Supposedly, in 814 Bishop Ratoldus had made the chapter exempt from the bishop's authority and directly dependent upon the patriarch of Aquileia. *CDV* 1 no. 104. This document, however, is clearly a falsification. See Pio Paschini, "Le vicende politiche e religiose del Friuli nei secoli nono e decimo," *Nuovo archivio veneto* 21 (1911): 423–28. In looking at the history of the chapter, however, it seems that this assertion of an exemption granted by Ratoldus sought to preserve an independent status the canons really had come to enjoy.

15. It is often asserted that the city of Verona had more than one baptismal church before the millennium. Supposedly the various churches where the bishops resided before the cathedral was finally established at Santa Maria Matricolare (San Procolo, Santo Stefano, and San Pietro in Castello) all retained baptismal rights. I have found, however, no documentary evidence to support this local tradition. For an example of a recent reassertion of this jurisdictional oddity, see Forchielli, "Collegialità," p. 44.

16. ". . . in tempore quadragesime sacerdotes et diaconi et uniuersi suburbani sacerdotes huius ciuitatis pascantur." *CDV* 2 no. 214. Bishop Rotaldus's gift of suburban tithes to the chapter also suggests this. The cathedral's control of the city and its immediate suburbs has also been demonstrated for Padua and Pisa. See Sante Bortolami, "Pieve e "territorium civitatis" nel medioevo: Ricerche sul campione padovano" in *Pievi, parrocchie, e clero nel Veneto dal X al XV secolo,* ed. Paolo Sambin (Venice, 1987), pp. 5–13; Ronzani, "L'organizzazione," pp. 52–53.

17. Ratherius, *Briefe,* pp. 76–77 (no. 16), quoted below.

18. Giles Gerard Meersseman, "Il codice XC della Capitolare di Verona," *Archivio veneto,* ser. 5, 104 (1975): 37. The richer documentation of Lucca in this period also indicates that cathedral

tion as a center for the instruction and formation of clerics, therefore, resulted in effective control of the diocesan clergy.

It was, in fact, the chapter that Bishop Ratherius blamed for the secular clergy's many failings in the tenth century. His letter of 966 to a priest in his diocese indicates that some secular clerics lacked the rudimentary knowledge required for their duties.

> You must hasten to prepare three creeds by memory, that is: the second creed (i.e. the collection of the apostles), which is found in the emended psalter; the one which is sung at mass; and that of Saint Athanasius, which begins "Whoever wishes to be saved." Whoever wishes, therefore, to be or be made or remain a priest in our parish should be able to recite these three to us by memory when soon he shall have been called hither before us.[19]

Ratherius also complained of his clergy's "fondness for women"—their "mulierositas"—and tried to bar married and concubinary priests from office.[20] The charters of the period confirm that the clergy's living arrangements differed little from the laity's. When Emperor Berengar I made a gift of the chapel of Nogara, it came with "the cleric named Leo with his wife and sons and daughters."[21]

Lest we dismiss the bishop's criticism as too harsh, his true sympathy for a large part of his clergy should be noted. While the few cathedral canons were extremely rich, the majority of the secular clergy were "pauperissimi."[22] Those in minor orders were especially needy and as a result,

---

chapters provided clergy for rural *plebes.* Cinzio Violante, "Pievi e parrocchie nell'Italia centrosettentrionale durante i secoli XI e XII," in *Le istituzioni . . . Diocesi, pievi, e parrocchie,* pp. 678–80.

19. ". . . trifarie parare memoriter festinetis, hoc est: secundum symbolum, id est collationem apostolorum, sicut in psalteriis correctis invenitur, et illam, que ad missam canitur, et illam sancti Athanasii, que ita incipit: Quicumque uult saluus esse.—Quicumque vult ergo sacerdos in nostra paroechia esse aut fieri aut permanere, illas tres memoriter nobis recitet, cum proxime a nobis huc vocatus fuerit." Ratherius includes in this letter a copy of the "Admonitio synodalis," a collection of very basic instructions for clerics. Ratherius, *Briefe,* pp. 125 (quote), 130–135 (no. 25).

20. Ratherius, *Briefe,* p. 81 et seq. (no. 16); pp. 160–61, 165 (no. 29); p. 183 (no. 33).

21. ". . . et quemdam clericum nomine Leonem una cum uxore et filiis ac filiabus suis . . ." *CDV* 2 no. 66. On the long and complex history of clerical marriage see Gabriella Rossetti, "Il matrimonio del clero nella società altomedievale," in *Il matrimonio nella società altomedievale* (Spoleto, 1977) 1: 473–567.

22. Ratherius, *Briefe,* p. 162 (no. 29). Appended to a sacramentary associated with Bishop

Ratherius noted, they were "hastening illegally to holy orders," presenting themselves for ordination before they were prepared morally or intellectually for priestly duties.[23] Ratherius tried to redress this problem by proposing a restructuring of the cathedral chapter, thereby removing the lower clergy from the chapter's control and giving them their own patrimony and seat at the urban church of Santa Maria Consolatrice.[24] Unsuccessful in this plan, he made donations to other churches (especially San Pietro in Castello) to alleviate the lower clergy's poverty.[25]

Ratherius saw all these problems—the poverty of the clergy, their intellectual and moral failings—as rooted in the institutionalized power of the cathedral chapter.

---

Ratherius are also two special masses for priests, one described as "Mass which a priest ought to sing for himself" ("Missa quam sacerdos pro se cantare debet"). Meersseman, L'orazionale, pp. 70–71.

23. "I took into consideration, therefore, those who have sustained the greater share of the Church's work and, indeed, endured the more severe poverty, so much so that they complained incessantly and, on account of their need, hastened illegally to holy orders so that they might find some sustenance, even if incurring great harm to their souls—for neither age allowed them, nor knowledge commended them, nor moral probity adorned them" ("Considerans itaque, qui maiorem in ecclesia laborem et fortiorem sustinerent adeo paupertatem, ut sine intermissione murmurarent et ob inopiam ad sacro ordines inlegaliter etiam accedere festinarent, ut aliquid ex his cum detrimento quoque animae maximo invenirent subsidii, cum nec aetas utique eos admitteret nec scientia commendaret nec morum probitas illustraret . . ."). Ratherius, "Urkunden," pp. 26–27.

24. This attempt came near the end of his last sojourn in Verona, in November of 967. After a long prologue decrying their poverty and the evils it brought, Bishop Ratherius gave to the priests of the urban churches and the subdeacons, acolytes, cantors, and doorkeepers of the cathedral their own patrimony, which included the church of Santa Maria Consolatrice and many other properties. This gift would have effectively removed the secular clergy from the power of the canons, who clearly recognized the threat. Toward the end of Ratherius's grant he speaks to the opposition who contributed to the defeat of his plan. "They maintain that I create a schism by removing these [lesser clergy] from the discipline of their superiors. I do not remove them from discipline, but I am eager to rescue them, if it were possible, from want and the temptation to neglect the service of God" ("Scisma, inquiunt, facis, dum eos a disciplina maiorum avertis—Non averto a disciplina; sed ab inopia eos et occasione servitium Domini neglegendi eruere, si esset possibile, gestio."). Ratherius, "Urkunden," p. 31. The bishop's plan failed chiefly because he tried to use lands that traditionally supported military retainers to endow the new institution for the minor clergy. Fritz Weigle, "Il processo di Raterio di Verona," Studi storici veronesi 4 (1953): 39–44; Fritz Weigle, "Ratherius von Verona im Kampf um das Kirchengut 961–968," Quellen und Forschungen aus italienischen Archiven und Bibliotheken 28 (1937–38): 21–34.

25. ASV, Fondo Veneto, no. 6533, no. 6534.

but these clerics [the canons] divide the goods bestowed upon the Veronese Church, which they ought to yield, among themselves according to whoever among them is more powerful and not according to the custom of other Churches (that is, to all the clergy of the Church) but, following their own will, only to deacons and priests. [They do this] so that thus enriched, of course, they may have the wherewithal to rebel against their bishop and so that they may dominate the rest [of the clergy]. They are able through this power, whenever they wish, to compel these [other clerics] to aid them. They [are also able] to have made them swear an oath of fidelity to another bishop [Milo], whom they have evidently gotten to go along with them, and if they do not obey, [these canons] are able to throw them out of the Church. [They do all this] so that they may acquire wives for their sons, husbands for their daughters, may have vineyards and fields, and finally may be able to be slaves of the sin of Mammon without interruption. What ought the subdeacons, acolytes and the rest of the orders of clerics do to live, to strive for the cause of the Church, to keep guard, to endure lashes to at least learn their letters when to the Apostle asking and saying, "What soldier in the field," in fact, "ever paid for his own rations?" no one shall yet have responded: "that one or that other one"? [26]

Clearly, the reform of the secular clergy in Verona required some institutional circumvention of the powerful cathedral chapter.

The means to achieve this first appeared under Ratherius. In the tenth century, three new *scole* were formed. All three churches where *scole* emerged—San Lorenzo in Sezano in 938, San Pietro in Castello in 951, and

---

26. ". . . sed ipsi clerici dividunt inter se, prout quilibet eorum potentior est, et non iuxta consuetudinem aliarum ecclesiarum omnibus ecclesie clericis, sed iuxta propriam voluntatem solis diaconibus et presbyteris, debent, que Veronensi ecclesie collata sunt, cedere, ut ditati videlicet habeant, unde contra episcopum suum valeant rebellare, et ut dominentur ceteris et ad sui auxilium per potestatem possint eos, cum volunt, compellere et iuramentum alteri, quem illi scilicet attraxerint, episcopo fidelitatis fecisse iubere et, si non oboedierint, de ecclesia eos eicere posse, ut habeant quoque, unde filiis uxores, filiabus adquirant maritos, vineas et campos, postremo unde mammone iniquitatis sine intermissione valeant deservire, subdiaconi, acoliti et ceteri in ordine clerici quid debent agere, unde vivere, pro qua re militare ecclesie, excubias custodire, flagella pro discendis litteris saltem perferre, cum interroganti apostolo atque dicenti: *Quis enim militavit suis stipendiis unquam,* adhuc nemo responderit: Ille vel ille?" The scriptural quotation is from the apostle Paul's reply to the Corinthians when they questioned their duty to support ministers (1 Cor. 9:7). Ratherius, *Briefe*, pp. 76–77 (no. 16).

Santo Stefano in 995[27]—were closely associated with the Veronese episcopate. San Lorenzo was founded by the Veronese bishop Audo in the ninth
century.[28] The church of San Pietro in Castello was the burial place of
several early bishops and, as we have seen, was a recipient of Bishop
Ratherius's support. Santo Stefano had been the episcopal seat from the
fifth to the eighth century.[29] These strong episcopal ties suggest some
attempt to increase the bishop's influence over the secular clergy through
the formation of new *scole*.

Were these new *scole* centers for the instruction and formation of clerics?
Several kinds of evidence suggest that they were. First, the year after
Ratherius's plan for reorganizing the clergy was defeated (968) he made
two gifts to San Pietro in Castello citing the needs of its "most destitute
clerics" (*clerici indigentissimi*). These needs, as we have seen, were also behind
his plan to remove the lesser clergy from the cathedral *scola*. San Pietro was
at the time of these gifts already calling itself a *scola*, and it seems to me that
Ratherius supported this institution as an alternative to setting up his own
center at Santa Maria Consolatrice to educate and support young clerics.[30]
Second, these new *scole* are described by notaries in the exact terms used
for the cathedral chapter: each is called a *scola sacerdotum* having a *custos et
rector*. Third, there is evidence for the presence of young clerics in minor
orders at these new *scole*. A witness list of 947 for San Pietro in Castello
reveals not only an archpriest, two other priests, an archdeacon, and two
deacons, but also five subdeacons and three acolytes.[31] Obviously, the
level of education young men would receive in these new *scole* would have
been more rudimentary than the resources of the cathedral would have
allowed. But considering Ratherius's dismal appraisal of the tenth-century
chapter, offering some basic education to more young clerics probably
seemed a timely alternative.[32] Bishop Ratherius judged his own efforts to

27. CDV 2 nos. 220, 247; ASVR, S. Stefano, no. 2.
28. CDV 1 nos. 194, 196, 197, 201, 219.
29. VerST 2: 9.
30. Notes 23–25 above. We know from Ratherius's earlier decree reforming the monastery of
Maguzzano that he saw the institution of the *scola* as a tool of reform. He replaced the corrupt
monks of Maguzzano and their abbot with a small *scola* of clerics led by an episcopally
appointed priest. The *scola* established there supported three priests, one deacon, one subdeacon, and several clerics. Ratherius, "Urkunden," pp. 22–25.
31. CDV 2 no. 236. Several clerics not in major orders also appear as witnesses to a charter of 963
concerning the *scola* of San Lorenzo in Sezano. ASVR, S. Maria in Organo, no. 34 app.*
32. Pierre Riché has found evidence of the training of clerics at rural *plebes* even earlier (in the
sixth century) and suggests that the practice began in Italy and spread to Gaul. His best

improve the Veronese clergy a failure, but the spread of *scole* he encouraged was to provide an institutional means for a real reform of the secular clergy in the eleventh and early twelfth centuries.

◫ Two areas of change are most striking in the development of the secular clergy over the eleventh and early twelfth centuries. First, institutional change slowly transformed their organization. Secular clerics increasingly formed *scole* and collegiate churches, and these new aggregates by the twelfth century came together to form two guild-like congregations. Second, new ideas about the secular clergy—about the appropriate ways for them to live and act, about their relation to lay society, and about the importance of their pastoral functions—informed and amplified these institutional changes. By the mid-twelfth century these new ideas produced higher expectations for the secular clergy but also greater esteem.

The institutional reorganization of the clergy is the most immediately apparent change revealed by Veronese charters. Over the eleventh and early twelfth centuries, numerous *scole* appear. The formation of these clerical communities was particularly intense in the city, but also occurred in the countryside. By 1021 there was a *scola* at the urban church of Santa Maria Consolatrice, and at Santa Maria Novella and San Giusto by 1035.[33] By 1055 there was a *scola* dedicated to Santa Maria, Sant'Agata e Santa Cecilia, and by 1083 another at San Siro.[34] *Scole* also were formed in rural parishes. The clergy of San Floriano in the Valpantena formed a *scola* by 1054,[35] and there was a *scola* at Cerea by 1061.[36]

Why were so many *scole* formed in the eleventh century? To understand this development we must first return to Bishop Ratherius's attempts at reform. The chief result of the canons' failure to support the minor clergy adequately, according to Ratherius, was that young clerics "hastened illegally to Holy Orders," before they were prepared intellectually or spir-

---

evidence, however, is from Gaul. Rural priests were instructed by the Council of Vaison (529) to take in lectors and teach them the Psalter, holy texts, and divine law. Riché, *Education and Culture*, pp. 128, 279–81.

33. ACV, I–5–IV (calp. mp n4); ASVR, S. Anastasia, no. 4.

34. ASVR, S. Maria in Organo, nos. 28, 52

35. ASVR, Orfanotrofio Femminile, no. 20.

36. ACV, III–6–3r (AC 60 m4 n12).

itually for priestly duties.[37] The bishop's complaint indicates that these clerics were finding benefices despite their inadequate training. The availability of positions for priests provided an incentive to young clerics to "hasten" to Holy Orders. A need for priests, then, seems to have contributed to the poor conditions of clerical education and formation in the diocese. This need for priests, as the number of new churches increased over the eleventh century, certainly encouraged the development of *scole*.

The demand for clergy to meet the needs of a rapidly expanding population also helps explain some of the abuses addressed by eleventh-century reform legislation. First, conciliar enactments suggest that "hastening" was still a problem: several councils restate the canonical minimum ages for the ordination of subdeacons (20), deacons (25), and priests (30). They also offer evidence that some circumstances legitimately warranted such "hastening." The Council of Rouen in 1074 restated the minimum canonical age for ordination to the priesthood as 30 years, but allowed that this requirement might be waived in cases of urgent need. Even then, however, bishops were exhorted not to ordain anyone under the age of 25.[38] Second, the need for clergy may offer an explanation for frequent conciliar exhortations to bishops not to accept priests in their dioceses without letters attesting their ordination.[39] Bishops were clearly accepting clerics not trained or ordained in their dioceses.

Although the formation of *scole* seems to respond to a need to train more priests, these institutions also offered the opportunity for fellowship advocated by reformers in order to promote both discipline and spiritual devotion in the clergy. They were communities as well as centers of education. Even churches not designated as *scole*, especially rural *plebes*, developed communities of secular clerics in the eleventh century.[40] While

37. Ratherius, "Urkunden," pp. 26–27.

38. "So that orders are given according to the decrees of the Holy Fathers. Namely, that no subdeacon be ordained before the age of 20, no deacon before 25, no priest before 30, unless there is great need. But even granting that, no priest should be ordained before the age of 25" ("Ut ordines juxta SS. Patrum statuta denter. Scilicet ut nullus ordinetur subdiaconus ante XX. annos, diaconus ante XXV. annos, presbyter ante XXX. nisi summa necessitate. Sed tamen presbyter nullus ordinetur ante XXV. annos"). Mansi 20 col. 400. The Roman Council of 1059 and the Council of Melfi in 1090 also repeated injunctions against ordaining clerics before they reached canonical age. Mansi 19 col. 915; 20 col. 723.

39. The Councils of Gerona (1068 and 1078), Rouen (1074), Winchester (1074), Rome (1078), Benevento (1091) all published canons with this prohibition. Mansi 19 col. 1071; 20 cols. 400, 508, 520, 739.

40. Archpriests appear at many of these rural churches, suggesting that the presence of several

the incidence of collegiality increases over the eleventh and early twelfth centuries, it is impossible to say if the newly founded clerical communities were living the kind of communal life advocated by reformers. We do not know if their members shared a common table, slept in a common dormitory, and celebrated the hours together. Certainly, in outlying *plebes*, which were usually responsible for several smaller village churches, a strict communal life would have been impractical. In the early Middle Ages, rural clerics were expected to come together only once a month on the Kalends. After a mass, they were to share a meal, sing hymns, have "religious conversation" and discuss "things that happen in their parishes."[41] A ninth-century manuscript in the Capitular Library containing a song for such a gathering suggests that the Veronese clergy were following this custom.[42] What became of this practice in the eleventh and twelfth centuries is unknown.

The documented reform of one urban church, however, reveals at least one compromise considered suitable for the life and work of secular clerics. In February of 1046, the Abbot of Santa Maria in Organo issued a series of directives to the secular clergy of a church subject to his monastery, Santa Maria Antica. With the approval of his monks and the "good neighbors" (*boni vicini*) of the church, he ordered the priests of Santa Maria Antica to eat and to sleep "communiter" in a room adjacent to their church during Lent. Only if they were outside of the city of Verona, or ill, or engaged in some activity not for their own enjoyment or benefit could they be excused.[43]

---

clerics required the elevation of one to a position of authority and leadership. Archpriests exchanging lands in the eleventh century were usually accompanied by other priests of their churches who acted as witnesses and surveyed the lands (see for example ASVR, S. Maria in Organo, no. 22 and S. Stefano, no. 11). Archpriests appear at the *plebs* of Santa Maria in the Valpantena as early as 1010, the *plebs* of San Zeno in Roverchiara by 1041, and the *plebs* of Santa Maria in Valle Fontense by 1060. ASVR, S. Maria in Organo, no. 44 app*; S. Anastasia, no. 5; Ospitale Civico, no. 53. Forchielli also finds archpriests at San Martino in Lazise, San Giorgio d'Illasi, and Sant'Andrea di Sommacompagna, "Collegialità," pp. 58–59.

41. Meersseman, Ordo fraternitatis 1: 113–21; quotes taken from ninth-century decree of Bishop Ricolufus of Soissons, p. 115.

42. Ibid. 1: 158–59.

43. The abbot ordered that "the priests of this church eat together communally in the room of this church during the holy days of Lent if they are in the city of Verona, unless they have remained due to illness or if some unfriendly person invited one or some or all of them to dinner. Similarly, I want them to lie in that room during the aforesaid holy days of Lent." ("hipsi ut presbyteri ipsius hecclesie . . . in sanctis quadragesimalis diebus communiter manducent ad

Our sources do not reveal whether other communities of secular clerics adopted similar arrangements. What we do know is that over the eleventh century *scole* and other churches of the secular clergy began to attract lay donors. Usually these donors lived near the church they patronized (like the *boni vicini* who supported the abbot's reforms), and often they asked the prayers of its clergy. These gifts suggest that lay persons perceived communities of secular clerics as worthy recipients of support and as worthy intercessors for their souls. Whether or not these clerics would have won the praise of Roman reformers, they appear to have won the confidence of local donors.[44]

The chronology of the formation of clerical communities is especially significant: these changes among the secular clergy occurred across the tenth, eleventh, and early twelfth centuries. The gradual pace of change is particularly important in assessing its causes. First, the gradual spread of *scole* parallels the multiplication of churches within the diocese. As instructional and formative institutions of the clergy, the new *scole* arose to meet the demand for clerics in a period of demographic expansion. Second, if the new confidence of lay donors in the secular clergy does denote some reformation of clerical life in the spread of clerical communities, then the chronology of that development suggests that clerical reform in Verona was a movement of local origin, not a reaction to Rome.[45] The spread of both *scole* and communities of clerics indicates continuity with tenth-century attempts at reform under Ratherius and a steady development

---

caminata ipsius hecclesie si ipsi presbyteri in predicta civitate veronensis fuerint nisi pro infirmitate remanserint aut aliquis inimicus aliquem eorum aut parte aut toti ad prandium invitaverit. Similiter volo ut ad caminata in predictis sanctis quadragesimalis diebus ipsi presbyteri iaceant . . ."). *ASVR*, S. Maria in Organo, no. 54 app*.

44. See Chapter 4 below.

45. Here, my findings concur with the important conclusions of Johannes Laudage. Using very different kinds of sources—canonical collections, synodal decrees, tracts, letters, and saints' lives—Laudage argues that a new consciousness of the priestly office had already emerged in the early eleventh century. This new awareness is evident in attempts to improve the intellectual and spiritual preparedness of the clergy, particularly in the promotion of communal life based on an apostolic model, and in emphasis upon canonical election. Laudage suggests that this new ecclesiastical self-understanding of the priesthood was an important root of the reform movement. I think he is absolutely right, and that the formation of *scole* in the Veronese diocese is another aspect of this new appreciation of the importance of the priestly office. I would emphasize, however, that this new consciousness did not emerge in a vacuum, but in response to the practical problems engendered by the rapid expansion of pastoral care. Johannes Laudage, *Priesterbild und Reformpapsttum im 11. Jahrhundert* (Cologne, 1984), especially pp. 304–10.

through the eleventh century. This reorganization of the secular clergy was not a sudden change accomplished during or after the investiture crisis, and it was certainly not imposed from outside the diocese. It may have been supported and influenced by reform currents in northern Italy. But if the adoption of collegiality is a mark of "reform," then the Veronese clergy began their reform well before papal pronouncements demanded it.

The fact that some reform was already underway by the mid-eleventh century is also important. It helps explain why Verona did not experience the violent clashes associated with the reform era in other cities. Local historians have interpreted the obvious loyalty to the emperor and the lack of popular risings against the imperial Church as a total lack of reform in the city.[46] Yet the spread of *scole* and clerical communities suggests a slow and moderate reformation of clerical life, despite Verona's imperial allegiance. The Veronese maintained their traditional alliance with the German emperors as well as a strong local ecclesiastical tradition.

The manuscripts of the Capitular Library, in fact, demonstrate that local ecclesiastical life developed independently of the city's political affiliations from the tenth century. Ties with south German monasteries were very strong in the era of Carolingian domination. The liturgical calendars, musical notation, and plainsong melodies used by the cathedral clergy show the influence of Reichenau and St. Emmeram, monastic centers that supplied several of Verona's bishops as well.[47] Although Verona continued to receive its bishops from north of the Alps, beginning in the tenth century its liturgical life was more influenced by Italian contacts. Cantors adopted Nonantolan and central Italian musical notation; they also used Italian plainchant melodies.[48] A liturgical calendar from Monza appears in an eleventh-century manuscript used at the cathedral, and manuscripts copied in the canons' scriptorium survive most numerously in Italian ecclesiastical collections.[49] Despite continued German political domination, the Veronese Church from the tenth century was decidedly Italian.

---

46. VerST 2: 145–49, 171.

47. James Matthew Borders, "The Cathedral of Verona as a Musical Center in the Middle Ages: Its History, Manuscripts, and Liturgical Practice," 2 vols. (PhD. diss., University of Chicago, 1984) 1: 199, 219, 274–75, 282, 392–93; Meersseman, *L'orazionale*, pp. 30–31, 54–55, 57, 66. Bishops Egino (780–803) and Ratoldus (803–840) were monks of Reichenau; Bishop Nottingus (840–844) had strong contacts with Mainz. Ederle, *Dizionario*, pp. 26–28.

48. Borders, "The Cathedral," 1: 282, 392–93.

49. Ibid. 1: 276 and Meersseman, "Il codice XC," pp. 28–34.

The independence of Veronese ecclesiastical life, however, was not isolation. If the reform of the secular clergy was occurring gradually from the tenth century, the chronology of several changes nevertheless indicates the influence of papal reform efforts. Which reforms advocated by Rome did the Veronese clergy adopt? Although there is no evidence of opposition to lay investiture within the diocese, other reform tenets made a deep impact upon the Veronese clergy. Generally, the reforming councils held at Rome from the 1050s aimed to purify the clergy and to delineate more clearly the sacred and the profane. The canons of these councils demanded, for example, that clerics should not charge fees for administering the sacraments, should not have wives, should not bear arms or follow worldly professions, and should not frequent taverns.[50] The intent was to produce a clergy more noticeably distinct in life and morals from the laity. Adherence to these canons is, of course, difficult to gauge. Veronese charters offer us evidence, however, that by the early twelfth century the clergy had a greater sense than before of membership in a distinct and separate ecclesiastical order. They also suggest that by the twelfth century there was either a decline in clerical marriage and concubinage or at least a greater reticence about it in documents.

Let us first consider the "mulierositas" of the clergy. Clerical marriage and concubinage were never completely stamped out. Verona's bishops throughout the Middle Ages had to repeat decrees against both.[51] But after 1122, the wives, concubines, and sons of priests disappear from notarial documents.[52] Couples such as "Toto priest of the church of Santa Maria outside the gate of San Zeno at the place called Fratta, and the woman Dodolenda, living in the city of Verona near the Arena" were commonly mentioned in notarial documents through the eleventh century.[53] Such

50. Mansi 19, cols. 245, 395; 21, col. 523.

51. Bishop Norandinus in 1219 forbade priests to have concubines; Bishop Peter della Scala (1290–1295) devoted one of his 89 synodal canons (no. 37) to clerical marriage; and Bishop Tebaldus III repeated this same canon in the early fourteenth century. Luigi Bellotti, "Gli statuti sinodali dei Vescovi Adelardo II (1188–1214) e Norandino (1214–1224)," in *Ricerche intorno alle costituzioni del capitolo della cattedrale di Verona nei secoli XIII–XV* (Venice, 1943), pp. 54, 59, 63.

52. The disappearance of clerical wives is not due to any broad change in how couples are described in notarial documents. The wives of laymen continue to appear in the same notarial formula.

53. "Toto presbyter de ecclesia sancte Marie sita est foris porta sancti zenonis ubi dicitur frata et Dodolenda femina [abitantes] in civitate verona prope arena . . ." ASVR, Ospitale Civico, no. 55 (1071).

couples do not appear after 1102.[54] References to sons of priests remain common for another two decades, and then become rare.[55] While this does not mean that clerical concubinage and marriage was eliminated, it does indicate that at least the principle advocated by the reformers was accepted.

Other changes in Verona's secular clergy are revealed in notarial formulas. Before the 1080s, priests in the Veronese diocese professed the law of their "race" or "tribe" (natio): Lombard, Salic, or Roman. In a document of 1082, however, a new clause appeared for the first time. Persenaldus, priest of the church of San Siro, declared that he lived by the Roman law "according to the order of the churches."[56] That an actual change of law was being required of priests is illustrated by the declaration of the priest Siginzo, "who used to profess by his race to live by the Lombard law, but according to the order of the churches he was seen to live by Roman law."[57] This profession of a different law, the law of the Church, evinces both a greater corporate sense among the clergy and a separation of the individual cleric from his past, his family and their law, when he received Holy Orders.[58]

54. Other examples: *ASV*, Fondo Veneto, no. 6756 (1020); *ASVR*, S. Stefano, no. 4 (1059); *ACV*, II–5–4r (AC 38 m2 n4) (1070); *ASVR*, SS. Nazaro e Celso, no. 630 (1102).

55. *ASVR*, S. Michele in Compagna, no. 3 app. (1088); S. Silvestro, no. 1 (1107); *ASV*, Fondo Veneto, nos. 6857 (1111), 6852 (1119); *ACV*, II–6–6r (AC 24 m3 n11) (1122); *ASVR* Clero Intrinseco, reg. 13 (Ist. Ant. Reg. I) fol. 19 (1124). The only other reference to the son of a priest I have found between 1124 and 1157 occurs in 1141: *ASVR*, S. Anastasia, no. 17.

56. ". . . professus sum secundum ordinem ecclesiarum lege vivere Romana," *ASVR*, Clero Intrinseco, reg. 12 (Ist. Ant. Reg. II), fol. 196.

57. "qui profitebat ex nacione sua lege vivere Langobardorum set secundum ordinem ecclesiarum lege vivere videbatur Romana," *ACV*, I–6–2r (AC 71 m3 n5). Although a sixth-century council and several Carolingian capitularies held that the Church followed the Roman law, by the tenth century many clerics (like those in Verona) were professing the laws of their nations. In the late eleventh century, however, clerics began using Roman law again, invoking a capitulary of Louis the Pious. Thus, in 1086 Bishop Rainulfus of Chieti prefaced an exchange of lands with "as is written in the law: let every ecclesiastical rank live and act according to the Roman law" ("sicut in Lege scriptum est: *Omnis ordo Ecclesiarum secundum Legem Romanam vivant, et faciant . . .*"). *RIS* 2.2: 1002. Simeon L. Guterman, "The Principle of the Personality of Law in the Early Middle Ages," *University of Miami Law Review* 21 (1966): 297–99. I thank Tom Head for this reference.

58. I have found no evidence that this profession of Roman law by the clergy was specifically advocated by reformers. None of the surviving canons of the reform era councils required it, but many of the canons for these councils are lost. Nor do the collections of canons circulating in Italy during this period mention it. Paul Fournier, "Les collections canoniques romaines de l'époque de Grégoire VII," *Mémoires de l'institut national de France—Académie des inscriptions et belles-*

Even the cathedral chapter, which Bishop Ratherius in the tenth century saw as the chief impediment to reform, had definitely adopted a communal life by the early twelfth century.[59] This process can be traced in the notarial clauses indicating where chapter documents were redacted.[60] These clauses through the early 1080s indicate that canons were still living in houses clustered around the cathedral. In 1079, for example, the archdeacon of the chapter, Isnardus, had a document concerning lands of the canons, drawn up "in the two-story house of the aforesaid Isnardus" ("in casa solariata predicti Isnardi").[61] By 1090, however, the archdeacon and other leaders of the chapter were having documents redacted not in their houses, but in their "rooms" (caminate).[62] Where were these rooms? A document of 1118 specifies the location: "in the canonry (canonica) of the holy Veronese church in the room of a deacon of that canonry."[63] Notarial designations stabilized in the 1120s: from this period on, the chapter's documents were redacted in the canonry or cloister of the Veronese

---

lettres 41 (1920): 271–395; The Collection in Seventy-four Titles, trans. and ann. John Gilchrist (Toronto, 1980), chaps. 138–59, 170–73 on priests; Anselm of Lucca, Collectio canonum, ed. Fridericus Thaner (Innsbruck, 1906) Liber VII, on the clergy, 2: 357–434. Perhaps the general recourse to Roman law by the eleventh-century reformers strongly linked reform to Roman law in the minds of local clerics. On the recourse to Roman law in the eleventh century, see Aloïs Van Hove, Prolegomena (St. Mecheln, 1945), chaps. 209, 216–19, 221, 223, 231; G. Le Bras et al., Histoire du droit et des institutions de l'Eglise en occident, volume VII: L'âge classique (1140–1378) (Paris, 1965), p. 168; DDC 4: 1505.

59. The chapter's patrimony was administered in common, but individual canons did hold personal property in addition to whatever they received from the chapter. The documents of the capitular archive reveal canons buying, selling, and donating their own property. A few examples: ACV, II–5–7r (AC 59 mp n2); III–7–3v (BC 44 mp n12) [copy in Muselli]; III–7–6v (AC 68 m5 n12); II–7–2r (AC 14 m5 n14). An extreme faction of the Gregorian party wanted to require canons to give up their personal property, but this position was never legislated. The Roman council of 1059 required only that the goods of the church be shared communally. Mansi 19 col. 898; Cosimo Damiano Fonseca, "Gregorio VII e il movimento canonicale: Un caso di sensibilità gregoriana," Benedictina 33 (1986): 11–23. The canons of Pistoia also adopted the communal life but retained personal property. See Milo, "From Imperial Hegemony," pp. 95–96.

60. The changes in these redaction clauses are not related to changes in formulary. Specific references to places where documents were redacted (in houses, outside gates, under porticos, etc.) occur across the eleventh and twelfth centuries. They are not associated with any particular type of document.

61. ACV, I–5–5v (AC 53 m2 n4).

62. Luigi Simeoni, "Antichi patti tra signori e comuni rurali nelle carte veronesi," AMAV 83 (1906–7): 54; ACV, II–6–4r (BC 37 m5 n9).

63. ACV, III–7–5r (BC 33 m5 n2).

Church. A document of 1120 reveals that this cloister had a refectory, and one of 1133 was drawn up "before the door of the canon's dormitory" ("ante ostium dormitorii canonicorum").[64] Archaeological excavations corroborate, in fact, that the cloister of the chapter dates from approximately the early twelfth century.[65] The chronology of the chapter's reform in Verona seems to be about average for northern Italian cities. The Paduan chapter's adoption of the communal life by the early eleventh century is quite precocious. Most cathedral chapters—like those of Pistoia, Florence, Bologna, Mantua, Vicenza, and Volterra—reformed in the second half of the eleventh century.[66]

In addition to coming together in new communities and to following the Roman law of the Church, the Veronese clergy exhibited an even more expansive sense of corporatism in the formation of urban and rural Con-

64. *ACV*, II–6–5v doc I, "in refectorium canonicorum;" I–6–4r (AC 12 mp n11) also mentions the refectory. For the dormitory, *ACV*, II–6–7r (BC 46 m3 n2), doc II; another reference, II–6–7v (AC 27 m4 n7).

65. Cinzia Fiorio Tedone, "Tombe dipinte altomedievali rinvenute a Verona," *Archeologica veneta* 8 (1985): 270–71. I think the changed architecture of the chapter's surroundings is more persuasive evidence of reform than changes in how the canons characterized themselves and changes in their administrative offices. Maria Venturini has argued (and Meersseman repeated) that the substitution by the mid-eleventh century of the term *canonica* for *scola sacerdotum* demonstrates the chapter's reform. Although this change in self-characterization in the chapter's documents may mirror reform efforts, it may also reflect a desire to distinguish the chapter from the growing number of other *scole* in the diocese. Venturini has also argued that the appearance of a *praepositus* in the eleventh century indicates reform. She equated the chapter's *praepositus* with the official responsible for provisioning the communal monastic *mensa*. A more common meaning for *praepositus* in the eleventh century, however, is an administrator of estates. The functions in which the Veronese chapter's *praepositus* appears support this interpretation: he surveyed the measurements of lands to be exchanged (or sent *missi* to do so) and he negotiated rental agreements. *ACV*, I–6–1r (AC 9 mo n–); I–6–2r (AC 71 m3 n5); III–7–3r (AC 38 m4 n10); II–5–1r (AC 21 m4 n9); I–5–2v (AC 70 mp n10); II–6–4r (BC 37 m5 n9). Maria Venturini, *Vita ed attività dello «scriptorium» veronese nel secolo XI* (Verona, 1930), pp. 45–46; Meersseman, *L'orazionale*, pp. 105–6.

66. For a few chapters, like those of Lodi and Aquileia, there is no evidence of the communal life until the mid-to-late twelfth century. For Pistoia, see Milo, "From Imperial Hegemony," pp. 87–88; for Florence, see George W. Dameron, *Episcopal Power and Florentine Society, 1000–1320* (Cambridge, Mass., 1991), p. 50; for Vicenza, see Giorgio Cracco, "Religione, Chiesa, pietà," in *Storia di Vicenza II: L'età medievale* (Vicenza, 1988), p. 382 note 142; for Aquileia, Padua, Lodi, Mantua, Bologna, and Volterra, see the articles by Spiazzi, Barzon, Caretta, Montecchio, Fasoli, and Cristiani in *La vita comune 2*: 131, 139, 151–53, 168–69, 196–97, 247. Bernold of Constance also attests that the communal life was spreading throughout the *regnum Teutonicum* in the late eleventh century. Alfred Haverkamp, *Medieval Germany 1056–1273*, trans. Helga Braun and Richard Mortimer (Oxford, 1988), p. 186.

gregations (the *Clerus Intrinsecus* and *Extrinsecus*). The Congregation of urban clergy was formed by the very beginning of the twelfth century and its rural counterpart by the century's close.

The urban Congregation first appears in a donation of 1102.[67] The early documentation of the Congregation reveals that it was headed by an archpriest assisted by several other officials called *primicerii*.[68] It also suggests some of the impulses behind its formation. Several of the churches whose clergy were most active in the Congregation were sites of well-established *scole*. Daniel, archpriest of San Pietro in Castello, appeared with the archpriest of the Congregation and its *primicerii* in a document of 1103.[69] Several early documents of the Congregation were drawn up at Santo Stefano.[70] Another church prominent in the Congregation's early history was San Giusto, the site of a *scola* by 1035.[71] The formation of the Congregation thus seems related to the ongoing spread of collegiality among the Veronese secular clergy and the establishment of *scole* to train clerics.

When documentation of the Congregation's membership appears, it is clear that it included the secular clergy of urban churches generally, but especially those exercising care of souls. Forty-nine of the fifty-nine churches inscribed as members by the early fourteenth century were parochial churches. Even parochial churches whose clergy were appointed by local religious houses—such as Santissima Trinità and San Giorgio in Braida—participated in the Congregation: care of souls brought them under the *Clerus Intrinsecus*. This composition and the chronology of its development suggest that one of the key forces behind the Congregation's formation was the devolution of pastoral care in the city from the cathedral to neighborhood parishes. Before the millennium, the care of

67. *ASVR*, Clero Intrinseco, reg. 13 (Ist. Ant. Reg. I), fol. 107. Biancolini cites a Ghisalberto in a document of 975 as the first archpriest of the Congregation; he finds no other archpriest until 1103. Several authors (Kehr, Mor, and most recently Forchielli) have repeated Biancolini's assertion that the Congregation had its beginnings in the tenth century, but none is able to cite this document of 975. I have found no mention of this archpriest Ghisalberto in the late tenth-century documents in the Archivio di Stato, the Biblioteca Capitolare, or the Vatican Archive. On the longevity of Biancolini's reconstruction, see Giulio Sancassani, "Aspetti giuridici nella vita ecclesiastica della città," in *Chiese-Ver.*, pp. 200–201.

68. In an exchange dated 1103, the archpriest Boniface was joined by the priests and *primicerii* Toto, Alboynus, and Winizo. In a rental agreement of 1116 there were also three *primicerii*: Toto, Dominicus, and Blanchus. *ASVR*, Clero Intrinseco, reg. 13 (Ist. Ant. Reg. I), fol. 17, 18, 107.

69. *ASVR*, Clero Intrinseco, reg. 13 (Ist. Ant. Reg. I), fols. 17, 18.

70. Ibid., and fol. 107 in the same register.

71. *ASVR*, S. Anastasia, no. 4.

souls throughout the city rested with the cathedral, but urban expansion over the eleventh century led to the emergence of parishes in the twelfth century. And when the boundaries of the urban parishes were defined in the late twelfth century it was the archpriest of the Congregation who was assigned the task.[72] This formation of parishes within the urban center occurred in other cities of the Veneto in the late eleventh and early twelfth centuries,[73] and the emergence of associations of the secular clergy was common in the wake of this division of the urban *plebs*. There was an association of the secular clergy at Treviso by 1078, one in Venice by 1105, and the "brotherhood of chaplains" (*fratalea cappellanorum*) is attested at Padua by 1136.[74]

The division of pastoral care among the urban clergy gave them more responsibility. Ultimately it gave them more power, and the Congregation became the institution through which this new power was exercised. The Congregation controlled appointments to churches,[75] and in 1185 Pope Urban III confirmed to the Congregation its "third share" (*tertia pars*) in the election of the bishop (the rural Congregation and the cathedral chapter held the other two thirds).[76] By forming the two Congregations, the major-

72. *ASVR*, Clero Intrinseco, reg. 12 (Ist. Ant. Reg. II), fol. 19.

73. This process is particularly well documented and studied for Padua. Sambin, *L'ordinamento parrochiale*, pp. 9–14, 23–29.

74. Antonio Rigon, "L'associazionismo del clero in una città medioevale: Origini e primi sviluppi della «fratalea cappellanorum» di Padova (XII–XIII sec.)," *Pievi, parrocchie e clero nel Veneto* (Venice, 1987), p. 103. See also Rigon's detailed study of this institution, *Clero e città*, pp. 21–22. Many of the functions exercised by these clerical Congregations in Italy (e.g., clerical appointments and discipline) were carried out by archdeacons in German dioceses. The development of the archdiaconate in Germany is roughly contemporary with the emergence of clerical Congregations. It is also associated with collegiate churches and the spread of communal life. See Lawrence G. Duggan, *Bishop and Chapter: The Governance of the Bishopric of Speyer to 1552* (New Brunswick, N.J., 1978), pp. 41–43; Karlotto Bogumil, *Das Bistum Halberstadt im 12. Jahrhundert*, (Cologne, 1972), pp. 186–94.

75. The late twelfth-century documentation of the Congregation reveals the election and investiture of archpriests to their churches. See *ASVR*, Clero Intrinseco, reg. 12 (Ist. Ant. Reg. II), fol. 103 for the election and investiture of the archpriest of Ognissanti in 1184.

76. Biancolini, *Chiese* 4: 545–47. This document is the first hint we have of the existence of the *Clerus Extrinsecus*. Castellazzi assigned this first indirect reference to 1202 based on Biancolini, but the 1185 bull preceding it clearly confirms the three shares in the episcopal election. The first direct reference to the rural Congregation does not appear until 1295. Laura Castellazzi, "Aspetti giuridici nella vita di chiese e monasteri del territorio in epoca medioevale," *Chiese-terr.*, pp. 316–324; the 1295 document recording the election of Bishop Bonincontro is published in A. Spagnolo, "Il clero veronese nella elezione del vescovo, 1080–1338," *AMAV* 84 (1907–8): 100–105. Other clerical congregations were not as successful in challenging cathedral chapters'

ity of the secular clergy kept the elite cathedral chapter from dominating diocesan government. With the development of the Congregations, the immense power of the cathedral chapter was finally effectively curtailed.

The voice the secular clergy gained in the diocese through the formation of the Congregations seems to me their most important function. Veronese historians, focusing on the later documentation of the urban Congregation, have stressed its confraternal character. Indeed, the fourteenth-century statutes of the Congregation provided for assistance to ailing members, their funeral expenses, and prayers for the departed. Like the guilds that provided these services for lay artisans, however, the Congregation also represented the interests of its members. It is the representation of these interests, especially against those of the cathedral chapter, which is foremost in the early documentation of the Congregation. Its archpriest, for example, was present with many clerics from urban churches at a legal judgment against the canons' claim to control the church of Sant'Alessandro in Quinzano.[77] The Congregation's right to participate in the election of the bishop and its direct control of several urban churches figures prominently in this twelfth-century documentation. Confraternity may have been sought by the Congregation's members, but these secular clerics also sought authority and representation within the ecclesiastical constitution of the diocese.

The secular clergy not only won these new jurisdictions, but also gained the approbation and support of the ecclesiastical hierarchy and the laity. The papal curia entrusted several disputes to the judgment of the Congregation's archpriest in the twelfth century. Pope Alexander III submitted a matrimonial case to the archpriest in 1176.[78] The Congregation's archpriest was also among the leading ecclesiastics Pope Lucius III asked to resolve a dispute between the monastery of Santa Maria in Organo and two of its subject churches.[79] Lay support for the secular clergy is demonstrated in donations to the institutions of the secular clergy: their scole, their churches, and their Congregations. Such donations became numerous only in the eleventh and twelfth centuries. In the early Middle Ages, the institutions of the secular clergy received support almost exclusively from

---

control over episcopal elections. See Antonio Rigon, "Le elezioni vescovili nel processo di sviluppo delle istituzioni ecclesiastiche a Padova fra XII e XIII secolo," *Mélanges de l'École française de Rome: Moyen Age–Temps Modernes* 89 (1977): 371, 385, 392–93, 404–5.

77. ASVR, S. Martino d'Avesa, no. 1.

78. Kehr, IP 7.1: 246.

79. Ibid., p. 278.

their own members. After the millennium, lay donors began to support these institutions.[80] By the mid-twelfth century, the secular clergy in Verona enjoyed greater support in their local community and greater respect and responsibilities in ecclesiastical governance.[81]

In sum, the secular clergy of the mid-twelfth century were very different from their early medieval forbearers. The Veronese clergy before the millennium were loosely organized around the cathedral chapter. The chapter was the only institution representing the secular clergy, and yet its canons were hardly representative: they were extraordinarily wealthy while most clerics were extremely poor. This elite chapter dominated the city's secular clergy and by the tenth century had produced a clergy ill prepared to administer pastoral care.

The expansion of pastoral care necessitated by a growing population underscored the need for change and encouraged the development of institutional forms to bring it about. The spread of *scole* slowly diminished the dominance of the cathedral chapter, tied the clergy more firmly to the bishop, and fostered communal life, as well as meeting the demand for clerics as the Church grew. These institutional developments and the new ideas of the reform era transformed the secular clergy. By the mid-twelfth century, the secular clergy were no longer dominated by the cathedral chapter. Although this institution remained prominent and powerful, the majority of the secular clergy was represented within the diocese by the new urban and rural Congregations. A large part of the clergy lived in clerical communities, either *scole* or collegiate churches. They professed a separate law and had accepted, at least in principle, the ideal of a life separate from and more rigorous than the laity's. They enjoyed greater support from the laity and assumed a prominent and respected role in the governance of the Veronese Church. The challenge of tremendous growth and expansion had been met with institutional creativity and reform.

80. Discussed in Chapter 4 below.

81. R. I. Moore also sees a connection between the increased importance of the clergy in the eleventh century and the expansion of settlement. He points out the social importance of having a church and a priest to form a "focus of social activity and organization" in new communities. See R. I. Moore, "Family, Community, and Cult on the Eve of the Gregorian Reform," *Transactions of the Royal Historical Society*, ser. 5, 30 (1980): 56–57, 60.

# 3  THE RELIGIOUS LIFE

**I**N addition to the secular clergy, the priests and clerics who attended to the care of souls, there were also those who took vows of poverty, chastity, and obedience and lived in special communities devoted to a full and lifelong practice of a Christian life.[1] These special seekers were called *religiosi*, the religious. Their lives were devoted to an ideal practice of Christianity; changes in their way of life are our best gauge of what medieval men and women thought a true Christian life entailed.

For the development of religious life in Verona, the mid-twelfth century was a turning point. The majority (90 percent) of new Veronese churches built in the great expansion of the eleventh and early twelfth centuries were in the hands of the secular clergy and primarily devoted to the care of souls.[2] Only 10 percent of the diocese's institutions were devoted to the religious life. After 1150 the number of foundations for the religious life increased dramatically. One third of the foundations in the second half of the twelfth and the thirteenth century were devoted to the religious life, and several old churches administered by secular clerics passed into the hands of new religious orders.

Although religious foundations in the century and a half after 1150 are more quantitatively significant than in the preceding century and a half, in

1. The latter came to be called the regular clergy because they usually lived under a rule. I employ here the definition of religious life used by R. W. Southern, *Western Society and the Church in the Middle Ages* (Harmondsworth, 1970), p. 214; this usage includes all the defining characteristics specified by canon law, DDC 7: 551.

2. These figures are drawn from the database of ecclesiastical institutions in Verona described in Appendix B. Before the millennium, only 16 of Verona's 130 ecclesiastical institutions were devoted to the religious life (12%). Of the institutions founded from 1001 to 1150, 13 of 124 (10%) were for religious. In the next century and a half, from 1151 to 1300, 26 of 76 foundations (34%) were devoted to the religious life. Table 2 shows the ratio of new religious institutions to all new ecclesiastical foundations by half-century over the Middle Ages.

Table 2  Percentage of new foundations devoted to the religious life, c. 750–c. 1500

| Years | No. of new foundations | No. devoted to religious life | % devoted to religious life |
|---|---|---|---|
| To 750 | 18 | 4 | 22 |
| 751–800 | 23 | 5 | 22 |
| 801–850 | 31 | 4 | 13 |
| 851–900 | 12 | 0 | 0 |
| 901–950 | 30 | 2 | 7 |
| 951–1000 | 16 | 1 | 6 |
| 1001–1050 | 27 | 3 | 11 |
| 1051–1100 | 34 | 5 | 15 |
| 1101–1150 | 63 | 5 | 8 |
| 1151–1200 | 36 | 11 | 31 |
| 1201–1250 | 29 | 12 | 41 |
| 1251–1300 | 11 | 3 | 27 |
| 1301–1350 | 11 | 4 | 36 |
| 1351–1400 | 8 | 2 | 25 |
| 1401–1450 | 21 | 4 | 19 |
| 1451–1500 | 18 | 6 | 33 |

this case numbers are not the whole story. In the period from 1000 to 1150 profound qualitative changes occurred in religious life: new types of religious institutions were founded and the popular conception of the religious life was radically altered. These changes in turn influenced the contemporary process of the codification of canon law and its formal definition of the religious life. Even in its fully developed form, the canon law recognized as religious not only those who took solemn, public vows but also those whose vows were less formal. As a result, the recognition of *religiosi* in any diocese was sometimes problematic and, since experiments in Christian living attracted the ardent, it could become an arena for determining the boundaries of orthodoxy. The changes in religious life in the century and a half following the millennium, then, prepared the way for and are crucial to our understanding of the great expansion of the religious life that marked the late twelfth and thirteenth centuries.

The religious life in early medieval Verona was spent under the Benedictine Rule;[3] a life lived mainly by men, outside the city walls. Of seventeen monasteries in the diocese before 1000, only three offered women the opportunity to lead the religious life; the rest were male houses. Half of these male monasteries were located in the suburbs of the city, the "monasteri cittadini" characteristic of Italian towns; half were in more remote sites in the countryside. Unlike male monasteries, and in deference to what was perceived as women's special need for protection, female houses were usually in or very near the city.[4]

Before the millennium, royal and imperial patronage played a decisive role in the development of monasteries, as it did generally for all ecclesiastical institutions in the early Middle Ages. Most Veronese monasteries were founded in the eighth and early ninth centuries, the heyday of Lombard and Frankish rule. Many were royal foundations. San Pietro in Moratica, San Tommaso Apostolo da Foro, Santo Stefano in Ferrariis were "monasterioli regalii."[5] The Lombard queen Ansa, "gloriosa coniux" of Desiderius, founded San Salvatore in Sirmione in the mid-eighth century.[6] Even those religious houses not founded by kings and emperors were the special recipients of royal patronage. The gifts bestowed upon the ancient abbeys of San Zeno[7] and Santa Maria in Organo[8] were considerable. San Fermo Maggiore also received imperial donations. Its abbot in 1186 recalled how Charlemagne had liberally endowed his monastery.[9]

As monasteries constituted only a small fraction of the ecclesiastical institutions of the diocese, so they also involved only a small number of

3. The Benedictine Rule came to dominate monastic life in Italy during the revival of monasticism that followed the conversion of the Lombard kings (late seventh–eighth centuries). Gregorio Penco, Storia del monachesimo in Italia dalle origini alla fine del medio evo (Rome, 1961), pp. 85, 122, 170–72. There is no evidence indicating exactly when Veronese monasteries adopted the rule, nor evidence of which rules or customs they used before Saint Benedict's.

4. Of these three female houses, one (San Michele) was in the countryside but only about a mile east of the city on the Via Postumia. The other two, Santa Maria in Solaro and San Tommaso Apostolo da Foro, were within the city walls. This placement of female houses was standard throughout Italy; see Francesca Bocchi, "Monasteri, canoniche, e strutture urbane in Italia" in Istituzioni monastiche e istituzioni canonicali in occidente (1123–1215) (Milan, 1980), pp. 274–76.

5. CDV 1 no. 147.

6. CDV 1 no. 53.

7. CDV 1 nos. 39, 117, 190; 2 no. 27.

8. CDV 1 nos. 25, 30; 2 nos. 11, 15.

9. Biancolini, Chiese 1: 329.

persons. A few large monasteries existed in Italy: in the eighth century there were about 500 monks at Novalesa near Turin; fifty at the Brescian monastery of Leno.[10] Verona's monasteries, however, were much smaller. Even the city's most prominent houses, San Zeno and Santa Maria in Organo, probably had about a dozen monks. In 838 the abbot of Santa Maria in Organo, Audibert, leased several pieces of land in the Val Veriaco to a patron of the monastery named Adelbert son of Adelbald. Eight monks signed the document along with the abbot and several lay witnesses.[11] When the abbot received a pledge of obedience from a subordinate monastery in 854, only five monks were present.[12]

While these lists may not be complete, even doubling or tripling the numbers they yield still indicates monasticism on a modest scale.[13] Rural monasteries offer some further indications of small congregations. When Bishop Ratherius reformed the monastery of Maguzzano near Garda (c. 966), he replaced its abbot and monks with only five clerics.[14] A monastery of this size clearly could be easily depopulated. The monastery near Malcesine founded in honor of the hermit saints Benignus and Carus may indeed have suffered this fate. Founded in the ninth century, it had no monks by the early eleventh century and had to be refounded.[15]

Our only evidence for female monasticism also indicates small congregations. In 745 two sisters, Autconda and Natalia, instituted a monastery for women in their home. The house was dedicated to the Blessed Virgin and placed by the founders under the tutelage of the abbot of Santa Maria in Organo. The wording of the charter indicates that at the time of the foundation, the two sisters were alone in their monastery and unsure that others would join them. They endowed it with their property,

> in order that, if the Lord shall give us other sisters, and a congregation of nuns shall have been formed for these, after our deaths [then] they may elect for themselves a spiritual mother who, following God and

10. U. Berlière, "Le nombre des moines dans les anciens monastères," Revue Bénédictine 42 (1930): 31.

11. CDV I no. 151. Two, Deusdei and George, were priests as well as monks. The others— Rodemari, Bonipertus, Domenator, Sicbertus, Lubaldus, and Peter—identify themselves simply as monks. All signed their own names.

12. CDV I no. 192.

13. For comparative figures, see Berlière, "Le nombre," 41 (1929): 231–61; 42 (1930): 19–33.

14. Ratherius, "Urkunden," pp. 22–25.

15. Biancolini, Chiese 2: 469–72.

the holy rule, may sustain and govern them. And let this abbess and the sisters always have power over all our property, administering it according to the rule. If a congregation shall not have been formed after our deaths, let our whole property be in the power of the church of Santa Maria outside of the gate of Organo. The abbot, who shall be there at that time, shall use [the property] for the office or for candles for the sacred oratory and from our property he ought to apportion [some] to the brothers and some to the poor and *famulis* who labor on this property.[16]

Autconda and Natalia were joined by others. The monastery had an abbess named Eufrasia in 839 who, together with her sisters, swore obedience to the abbot of Santa Maria in Organo in 854.[17]

Several things should be noted about the small number of monasteries and those who served in them, and the crucial role of royal and imperial patronage in making possible even these few. First, the economy of early medieval Verona seems to have allowed very few to leave the world for a life of prayer. Second, the diocese itself could not have supported even so few without the assistance of emperors and kings. The pursuit of the religious life in the early Middle Ages was a luxury, and one afforded to few.

If the monks were few, however, their cultural contributions were considerable. The monastery had a school, library, and scriptorium by the eighth century.[18] As already noted, the cathedral *scola* was also an important cultural center. But it was a monk of San Zeno, Coronatus, who wrote the beautiful life of the city's patron that is considered its most distinguished piece of medieval Latin literature.[19] Just as in other monasteries in early medieval Europe, Verona's monks kept classical learning alive. A poem written by a monk of San Zeno recalls the pleasures of reading Juvenal and

---

16. "Eo scilicet ordinem ut sit nobis dominus alias sorores dederit et congregatio monacharum istis facta fuerit post obitum nostrum exemetipsas sibi elegant matrem spiritalem qui eas secundum Deo et sanctam regulam foueat atque gubernet et cuncta nostra substantiam regulariter disponendi in ipsius abbatisse uel sororum per omnia permaneat potestatem. Et si congregatio hic facta non fuerit post obitum nostrum omnis pecunia nostra sit in potestatem ecclesie sancte Marie sita foris portam Organi et abba qui pro tempore fuerit ipse disponat de oficio uel luminaria sancti oratorii et de pecunia nostra quid a fratribus uel quid ad pauperibus seu famulis qui cum ipsam pecuniam laborauerint debeat pertinere." CDV I no. 33.

17. CDV I nos. 153, 192.

18. VerST 2: 358–59.

19. VerST 2: 363–70.

Terence: "Their joking and witty words / Made us burst out laughing."[20] San Zeno's poets also applied classical style and conceits to religious topics, writing verses on spiritual dangers and hymns celebrating pilgrimage to Rome.[21]

While the early medieval manuscripts of San Zeno and the dispersion of Veronese manuscripts throughout Europe suggest far-ranging intellectual ties, the institutional bonds of Veronese monasteries were decidedly local. If there were ties to other monasteries, they were to other Veronese houses. San Zeno controlled San Pietro in Moratica and Santa Maria in Organo the smaller monasteries of Santa Maria in Gazzo and Santa Maria in Solaro.[22] Only one house, the "monasteriolo" of San Salvatore in Sirmione, was under the tutelage of a monastery outside the diocese. In 774 Charlemagne had donated the monastery to Saint Martin of Tours.[23]

Small but influential, Veronese monastic institutions were deeply rooted in the local community. Although there were differences among them—in location, wealth, and prestige—what they had in common was more important. All of these institutions shared a single vision of the religious life and labored under a single rule in their pursuit of holiness. Their place in society was well defined and preeminent. Both the unified vision and the preeminent position of Benedictine monasticism, however, were vigorously challenged in the century and a half after the millennium.

Some historians have perceived the major change in the regular life in this period to be a "crisis" of Benedictine monasticism.[24] According to this interpretation, the crisis had two aspects. First, traditional Benedictine monasteries had, by the eleventh and twelfth centuries, become

20. "Sepe suis verbis iocundis atque facetis / Nos quae fecerunt risum depromere magnum"; *VerST* 2: 397.

21. *VerST* 2: 397–99.

22. *CDV* 1 nos. 190, 228, 33.

23. *CDV* 1 no. 53.

24. On the emergence of this interpretation, see John Van Engen, "The 'Crisis of Cenobitism' Reconsidered: Benedictine Monasticism in the Years 1050–1150," *Speculum* 61 (1986): 271–72. The key articles in its development are Charles Dereine, "Odon de Tournai et la crise du cénobitism au XIe siècle," *Revue de moyen age latin* 4 (1948): 137–54; Jean Leclerq, "Le crise du monachisme aux XIe et XIIe siècles," *Bulletino dell'Istituto storico italiano per il medioevo e Archivio Muratoriano* 70 (1958): 19–41 [a translation may be found in Noreen Hunt, ed., *Cluniac Monasticism in the Central Middle Ages* (London, 1971), pp. 217–37]; Norman F. Cantor, "The Crisis of Western Monasticism, 1050–1130," *American Historical Review* 66 (1960): 47–67.

phenomenally wealthy and, in the eyes of many, decadent. Those whose strong ascetic and eremitic religiosity left them discontented in traditional Benedictine monasteries founded new institutions for the religious life: the Cistercian, Vallombrosian, and Camaldoli congregations, and houses of regular canons. Second, the Black Monks lost their preeminent position in western culture, society, and government. Was there such a "crisis" in Veronese monasticism in the eleventh and twelfth centuries?

The argument for the decadence of Benedictine monasticism is based upon evidence of the emergence of new reforming institutions and the criticisms of the old monasticism made by the advocates of these new institutions.[25] New institutions of the religious life did emerge in Verona in the eleventh and twelfth centuries; but if their supporters were critical of the city's Benedictine monasteries, they did not record and preserve their criticisms for posterity. How, then, can we assess the vitality or decadence of Benedictine monasticism in Verona after the millennium? Veronese sources offer us both negative and positive evidence.

Let us first consider the negative evidence. Whatever the state of life within their cloisters, Veronese Benedictine houses were not closing up for lack of recruits or resources. Most of the monasteries founded before the millennium were still in existence in 1150. The invasions of the tenth century destroyed several churches and abbeys, but most were quickly rebuilt. In 951 the Magyars, that "gens crudelissima," burned the suburbs of Verona, destroying the monastery of San Zeno and the churches of San Procolo, Santo Stefano, and Santi Nazaro e Celso.[26] San Zeno was rebuilt

25. Van Engen has argued that the attacks of the critics of Benedictine monasticism "were not quite so numerous as their present prominence might suggest" and that these critics, being in the position of defending their fledgling institutions, were hardly objective. Van Engen, "The 'Crisis of Cenobitism'," p. 273.

26. Ratherius reported that "the churches of this land in every direction [are] either completely demolished or in large part destroyed" ("ecclesiae istius patriae passim aut penitus dirutae aut ex magna parte distructae"). Vittorio Cavallari, *Raterio e Verona* (Verona, 1967), p. 31. A more detailed account of the destruction appears in a manuscript of the Capitular Library: "In 951 that most cruel race of the Magyars had burned the suburbs of Verona; they burned the churches of San Zeno Maggiore of Verona, San Procolo, Santo Stefano, and Santi Nazaro e Celso. And the abbot and monks of the aforesaid monastery of San Zeno—fearing lest the holy body of the confessor and bishop of Verona, Saint Zeno, be carried off—secretly took the body of the said Saint Zeno with a chalice and cross of solid gold embellished with gems (objects of great value and worth that King Pippin had given to this monastery). They carried the body of Saint Zeno to the church of Santa Maria Matricolare and buried it in the sacristy of this church." ("Dum Ungararorum gens crudelissima Veronam incendissent in suburbiis. Nam combuserunt ipsi ecclesias sancti Zenonis maioris Veronae, Et sancti Proculi, sancti Stephani et

with the help of Bishop Ratherius, who also restored and reformed the abbey of Maguzzano.[27] Only the monasteries of San Tommaso al Ponte Pignola and Santo Stefano in Ferrariis seem to have permanently succumbed to the violence of the age; neither is documented after the tenth century.

Not until the thirteenth century, in fact, is there evidence of Benedictine institutions dying out. Donations slowed in the late twelfth century. The same scramble for economic resources that limited the foundation of new institutions at that time hurt the patrimonies of Benedictine houses.[28] The number of monks also declined. The death of abbot Peter in 1291, for example, left only one monk at San Zeno. San Pancrazio was deserted in 1294. And the "few monks" at San Fermo were stated as one of the reasons the cloister and church were ceded to the Franciscans in 1261.[29] Institutional collapse did characterize Benedictine monasticism in the thirteenth century, but not in the eleventh and twelfth.

There is, then, little evidence of Benedictine institutions faltering. There is also little evidence of decadence in the religious life. Only in two instances did Veronese bishops intervene to reform monasteries. In 966 Bishop Ratherius reformed the abbey of Maguzzano, casting out its concubinary abbot and monks,[30] and a century and a half later Bishop Bernard reformed San Giorgio in Braida.[31] We will return to examine the case of San Giorgio in detail, but now let it suffice to note that there were no other complaints of scandal. The lack of reform is, of course, in no way evidence of virtue. But since Verona's twelfth-century bishops were eager to exert their authority over institutions and showed themselves to be sensitive to

---

Sancti Nazarii et Celsi, Et dominus abbas et monachi monasterii dicti sancti Zenonis timentes ne corpus sacrum sancti Zenonis confessoris atque pontificis Verone raperetur, furtive tulerunt corpus dicti sancti Zenonis cum calice uno et cruce aurea tota, cum gemmis ornata, precii et valoris, Que rex Pipinus detulerat ipsi monasterio, Et portaverunt ad ecclesiam beate Marie Virginis matricularis, Et sepelierunt illud in secretario ipsius ecclesie"). Lorenzo Tacchella, "Le origini dell'abbazia dei SS. Nazario e Celso di Verona," *Studi storici veronesi* 20–21 (1970–71): 8.

27. Ratherius, "Urkunden," p. 23: "a little monastery burned down by the Magyars" ("incenso ab Ongariis coenodobiolo").

28. Andrea Castagnetti, "Aspetti politici, economici, e sociali di chiese e monasteri dall'epoca carolingia alle soglie dell'età moderna," in *Chiese-Ver.*, pp. 64–66.

29. Andrea Castagnetti, "I possessi del monastero di S. Zeno di Verona a Bardolino," *Studi medioevali*, ser. 3, 13/1 (1972): 131; Biancolini, *Chiese* 2: 482 and 1: 334.

30. Ratherius, "Urkunden," pp. 22–25.

31. ASV, Fondo Veneto, no. 6886.

rumors of scandal in other instances, it seems unlikely that flagrant abuses were being ignored.

If there is little evidence of decadence and decline in Veronese Benedictine monasticism, there is a great deal of positive evidence for the continued popularity and vitality of the Benedictine life through the mid-twelfth century.[32] Eleven new Benedictine monasteries were built between 1000 and 1150 (nine for men and two for women[33]). Most of these houses are mentioned only in passing in the documents that survive: a small group of monks at the church of San Mauro in Saline,[34] a monastery on the river Mincio cataloged among the possessions of the Veronese episcopate,[35] and a new foundation at Nogara supported by the monks of Nonantola.[36] Some monks, as was common in the eleventh century,[37] were propelled out of their houses by a desire to emulate the Desert Fathers. In 1027 a Veronese notary described a piece of land as bordered on the north by an encampment of hermits, *eramites sancti Benedicti*.[38]

Some of the new foundations were proprietary monasteries built by local noble families. The monastery of Santo Stefano donated to Cluny by Albert of Bonavigo and his son Henry was surely such a private foundation.[39] The most successful new monasteries, however, appear to have

32. Monastic foundations in nearby Padua were as numerous. Fourteen new houses emerged in the eleventh and twelfth centuries. As in Verona, some were episcopal foundations, others proprietary monasteries built by leading families. Giannino Carraro, "I monasteri benedettini della diocesi di Padova," *Benedictina* 35 (1988): 91–92, 122.

33. The founders of neither of these new female houses are known. In 1081 an inscription records the foundation of Santa Maria delle Vergine in Campo Marzio. San Pancrazio, a house subject to the older convent of San Michele, is first documented in 1133. Biancolini, *Chiese* 2: 748–49; 4: 700–701. In addition to new foundations, older monasteries for women grew in wealth and prestige. San Michele in Campagna, founded before the millennium, received numerous donations in the eleventh century. Among the rights acquired by the nuns was that of holding an annual fair; the revenues derived from this fair made San Michele a wealthy and powerful monastery in the twelfth century. Valeria Monese Recchia, "Aspetti sociali ed economici nella vita di un monastero benedettino femminile, S. Michele in Campagna di Verona dal secolo XI al periodo ezzeliniano," *Archivio veneto*, ser. 5, 98 (1973): 5–54.

34. BC, Mss. Lodovico Perini, b. 26, document dated 25 September 1145; Biancolini, *Chiese* 3: 320–21.

35. Pighi, "Cenni," p. 152.

36. Kehr, IP 7.1: 301.

37. Henrietta Leyser, *Hermits and the New Monasticism* (London, 1984), pp. 18–37.

38. ASV, Fondo Veneto, no. 6762.

39. Auguste Bernard and Alexandre Bruel, *Recueil des chartes de l'abbay de Cluny*, 6 vols. (Paris, 1876–1903), 5: 86–87 (no. 3736). These donors—"Albert, son of the deceased Hubert of Bonavigo . . .

been episcopal foundations.[40] The monastery of Santi Pietro e Vito di Calavena emerged in the remote mountains northeast of the city in the mid-eleventh century.[41] Around the same time, a monastery was built at the church of Santi Nazaro e Celso just beyond the city's walls.[42] Foundation charters do not survive for either house, but both had strong early ties to the Veronese episcopate. Bishop Walther (1037–55) had built a castle at Calavena,[43] and one suspects that he may have had a hand in founding the monastery too. The jurisdiction of the abbey was confirmed to the see in 1145.[44] San Nazaro received significant support from the bishop in its early years. In 1036, "considering the church of the holy martyr of Christ Nazaro destitute of its own means to be restored by the brothers gathered there," Bishop John made a sizable donation to the monastery "in order that there may always be a house of monks there."[45] The locations

---

with my son Henry"—do not appear in other documents of the period. The three generations of names follow a pattern recurrent in the comital San Bonifacio family, but these donors professed Roman (not Salic) law.

40. Verona is not unusual in this regard. See Geo Pistarino, "Monasteri cittadini genovesi," and Pietro Zerbi, "I monasteri cittadini di Lombardia," both in Monasteri in alta Italia dopo le invasioni saracene e magiare (sec. X–XII), (Turin, 1966), pp. 248–49 (Genoa), 287 (Milan), 295–97 (Brescia), 309–11 (Como); Giovanni Tabacco, "Vescovi e monasteri," in Il monachesimo e la riforma ecclesiastica (1049–1122) (Milan, 1971), pp. 106–13; Karlotto Bogumil, Das Bistum Halberstadt im 12. Jahrhundert (Cologne, 1972), pp. 63–76, 101.

41. The first document to mention the monastery was an exchange of lands in 1068. The abbot Bonus signed the charter along with seven monks. Castagnetti, Kehr, and Biancolini all place the monastery's foundation in the early twelfth century and name Pellegrinus as its first abbot. They cite a document of 1133 (ASVR, SS. Nazaro e Celso, no. 318, 21 March 1133) as the monastery's first. The document here cited, enacted at the monastery in June of 1068, is in the Capitular Archive: ACV, I–5–5r (AC 59 m4 n8). Biancolini, Chiese 2: 568–69 and 4: 714; Andrea Castagnetti, "Aspetti economici e sociali di pievi rurali, chiese minori, e monasteri (secoli IX–XII)" in Chiese-terr., p. 122; Kehr, IP 7.1: 295.

42. Lorenzo Tacchella, "Le origini dell'abbazia dei SS. Nazario e Celso di Verona," Studi storici veronesi 20–21 (1970–71): 13–14.

43. An inscription, now at Museo Castelvecchio, was erected by the bishop along with the castle: "In the year of our Lord 1040, this castle was raised at the sole expense of Bishop Walther" (AN. DNI. MXL / SVPTV. WALTEII. EPI / HOC. CASTELLV / EREXIT A SOLO). Gianni Faè, Badia Calavena (Verona, 1964), pp. 6–7, and Biancolini, Chiese 2: 571.

44. Pighi, "Cenni," p. 155.

45. ". . . considerans ecclesiam sancti martyris Christi Nazarii destitutam de propriis facultatibus restaurari statutis ibi fratribus, ut in perpetuum sit monachorum habitatio . . ." ASVR, SS. Nazaro e Celso, no. 434; Tachella, "Le origini," pp. 74–75. The bishop gave two-thirds of the manor of Corliano and several other holdings.

of both monasteries' patrimonies also suggest episcopal involvement.[46]

Both these traditional Benedictine foundations were highly esteemed within and beyond the local community. Pope Lucius III, just before his death in 1185, made the difficult trek to Calavena to consecrate a new church there.[47] He also took the monks under his protection.[48] San Nazaro received gifts from a wide spectrum of donors: emperors;[49] Verona's comital family, the San Bonifacio, and other local nobles;[50] the notarial and judicial families of the city;[51] artisans;[52] persons living near the monastery,[53] and donors from communities where the monastery held lands.[54] Pope Adrian IV in 1158 took the monastery under the protection of the Holy See.[55] And when a German baron returning from the second crusade was on his deathbed, he called on the abbot of San Nazaro to hear

46. Calavena is on the northwest frontier of the diocese and the patrimony of San Nazaro on the ill-defined western border with Vicenza. Both patrimonies are also strategically located around the stronghold of the San Bonifacio family, which at the time of both these foundations was just securing its hold on the Veronese countship. The foundations of both monasteries seem to be part of episcopal efforts to expand the see's influence in the border regions of the diocese and to check the rising power of the San Bonifacio. Other bishops were pursuing similar strategies in the eleventh century; see George W. Dameron, *Episcopal Power and Florentine Society, 1000–1320* (Cambridge, Mass., 1991), pp. 32–35, 52–53; Pistarino, "Monasteri cittadini genovesi," pp. 249, 259; Tabacco, "Vescovi e monasteri," pp. 109–11. Episcopal support of the suburban monasteries San Nazaro and San Giorgio in Braida (discussed below) may also have been an effort to counterbalance the power of the cathedral canons in the city. For examples of this in Mantua, Modena, and Reggio Emilia, see Paolo Golinelli, *«Indiscreta sanctitas.» Studi sui rapporti tra culti, poteri, e società nel pieno medioevo* (Rome, 1988), pp. 72–77.

47. Faè, *Badia*, pp. 8–9.

48. Kehr, IP 7.1: 296.

49. ASVR, SS. Nazaro e Celso, nos. 40 and 42; Tachella, "Le origini," pp. 75–76, 82–84.

50. Count Albert, his brother Mainfred, and their mother, Richelda, ceded their rights in Corliano. ASVR, SS. Nazaro e Celso, no. 437; Tachella, "Le origini," pp. 79–80. The widow and sons of the viscount Walfred and the "nobilissima femina" Richarda also made gifts: ASVR, SS. Nazaro e Celso, nos. 914 and 314.

51. The "iudex" Sentichus and his brother gave the monastery a piece of land in 1090, and in 1118 a "vicedominus" and his sons donated lands in the Val d'Illasi: ASVR, SS. Nazaro e Celso, nos. 1679 and 806.

52. ASVR, SS. Nazaro e Celso, no. 915.

53. Especially those living in the neighborhood outside the Porta Organo: ASVR, SS. Nazaro e Celso, nos. 628, 641, 2232.

54. In Montorio, ASVR, SS. Nazaro e Celso, nos. 967, 1534; in Colognola, nos. 313, 314, 315, 317; in Lavagno, nos. 627, 629, 630, 631.

55. Tachella, "Le origini," pp. 85–86.

his confession and entrusted to the monastery the relics of Saint Blaise which he had acquired during his years in the Holy Land.[56]

Another mid-eleventh-century foundation with episcopal support, the monastery of San Giorgio in Braida, did not fare as well as Calavena and San Nazaro. Its failure, however, impugns not Benedictine monasticism but papal-imperial politics. The foundation had an auspicious start. Its founder Cadalus was a cleric from a wealthy Veronese family[57] who was trained in the cathedral chapter and had served Bishop Walther as *vicedominus*.[58] In 1046, just after having been made bishop of Parma, Cadalus returned to Verona, secured a site on the banks of the Adige from Bishop Walther, and arranged for a monastery to be built.[59] He endowed the house with his substantial family inheritance and carefully provided for the spiritual and material well-being of the monks. Cadalus insisted that the monks should elect their abbot from among themselves; no one from outside the community should be made abbot. He placed the monastery under the protection of the bishop but explicitly stated that the bishop had no power over it and could not alienate any of its lands either through leases or benefices.

Subsequent developments in the career of San Giorgio's founder seem to have impeded the development of the monastery. When Pope Nicholas II died in 1061, one group of cardinals nominated Cadalus to the Holy See. This faction, following Nicholas's own decree on papal elections, sought out the emperor for his consent to the nomination. Meanwhile, another faction nominated Anselm, bishop of Lucca, and enthroned him as Pope Alexander II. A month later, having received the emperor's endorsement,

---

56. Tachella, "Le origini," pp. 88–89.

57. Cadalus was from a family of castellans in the Veronese *contado*. His grandfather was one of the inhabitants of the castle at Calmano; another branch of the family held the castle of Sabbion. Cadalus's father, Ingo, acquired a house in Verona in 1005 and in one document was styled viscount. With his two brothers, Erizo and John, Cadalus acquired a significant amount of property in the area between Lonigo, Cologna, and Orti in the early eleventh century. Vittorio Cavallari, "Cadalo e gli Erzoni," *Studi storici veronesi* 15 (1965): 63, 154–58.

58. The future bishop of Parma first appeared in a document of the Veronese chapter in 1028 identified as "clericus." In 1030, he was a subdeacon; by 31 July 1034, he had been ordained a deacon. Cadalus remained a deacon for several years, but also served as the bishop's *vicedominus*, a chief administrator, from 1041. This position gave him firsthand experience in the administration of the diocese. By 1045 Cadalus had been ordained a priest and made bishop of Parma. *ASV*, Fondo Veneto, nos. 6764, 6766, 6769, 6770, 6771, 6772, 6791; Cavallari, "Cadalo," pp. 95, 116–24, 130–32.

59. *ASV*, Fondo Veneto, nos. 6792 and 6793; Cavallari, "Cadalo," pp. 133–40.

Cadalus was made Pope Honorius II. Neither election was strictly canonical, but three years later Alexander triumphed.[60] Before Cadalus's election,
San Giorgio had received a grant of imperial protection, donation of a mill
from Verona's bishop, and a quitclaim from Cadalus's Lombard relatives.[61]
Only two documents illumine the period of Cadalus's pontificate; both
concern his relatives. The first coincides with his election as pope and
records a promise by three cousins to stop their molestation of the monastery's lands. The second, executed a year later by one of these cousins, is in
the form of a donation but is more likely a renunciation of claim to a piece
of San Giorgio's property.[62] More than a decade of documentary silence
follows these.

Many historians, following the "Gregorian" victors, have judged Cadalus
harshly. On the evidence of several caustic letters by Peter Damian,[63]
Cadalus has been characterized as an example of the kind of corruption the
reformers fought.[64] This characterization is neither fair nor particularly
helpful for understanding the eleventh-century Church. Cadalus was,
surely, ambitious. Considering his family's social pretensions, it would be
surprising if he were not. This is, in fact, the charge that reverberates
through Damian's denunciation: he chides Cadalus for succumbing to
aspirations and allowing himself to be used by the emperor to sow dissen-
sion in the Church.[65] But Cadalus was not a simoniac nor a "heresiarch." It
was Anselm of Lucca, not Cadalus, who had to purge himself of accusations of simony at the Council of Mantua in 1064.[66] At worst, Cadalus was a

60. Cavallari, "Cadalo," pp. 97–98, and Uta-Renate Blumenthal, The Investiture Controversy (Philadelphia, 1988), pp. 92–98; Michael Stoller, "Eight Anti-Gregorian Councils," Annuarium historiae
conciliorum 17 (1985): 254–63.

61. MGH DD 5: 406–7 (no. 298); ASV, Fondo Veneto, nos. 6805, 6800.

62. ASV, Fondo Veneto, nos. 6809, 6812; Cavallari, "Cadalo," pp. 69–72.

63. Peter Damian, Die Briefe des Petrus Damiani, ed. Kurt Reindel, 3 vols. (Munich, 1988), 2: 515–72
(nos. 88 and 89, to Cadalus) and 3: 384–92 (no. 120, to Henry IV).

64. Notably P. Cenci, "Documenti inediti su la famiglia e la giovinezza dell'Antipapa Cadalo,"
Archivio storico per le province parmensi n.s. 23 (1923): 94–95. But see also Cavallari's careful disman-
tling of Cenci, upon which my discussion is based. Cavallari, "Cadalo," pp. 94–101.

65. ". . . why do you, with your ambition (namely, that of a single man), throw the whole
Church of Christ into disorder?" (". . . totamque Christi aecclesiam tua unius videlicet hominis
ambitione confundas?") Damian demanded of Cadalus. He continued, likening Cadalus to a
sword sundering the Church: "And so in this way you who had been a son of the holy Church
were made a sword used against her" ("Hoc itaque modo qui sanctae aecclesie fueras filius,
adversus eam factus es gladius"). Damian, Briefe 2: 522 (no. 88).

66. Damian made subtle accusations of simony in his denunciations of Cadalus: Damian, Briefe

rather traditional churchman: not particularly ascetic in his personal piety, but a man who freed his slaves and gave them land;[67] a supporter of episcopal dignities and prerogatives; a generous donor to traditional ecclesiastical institutions. His family's ties with the emperor predisposed him to support Henry's right to a role in episcopal and papal elections, and in the 1060s this was not a reactionary position. In Cadalus's recent memory, Henry III had brought good and pious men to the Holy See.[68] No doubt Cadalus saw his own candidacy as the continuation of these reforms.

The failure of San Giorgio to attract monks may be read as some censure of Cadalus himself or his involvement in the schism. But it seems equally likely that fears about the monastery's future made it seem a poor risk for a lifelong vow. San Giorgio's lands bordered on significant holdings of the house of Canossa, and Countess Beatrix was an avid supporter of the Roman faction.[69] The security of the monastery's patrimony may well have been in question. When a Benedictine congregation finally did appear at San Giorgio in the 1070s, one of its first acts was to seek protection for its holdings.[70]

Ongoing conflict between the emperor and Rome also adversely affected the development within Verona of new congregations of Benedictines advocating a stricter interpretation of the rule. Under Countess Matilda, Canossan power was concentrated on the southern border of the diocese and ripe for expansion into the Veronese plain. Reformed monasteries were one of the most effective ways Matilda and her allies spread

2: 531 (no. 88); 2: 533–35 (no. 89). The Council of Mantua, however, condemned Cadalus as a schismatic, not a simoniac. Peter Damian was present at the council. Mansi 19, cols. 1029–31; Cavallari, "Cadalo," pp. 94, 99.

67. ASV, Fondo Veneto, no. 6844.

68. From 1046 to 1048 the emperor was able to wrest the papacy from the control of local factions. He elevated two short-lived German clerics as Popes Clement II and Damasus II, finally succeeding with the elevation of his cousin, the reformer Bishop Bruno of Toul, as Pope Leo IX.

69. See the map appended to Thomas Groß, *Lothar III. und die Mathildischen Güter* (Frankfurt am Main, 1990). San Giorgio's patrimony was concentrated north and east of the Adige on the plain (around Cologna Veneta, Lonigo, Bonavigo, Sabbion, and Carpi). Just to the south and west of the Adige (especially between the Adige and the Po) were numerous lands of the house of Canossa. Canossan interests in extending influence northward are clear. In the 1070s Countess Matilda supported the foundation of a Vallombrosian house in Verona, and in the early twelfth century the Veronese counts, the San Bonifacio, became her vassals.

70. In a *placitum* on 13 March 1077 in Verona, Abbess Richarda of San Giorgio begged that the emperor's ban might protect her, her advocate, her monastery, and all its goods. Manaresi, *Placiti* 3: 340–41 (no. 440).

their influence,[71] and fear of this political infiltration, not hostility to reform, is what frustrated the spread of new reformed foundations. In the early 1070s there was support within the city for a Vallombrosian foundation. John Gualbert (c.990–1073), the Florentine monk who inspired the strict Vallombrosian interpretation of the rule, was still alive and had already acquired a reputation for sanctity through his bold promotion of reform.[72] Enthusiasm for his ideas and uncertainty in the local political climate allowed the cornerstone of the church and monastery of Santissima Trinità to be set in 1073.[73] At this time Henry IV was politically weak, beset by revolts in Germany, and far from Verona. The city's bishop, Bruno, accepted the *pallium* from Rome, and a visit from Countess Matilda of Tuscany.[74] In August of 1073, she ceded some contested lands to San Zeno and, according to local tradition, founded the church of Santissima Trinità.[75] But in 1077, after Henry had regained political initiative by his surprising reconciliation at Canossa, work on the church came to a halt.[76]

Construction did not begin again until political tensions were resolved, and this took quite some time. The Veronese Count Albert of the San Bonifacio came to a reconciliation with Matilda and Pope Pascal II in 1106. Both were present in the city at that time, but apparently the unfriendly climate within the city forced the countess and the pontiff not only to leave, but also to abandon plans to proceed north to Germany through Veronese territory. The pope gave up plans to seek out Henry V in Germany and went to France instead.[77] Despite the reconciliation of its count, Verona was not completely reconciled with the papal party until the emperor made peace in 1111.[78] Only after this settlement of political tensions

71. The influence exerted by the monasteries of Farfa and Fonte Avellana opened most of the Marches to the papal party. Elisabetta Archetti Giampaolini, *Aristocrazia e chiese nella Marca del centro-nord tra IX e XI secolo* (Rome, 1987), pp. 269–85.

72. Gualbert had also recently (1068) driven the simoniac bishop of Florence from his see. On the history of Gualbert and the Vallombrosian congregation see B. Quilici, *Giovanni Gualberto e la sua riforma monastica* (Florence, 1943); on his successful political struggle in Florence, see Dameron, *Episcopal Power*, pp. 51–55.

73. Nicola Vasatura, "L'espansione della congregazione Vallombrosana fino alla metà del secolo XII," *Rivista di storia della Chiesa in Italia* 16 (1962): 456–85.

74. Ughelli, *IS*, 5: 767–68.

75. Ibid.; Mario Carrara, "Novecento anni di vita sul Monte Oliveto," in *SS. Trinità in «monte oliveto» di Verona* (Verona, 1974), pp. 46–47.

76. Carrara, "Novecento anni," p. 47.

77. Andrea Castagnetti, *La Marca Veronese-Trevigiana* (Turin, 1986), pp. 37–38, 43.

78. Ibid., p. 43.

did work on Santissima Trinità begin again. It seems significant, moreover, that the first donation to support the renewed construction of the Vallombrosian church and monastery came from the d'Este family so often cited as mediators in the papal-imperial struggle. The Marquis Adalbert Azzo d'Este in 1077 was one of those at the side of Pope Gregory VII at Canossa who urged the pontiff to have mercy upon Henry IV.[79] In 1115 it was the Marquis Falco d'Este, son of Adalbert Azzo, who donated lands and pasture rights to the church and monastery of Santissima Trinità.[80] The establishment of a monastery of the reformed Vallombrosian congregation in Verona was, indeed, the fruit of political mediation. The church and monastery were finally consecrated 12 January 1117.[81]

Ties with Benedictine reform movements north of the Alps, on the other hand, did not occasion controversy.[82] The ancient Veronese monastery of Santa Maria in Organo established ties with the south German house of Benediktbeuern in the mid-eleventh century.[83] At the instigation of Emperor Conrad II, the royal abbey of Benediktbeuern had been reformed in 1031. A new abbot and twelve monks were sent from Tegernsee, a monastery itself reformed in 982 under the influence of Saint Emmeram in Regensburg.[84] Within a decade of Benediktbeuern's reform, its influence was radiating further south. By 1041, Santa Maria in Organo had received a new abbot, Ingelbero, from Benediktbeuern.[85] Unfortunately, no documentation illumines Abbot Ingelbero's impact on monastic life

79. Ibid., p. 36.

80. Gloria, CDP 2: 58–59 (no. 71). A note at the bottom of the witness list of this document indicates that the monks were already present in 1115: "Hoc fuit actum post ingressus fratrum in predicto monasterio sex dies minus tredecim mensium."

81. Annales Sanctae Trinitatis, MGH SS, 19: 2.

82. While membership in the Vallombrosian congregation entailed strong, well-defined ties outside the diocese, the reforming monasteries of south Germany were much more loosely organized. They followed the traditional pattern of brief associations with other houses, usually for the life of an abbot, and then let the associations lapse. There is, for example, no evidence that Santa Maria in Organo continued to have any ties with Benediktbeuern after the tenure of Abbot Ingelbero. For these kinds of relations between monasteries and reform, see Constance B. Bouchard, "Merovingian, Carolingian, and Cluniac Monasticism: Reform and Renewal in Burgundy," Journal of Ecclesiastical History 41 (1990): 365–88.

83. Kassius Hallinger, "Progressi e problemi della ricerca sulla riforma pre-gregoriana," in Il monachesimo nell'alto medioevo e la formazione della civiltà occidentale (Spoleto, 1957), p. 272; Romuald Baurreiss, Kirchengeschichte Bayerns (St. Ottilien, 1949–70) 2: 32, 112.

84. St. Emmeram, in turn, had strong ties with Gorze. Kassius Hallinger, Gorze-Kluny (Rome, 1950) 1: 129–31, 133–36, 158–59.

85. ASVR, S. Maria in Organo, no. 23; Chronicon Benedictoburanum, MGH SS, 9: 226 (lines 33–35).

within Santa Maria's cloister. A decree of 1046, however, does show Ingelbero instituting reforms at an urban church under the jurisdiction of the
monastery,[86] and one suspects a similar increase in rigor had already taken
place at the mother house.

None of these developments in the Benedictine life in Verona, however,
suggest a "crisis" of monasticism. Not only did Benedictine houses
founded before the millennium survive, but new monasteries, both male
and female, were founded in the city and in the countryside. They received
strong support from the Veronese see and from local donors. Benedictine
reform movements also took root in the city, but their development was
very strongly influenced by papal-imperial politics.

Clearly, Veronese evidence suggests a modification of the crisis thesis.
While traditional Benedictine monasticism was not in decline in Verona in
the eleventh and twelfth centuries, new interpretations of the religious life
nevertheless were developing. The emergence of new kinds of institutions
for the religious life surely did signal an end to the preeminence the Black
Monks had enjoyed in the early Middle Ages. But even these new interpretations of religious life owed much to monastic ideals.[87] The life of Saint
Gualfardus (d. 1127) illustrates these continuities.

Gualfardus came to Verona from Augsburg with a company of merchants. Seeing what an agreeable place Verona was, Gualfardus remained
in the city when the rest of his company returned to Germany. He worked
as a saddler outside the city walls and, "chaste as the snow, inflamed with
charity, sober in his humility, free of anger, great in constancy, long-
suffering by virtue of his patience, compassionate with pity," he began to
give whatever he earned to the poor and destitute.[88] His desire for eternal
life and his longing to flee the vanity of this world, however, prompted him
to leave the city secretly and go off into the forest of Saltuclo (not far from
Verona on the Adige). He lived an austere and holy life there for twenty
years.

There came a time, however, when it was pleasing to God that the works
of blessed Gualfardus be made known to men. So the Lord pointed out the
holy man to certain sailors navigating on the Adige and they took him on
their boat to the city. There Gualfardus went to several churches doing

86. *ASVR*, S. Maria in Organo, no. 54 app*.

87. André Vauchez, *Les laïcs au Moyen Age* (Paris, 1987), pp. 97–101.

88. ". . . castitate niveolus, caritate flammeolus, modestia sobrius, ira vacuus, constantia
magnanimus, patientiae virtute longanimis, miseratione compatiens . . ." *Vita S. Gvalfardi solitarii*,
*AASS* April 3, 828E.

good works. He stayed for awhile at San Pietro in Monastero (near the cathedral); then, after a flood of the Adige, he went to the Vallombrosian church of Santissima Trinità. Finally, he took up residence at the church of San Salvar, where he lived in a tiny cell, in constant prayer and fasting, for ten years. People began to flock to the holy man: he cured the sick of fevers and fatigues, gave sight to the blind, cast out demons, and healed cripples. Even nature recognized the virtue of Gualfardus. When he went down to the Adige to wash his hands and fill his cup, fish would come to him. They would touch his hands and swim into his cup, not wanting to be put back into the river when he rose to leave.[89] After his death, miraculous cures of all kinds occurred at his tomb.

Gualfardus spent most of his life as a hermit and a recluse. Both his flight into the woods and his life of austerity in the cell at San Salvar would have been entirely comprehensible to those who lived under Benedict's rule. But Gualfardus began his religious life caring for the poor outside the city walls, and having been sent back to the city by God, he ended his life curing the sick, the crippled, the blind, and the deranged. These acts of mercy, which captivated his contemporaries, signal a new focus in religious life. While Gualfardus's sojourn in the wilderness recalls the tradition of Saint Antony, his compassion for the poor, and even the fish touching his hands, presage a new spirituality, one usually attributed to the great mendicant orders of the thirteenth century. These new visions of the religious life were well established in Verona by 1150.

The subsequent history of Cadalus's troubled monastic foundation provides a good example of the new kinds of religious life which emerged in the early twelfth century. Although founded in 1046, it was not until after Cadalus's death that a monastic community appeared at San Giorgio in Braida. In a document of 1075 an abbess, not an abbot, is named.[90] Richarda governed the monastery from 1075 to at least 1096. She rented, exchanged, and sold its lands and received donations. She also sought and received renewed imperial support.[91] A charter of 1096 also reveals that the church of San Giorgio had been designated a *plebs* and that it

89. Ibid., 829A–B.
90. *ASV*, Fondo Veneto, no. 6818.
91. *ASV*, Fondo Veneto, nos. 6821, 6822, 6827, 6835, 6836, 6837, 6841, 6842, 6843.

was being administered by a *scola* of secular clerics headed by an arch-priest.[92]

This community of cloistered women and the adjacent *scola* of secular clerics appears to have coexisted without problems under the leadership of the Abbess Richarda. After her death, difficulties seem to have arisen. A charter of November 1101 recorded Amharda as abbess, and then from 1109 to 1111, Armengarda. Suddenly in 1113 there was an abbot, Martin.[93] The next document concerning the monastery gives the first evidence of the bishop's intervention to reform the house. On 22 July 1121 Charles, the son of the monastery's longtime advocate Godo, was forced to renounce advocacy of the monastery and his fief into the hands of Bishop Bernard. The reason given was the "very, very great evil which he very frequently committed against the venerated place of San Giorgio in Braida, and, finally because of the great plunder of mares which he had driven to Sabbion."[94]

Weak and changeable leadership after the death of Richarda seems to have allowed the supposed protectors of the monastery to take advantage of its patrimony. This was exactly the sort of lay behavior that Cadalus's foundation charter had tried to deter. A series of inventories of the lands of San Giorgio dating from this period indicate the first task facing the new leadership: the reconstitution of the monastery's patrimony.[95] Aided by a grant of tithes from the bishop, Peregrinus, the reformer hand-picked by the bishop to lead the monastery, began buying property and arranging advantageous exchanges of lands with other religious houses to accomplish this task.[96]

The formal charter outlining Bishop Bernard's reform of the monastery, however, alludes not only to temporal disarray, but also to moral decay. He characterized the house as "having been destroyed" in both a spiritual and

92. ASV, Fondo Veneto, no. 6843; also published in Andrea Castagnetti, *La Valpolicella dall'alto medioevo all'età comunale* (Verona, 1984), pp. 193–194 (no. 38).

93. ASV, Fondo Veneto, nos. 6848, 6853, 6854, 6858, 6859.

94. "propter nimiam maliciam quam contra venerandum sancti Georgii in braida locum sepissime fecerat, ad ultimum propter maximam equarum praedam quam in Sabulone exercuerat." ASV, Fondo Veneto, no. 6876. Parchments no. 6877 and 6894 are also refutations of fiefs and judicial rights from this same period.

95. ASV, Fondo Veneto, nos. 6874, 6895.

96. ASV, Fondo Veneto, nos. 6880, 6886; purchases: nos. 6890, 6898, 6905, 6909, 6910, 6911, 6915, 6916, 6917, 6920; exchanges: nos. 6908, 6919, 6921, 6922. The reform of San Giorgio also sparked numerous donations: nos. 6881, 6888, 6891, 6893, 6899, 6912, 6928 (all during the tenure of Peregrinus).

temporal sense. "First," the bishop explained, "it had been a monastery of women and afterwards of monks. But in either case it was a brothel of Venus, a temple of the devil more than of God."[97] The bishop's solution to this problem, however, is most important. He did not turn to a "reforming" order, or any revamping of Benedictine monasticism at all, despite the stated wishes of the founder eighty years earlier that there should always be a house of Black Monks there. "Having therefore expelled the blasphemers of God from that place," wrote Bernard, "I ordained religious clerics in it who, by the grace of God, lead the celibate life of canons and observe the canonical rule." He named Peregrinus as "praepositus" of all the brothers serving God there.[98] In order to reform San Giorgio, Bernard instituted a house of regular canons.

What sort of religious life did these canons lead? How did it differ from Benedictine monasticism? "Nothing," Giles Constable observed, "is more difficult to define than a canon."[99] The difficulty lies in variations in practice as well as in the imprecision with which contemporaries described them. Bishop Bernard, like other contemporaries, gives us only rather vague outlines. As noted above, they lived under and had the right of electing a *praepositus*. They observed a "canonical rule." According to this rule, they said Matins and the rest of the Hours and at these times they were allowed to ring bells. Bernard also relinquished authority over the temporal goods of the house, "in order that they may serve God more freely."[100]

To which "canonical rule" was Bernard referring? Most regular canons were identified as living by the Rule of Saint Augustine, but each congregation usually adopted a set of canonical "institutes" (*ordines* or *consuetudines*) as well. Several of these sets of guidelines for houses of regular canons were

---

97. "Fuerat enim quondam & prius puellarum et post modum monachorum cenobium set in utrisque veneris prostibulum diaboli pocius quam Dei existerat templum." *ASV*, Fondo Veneto, no. 6886.

98. "Expulsis ergo ex inde Dei blaspematoribus religiosos in ibi clericos ordinavi qui Dei gracia canonicorum celibem ducunt vitam & regulam observant canonicam, Dei igitur amorem et dilecti filii nostri peregrini venerabilis presbyteri eiusdem ecclesie prepositi omniumque fratrum congregacionis . . ." Ibid.

99. Giles Constable, "The Study of Monastic History Today," in Vaclav Mudroch and G. S. Couse, *Essays on the Reconstruction of Medieval History* (Montreal, 1974), p. 32; rpt. in *Religious Life and Thought* (11th–12th centuries) (London, 1979); Christopher Brooke has also recently stressed the difficulty in distinguishing regular canons from monks: "Monk and Canon: Some Patterns in the Religious Life of the Twelfth Century," *Studies in Church History* 22 (1985): 109–29.

100. *ASV*, Fondo Veneto, no. 6886.

in circulation in the early twelfth century originating in the most successful foundations. Institutes from the houses of Saint Victor in Paris, Saint Ruf in Avignon, the canons of Saint John Lateran, and those of the Ravennese house of Santa Maria in Porto offered specific injunctions for the ordering of the religious life of canons.[101] In 1132 a bull of Innocent II described the canons of San Giorgio in Braida as living by the Rule of Saint Augustine.[102] In 1186 Urban III's bull confirmed at San Giorgio "the canonical order according to the Rule of Blessed Augustine and the institutes of the brothers of Porto."[103]

It is not surprising that the canons of San Giorgio should have looked to those of Santa Maria in Porto for a successful model of religious life. Of the most famous early foundations, the canons of Porto at Ravenna were the closest geographically and therefore probably the best known to the Veronese. The founder of Santa Maria in Porto had just died at around the time of the reform of San Giorgio. Peter of Onesti (also called Peter de Honestis or Peter the Sinner), founded the canons of Porto in 1096. Just before his death in 1119, his rule had been confirmed by Pope Paschal II (1117).[104] This rule was clearly meant to be used in conjunction with that of Saint Augustine, given the varying degrees of detail and generality on different topics. Taken together, what sort of religious life did these rules define? How was it different from the religious life of the Black Monks?

The lives outlined by these canonical rules and the Rule of Saint Benedict differ only subtly. Both prescribe a liturgical life organized around the Hours. The cycle of Hours used by the canons seems only slightly less time-consuming than the Benedictine. The Rule of Porto lists seven Hours to the Benedictine eight, eliminating Prime.[105] The number of psalms, hymns, and readings outlined in the Augustinian rule is slightly less than in

101. Carlo Egger, "Le regole seguite dai canonici regolari nei secoli XI e XII," *La vita comune del clero nei secoli XI e XII* (Milan, 1962) 2: 9–12. See also Reginald Grégoire, *La vocazione sacerdotale: I canonici regolari nel medioevo* (Rome, 1982), pp. 29–37.

102. *ASV*, Fondo Veneto, no. 6901; Kehr, IP 7.1: 260.

103. Kehr, IP 7.1: 264. The earliest house of regular canons in Venice, Santa Maria della Carità, also appeared in 1121, and it too adopted the rule of Santa Maria di Porto. Antonio Fabris, "Experienze di vita comunitaria: I canonici regolari," *La chiesa di Venezia nei secoli XI–XII*, ed. Franco Tonon (Venice, 1988), p. 76.

104. L. Holstenius, *Codex regularum monasticarum et canonicarum*, 6 vols. (Augsburg, 1759) 2: 138–75. For the history of Santa Maria in Porto, see Carlo Egger, "Canonici regolari di Santa Maria in Porto," *Dizionario degli istituti di perfezione* (Rome, 1974–) 2: 147–48.

105. Holstenius, *Codex* 2: 162 (book 3, chap. 1).

the Benedictine.[106] Beyond the liturgical life of the Hours, how did the canons spend their time?

They seem not to have cultivated learning as much as the Black Monks. Chapter 18 of the first book of the Rule of Porto does not assume an entirely literate congregation and treats the hubris of the learned as a real danger. Entitled "If those, who are literate, should dare to teach something," the chapter asserts:

> If some fittingly humble canons, not arrogant according to the degree of their knowledge of erudite letters, and full of knowledge of divine scripture, thus are able to offer something useful to others, and the prior shall have approved it as just and seen it as necessary, with all kindling of hatred and jealousy at once removed, let him allow them [to teach], or urge them to labor in those things whose knowledge he will have seen as more necessary and useful.[107]

Literacy is here viewed as a potent incitement to sin, leading to pride, envy, and hatred. So great is this danger, it seems that learning should not be pursued for its own sake. Unlike our monks of San Zeno who delighted in the classical authors, the canons of San Giorgio allowed only what learning was necessary and useful.

Wary of erudition, the regular canons seem to have devoted themselves instead to the service of others in the world. In his prologue to the rule, Peter of Onesti described exactly what the apostolic life of the canons should be. He called his followers to abandon the business of the world,

---

106. The standard night offices in both are at least twelve psalms, although the Augustinian Rule shows more seasonal variation (the year is divided into three parts each requiring a different number of psalms; in the Benedictine Rule the year is divided only into two periods, November to Easter and Easter to November). Lauds is considerably longer in the Benedictine Rule. It consists of four psalms, two canticles, Lauds, one lesson, a hymn, a benediction, the Kyrie, and the Lord's Prayer. In the Augustinian Rule, Lauds is simply three psalms. The rest of the hours in the Augustinian Rule usually include three psalms, a reading, and a closing prayer, whereas the Benedictine Rule requires a hymn, versicles, and the Kyrie. Benedict of Nursia, *Regula monachorum*, ed. Cuthbert Butler (Fribourg, 1927), pp. 41–53, chaps. 8–18; Adolar Zumkeller, *Augustine's Ideal of the Religious Life*, trans. Edmund Colledge (New York, 1986), pp. 283–300, "The Rule." See also Grégoire, *La vocazione*, pp. 85–101.

107. "Si qui Canonicorum humilia sentientes, non arrogantiam habentes in tantum fuerint litteris eruditi, & divinarum Scripturarum scientia pleni, ut inde aliquid utilitatis aliis aufferre valeant, & Prior justum probaverit, & necessarium viderit, omni prorsus invidiae & odii fomite remoto concedat eis vel praecipiat in his laborare, quorum scientiam magis necessariam, utilemque prospexerit." Holstenius, *Codex* 2: 148 (book 1, chap. 18).

the "negotia saeculi." But Peter's idea of abandoning the world is markedly different from the Benedictine notion. He continued,

> Therefore let them love fasting, let them comfort the poor, let them gather in guests, let them clothe the naked, let them visit the sick, let them bury the dead, let them serve the oppressed, let them console the sorrowful, let them weep with the weeping, rejoice with the joyful, let them not forsake charity, if possible let them have peace with all, let them fear the day of judgment, let them desire eternal life above all, let them put their hope in God, let them put nothing before the love of Christ, let them obey the orders of their prelates in all things, let them comply with their own bishop in all things according to the canonical institutes, and finally, let them devote work to spiritual teachings, readings, psalms, hymns, canticles and let them persevere unfailingly in the exercise of all good works.[108]

The very order of these exhortations is revealing. The liturgical life—spiritual doctrines, psalms, hymns—comes last, even after obeying the bishop and other prelates. Highest on Peter's list of apostolic callings is fasting, caring for the poor, clothing the naked, and visiting the sick. These acts of self-denial and charity are ranked even before the general exhortations to seek eternal life and put Christ before all. There is, in fact, a strong orientation toward the world and its problems in the canons' idea of abandoning the world.

These ideals seem particularly well suited to San Giorgio's location and circumstances. Its church was the *plebs* in a growing suburban neighborhood, along the road north to Trent outside the Porta Santo Stefano. Charters drawn up at San Giorgio give us a glimpse into this neighborhood served by the new regular canons. It was full of millers and dyers working along the river, with builders and artisans along the road to the city and the narrower streets veering off it.[109] Many of its inhabitants labored in trades

---

108. "Ament praeterea jejunium, pauperes recreent, hospites colligant, nudos vestiant, infirmos visitent, mortuos sepeliant, tribulantibus subserviant, dolentes consolentur, cum flentibus fleant, cum gaudentibus gaudeant, charitatem non derelinquant, pacem, si fieri potest, cum omnibus habeant; diem judicii timeant, vitam aeternam per omnia concupiscant, spem suam Deo committant, amori Christi nihil praeponant, Praelatorum suorum imperiis per cuncta obediant, proprio Episcopo in omnibus secundum Canonum institutionem obtemperent, postremo spiritualibus doctrinis operam tribuant, lectionibus, Psalmis, Hymnis, canticis et ceterorum bonorum operum exercitiis jugiter insistant." Holstenius, *Codex* 2: 143.

109. The charters of San Giorgio are teeming with workers of all sorts: millers (*molinarii*): ASV,

related to transit: blacksmiths, saddlemakers, and shoemakers.[110] Butchers appear frequently, their bloody line of work relegated to neighborhoods outside the city.[111] It was in the same type of suburban quarters, among workers and the poor, that the mendicants would settle in the thirteenth century. Already in the early twelfth century, however, the regular canons of San Giorgio dedicated themselves to a life of charity beyond the city walls.

Scholars are correct in pointing out that what distinguished the regular canons from the Benedictines was a difference of emphasis.[112] While retaining many elements of the traditional religious life, they shifted its focus. Moreover, as we have seen, the Veronese saw this shift in focus embodied in the regular canons as particularly suited to the work of reform. In this they seem inclined to agree with Peter the Venerable that "In the religious life it is easier to found than to restore, to make something new than to repair what has existed for a long time."[113]

As a new interpretation of the religious life, the orientation of the regular canons toward the world reveals a new direction in medieval spirituality. This new direction is even more clearly evident in the emergence of another type of institution for the religious life, the leper hospital.

---

Fondo Veneto, nos. 6982, 6996, 7002; dyers (*tinctores*): nos. 6973, 6997, 6998, 7011; craftsmen (*fabri*): nos. 6560, 6974, 6995; masons (*murarii*): nos. 6983, 7013.

110. blacksmiths (*ferrarii*): ASV, Fondo Veneto, nos. 7000, 7015; a saddler (*sellarius*): no. 6560; shoemakers (*calcearii*): nos. 6995, 6996.

111. butchers (*beccarii, masselli*): ASV, Fondo Veneto, nos. 7008, 7009, 7019, 7020.

112. Caroline Walker Bynum has characterized this distinction as "the quality of their [the canons'] sense of responsibility for the edification of their fellow man." "The Spirituality of the Regular Canons in the Twelfth Century: A New Approach," *Medievalia et Humanistica* n.s. 4 (1973): 19–20. R. W. Southern contrasted the Benedictine achievement of bringing "order into whole countrysides on a grand scale" and of imitating "a supernatural order in the midst of flux" with that of the regular canons, who "picked up the broken pieces in an already settled world." *Western Society*, p. 244. The new emphasis on poverty in the institutes of the regular canons, however, had important ideological implications, especially relating to the rise of the mendicant movements a century later. See Cosimo Damiano Fonseca, "La povertà nelle sillogi canonicali del XII secolo: Fatti istituzionali e implicazioni ideologiche," in *La povertà del secolo XII e Francesco d'Assisi* (Assisi, 1975), pp. 151–77. See also Grégoire, *La vocazione sacerdotale*, pp. 38–48, 124–45.

113. "Nam sicut nouit sapientia uestra, in negotio religionis facilius possunt noua fundari quam uetera reparari," *The Letters of Peter the Venerable*, 2 vols., ed. Giles Constable (Cambridge, Mass., 1967) 1: 43 (no. 23).

There were institutions in early medieval Verona, the *xenodochia*, that cared for the sick and the poor. These institutions, however, differed in a fundamental way from the new hospitals of the *malsani* (or lepers, also called *leprosi*) which emerged in the twelfth century.[114] The *xenodochia* of the early Middle Ages were adjuncts to religious institutions. They were nearly always physically separate from the church or monastery controlling them and juridically distinct, having their own patrimonies. They constituted only a part, and usually a minor part, of the religious life of the controlling institution.[115] The leper hospitals of the twelfth century, in contrast, were themselves religious houses, with a religious life completely devoted to the poor and sick. They were a new type of institution representing an entirely novel interpretation of the religious life.

Most early medieval *xenodochia* were founded by clerics, usually by leaving in their wills a house to be given over to the care of the poor. In 844, for example, the archdeacon Pacificus ordained in his will that his house in Quinzano should be made into a *xenodochium*. He instructed that on the anniversaries of his and his sister's deaths 140 paupers and twelve priests

114. The proliferation of hospitals was a broadly shared characteristic of the spirituality of the central Middle Ages. These foundations were often the work of lay confraternities. Thus, Giles Gerard Meersseman describes the development of hospitals as part of a multifaceted confraternal movement that became particularly strong after the eleventh century. Giles Gerard Meersseman, *Ordo fraternitatis*, 3 vols. (Rome, 1977) 1: 136–49. More recently, André Vauchez has linked the origins of lay confraternities to a more positive valuation of penance in religious life, diffused among the laity by hermits and reformed Benedictine congregations. See above, note 87.

But the origins of hospitals were remarkably diverse. Some were founded by monasteries, bishops, or urban churches; others by individual patrons and lay confraternities. A few of these do not differ markedly from early medieval *xenodochia*. But most, and especially leper hospitals, tended to be more independent than the *xenodochia*. Pierre De Spiegeler, *Les hôpitaux et l'assistance à Liège (Xe–XVe siècles)* (Paris, 1987), p. 147; John Hine Mundy, "Charity and Social Work in Toulouse, 1100–1250," *Traditio* 22 (1966): 203–87, especially p. 239 on leper hospitals; Joseph Avril, "Le IIIe concile du Latran et les communautés de lépreux," *Revue Mabillon* 60 (1981): 21–35. Several sets of statutes and regulations for leper hospitals are published in Peter Richards, *The Medieval Leper and His Northern Heirs* (Cambridge, 1977), pp. 123–43.

115. A *xenodochium*, in classical usage, was a hostel for travelers. By the eighth century, however, this word was used to designate a place that not only assisted pilgrims but also cared for the poor, widows, and orphans. In the ninth and tenth centuries, *xenodochia* founded as independent institutions increasingly came under the jurisdiction of larger ecclesiastical entities, and their ministries became adjuncts to the missions of the monasteries and chapters that controlled them. Vittorio Fainelli, "L'assistenza nell'alto medioevo: I xenodochi di origine romana," *Atti del Reale istituto veneto di scienze, lettere, ed arti* 92/2 (1932–33): 918–24.

ought to be fed with bread, vegetables, meat, and wine. Pilgrims were also to be fed on these occasions, and on each Saturday during Lent a certain amount of food was to be distributed to the poor.[116] The priest Rado in 774, Bishop Notker in 921, and the deacon Dagibert in 931 also willed that *xenodochia* be established in their houses.[117] Others were founded by the nobility: a charter of 837 mentioned two royal *xenodochia* in the city of Verona[118] and in 908 the Veronese Count Anselm founded a *xenodochium* "for the feeding of Christ's poor."[119]

Monasteries administered some *xenodochia*, but most were under the care of the cathedral canons. Santa Maria in Organo administered at least three, and San Zeno and San Fermo each supervised one.[120] This latter *xenodochium*, however, passed from San Fermo to the canons around the millennium. The canons also administered the *xenodochia* founded by Pacificus, Notker, Dagibert, Gotefredus, Aldo, and Arduin and one located at San Giovanni in Valle.[121] The supervising institutions would assign one or two of their members to look after the *xenodochium*. In August of 1114, for example, a priest and cathedral canon named Ilderadus was *praepositus* of the *xenodochium* at San Giovanni in Valle. Zeno, a subdeacon of the cathedral was "custos et rector" of the same *xenodochium* in December of that year.[122]

The care of the poor and sick in the *xenodochia* was only part of the work of the institutions that controlled them and never involved all of the institutions' members. The leper hospitals founded in the twelfth century were, in contrast, independent institutions, totally devoted to the care of the poor and sick. These institutions, in their dedication to the most vulnerable and reviled members of Christian society, most clearly express the new spirituality emerging in the twelfth century.

Several leper hospitals were founded in Verona along the Adige outside

---

116. *CDV* 1 no. 176.

117. *CDV* 1 no. 50, 2 nos. 177 and 214.

118. One at the gate of San Fermo and another called Calaudustra. *CDV* 1 no. 147.

119. *CDV* 2 no. 88.

120. One of Santa Maria in Organo's was in the city at Cortalta, originally founded by Lupo, and another was near the monastery. Fainelli claims the monastery held the *xenodochium* founded by Notker, but the bishop clearly placed this foundation under the care of the cathedral canons. By 987, however, the monastery did control the *xenodochium* of San Siro. *CDV* 1 no. 178; *ASVR*, S. Maria in Organo, no. 38; *ACV*, III–5–4v (/C 8 m2 n5). For those controlled by San Zeno and San Fermo, *CDV* 1 nos. 172, 50.

121. *CDV* 1 no. 176, 2 nos. 177 and 214; *ACV*, II–4–7v (BC 20 m2 n2), II–4–7v (AC 38 m5 n4); I–5–5r (BC 36 m5 n10), III–6–4v (AC 28 m2 n3).

122. *ACV*, I–6–3r (AC 52 m2 n14) and I–6–2v (AC 31 m2 n1).

the city walls during the twelfth century. Santa Croce was the earliest, founded by the fourth decade of the twelfth century. The lepers of Santa Croce first appear in a document of 1136 when a certain Crescentius bought them several pieces of land. Their hospital was located outside the city, "below San Fermo."[123] By 1141, it had its own oratory: Bishop Tebaldus consecrated the church "of the poor and infirm brothers of the hospital of the Holy Cross [Santa Croce] and of holy charity" on Sunday, 6 April.[124]

Lands were purchased for the hospital through a *missus* or *nuncius*; lands were donated to the *fratres*, or brothers of the hospital. The most revealing documentation for the early organization of the hospital, however, stems from a disagreement requiring the intervention of the bishop in 1146. Contention had arisen between a certain Lord Hugo, whom Bishop Tebaldus had appointed to administer the hospital, and the lepers who were there. The lepers claimed that they "ought to rule and divide the goods and alms which God and men gave." But the bishop, "knowing their badness, their plotting, and the fornicating going on among some of them, which had even created and generated children," said that they did not have the right to administer the goods of the hospital. They had only the right always to be fed and cared for there as paupers and guests. Tebaldus gave the rectors and administrators of the hospital the right to punish, excommunicate, and expel any who entered into plots or fornicated.[125]

This dispute reveals several things. First, there were obviously both male

123. *ASVR*, Istituto Esposti, no. 1 and S. Silvestro, no. 2. After I completed the archival research for this study, a collection of documents relating to Veronese leper hospitals was published by A. Rossi Saccomani, *Le carte dei lebbrosi di Verona fra XII e XIII sec.* (Padua, 1989).

124. *ASVR*, S. Silvestro, no. 5 app. The development of Santa Croce follows a pattern similar to other leper hospitals. Lepers seem to have gathered together on unoccupied lands outside a city gate where they attracted the assistance and alms of those entering and leaving the town. A loose network of those assisting the lepers usually developed into a confraternity. The establishment of a chapel or the assignment of a chaplain brought the community under episcopal supervision. De Spiegeler, *Les hôpitaux*, pp. 57–60, 105–110.

125. "De lite et controversia qua vertebatur inter dominum Ugonem quem dominus Thebaldus venerabilis veronensis episcopus de regimine et ministratione investiverat et inter leprosos qui ibi aderant necnon et nutriebantur. Dicebant quam regere ministrare ac dividere volebant et debebant bona et elimosinas quas Deus et homines dabant et dederant. Cognita autem idem dominus episcopus illorum nequitia et coniuratione et fornicatione a quibusdam inter eos factam et etiam filios concreasse vel generasse, . . . statuit et precepit ut leprosi qui in hospitalis ecclesie sancte [crucis et sancte] caritatis sunt vel erunt numquam habeant licentiam dominandi ministrandi neque iubendi sed ibi semper in pauperes et hospites ale[va]ntur et nutrientur." *ASVR*, Istituto Esposti, no. 4".

and female lepers in the hospital! Second, in this document and other early records of the hospital, the only distinction made is between the "leprosi" and the administrators. This implies that the "brothers and sisters" were the lepers. The designation of those who act on their behalf also bears out this interpretation. Crescentius was identified interchangeably as "treasurer" (*massaro*) of the *malsani* and "treasurer of the brothers in the place of and in the name of the *malsani*."[126] That the lepers felt entitled to administer and divide the goods of the hospital was understandable: donations were addressed to "you, the brothers of the hospital of the *malsani*."[127]

The situation became no clearer as the confraternal character of the house intensified in the second half of the twelfth century. By the 1160s both the lepers and those who assisted them were called brothers and sisters, and a remarkable document of 1164 reveals the acceptance of a couple into a confraternal relationship with the house. On a Monday in June Count Riprandus of the Gandolfingi dal Palazzo and his wife Garscenda made a sizable donation to the hospital. The following day, in the church of Santa Croce and in the presence of "many lepers," the count and countess "were accepted as brother and sister of the house of the lepers."[128] Donations and sales continued to be made to the brothers and sisters of the hospital, and in the early thirteenth century the lepers again protested that they owned the property given to Santa Croce.[129]

Throughout the twelfth century the hospital was run by lay persons. Not until 1156 do we find a cleric associated with Santa Croce. This priest, named Lemizo, was a constant witness to the transactions of the house from 1156 to his death in 1171.[130] Lemizo, however, appears only as a witness: the business of the house was still being transacted by lay persons.[131] In addition to Crescentius mentioned above, a certain Adam son

126. *ASVR*, Istituto Esposti, nos. 5, 6, and 1 app.
127. "Vos fratres ospitalis malsanorum per misso vestro . . ." *ASVR*, Ospitale Civico, no. 75 (document 2).
128. ". . . in ecclesia sancte crucis ante malsanos predictos multos, dominus Riprandus et eius uxor suscepti sunt in fratrem et sororem domus malsanorum" *ASVR*, Instituto Esposti, no. 9.
129. In the early thirteenth century the bishop and the commune forced the lepers of various small hospitals to join the hospital of SS. Jacopo e Lazaro della Tomba. The lepers resented being deprived of the property given to them, "malsanis et pro malsanis". See Giuseppina de Sandre Gasparini, "L'assistenza ai lebbrosi nel movimento religioso dei primi decenni del duecento veronese: Uomini e fatti," *Viridarium floridum* (Padua, 1984), pp. 25–59.
130. *ASVR*, S. Silvestro, no. 9 app.
131. Only at the very end of the twelfth century do priests begin to act in the name of the *malsani*. In 1183 a priest named Crescentius bought a piece of land for the church (*pro ecclesia*) but

of Sparello bought lands as a *misso* of the *malsani* in 1141.[132] A document of 1149 styled John as "gastaldus" of the *malsani* of Santa Croce and "gastaldus" of the poor.[133] By the 1160s the hospital had a "custos et rector," a *gastaldus*, a treasurer (*massarius*), a warehouse keeper (*canevarius*), a keybearer (*clavigerus*), and a notary.[134] By the end of the twelfth century these lay persons assisting the lepers were called *conversi*.[135] Just as the lay *conversi* of Benedictine monasteries hoped to share in the spiritual benefits of the monks by supporting their religious life, so these lay persons hoped to share the spiritual benefits of the poor lepers by supporting them.

This suggests a very different notion of the religious life. To be poor and infirm was a religious life, a Christ-like life. While the monks of the early Middle Ages lived a religious life by leaving the world and praying, the lepers of Santa Croce lived a religious life by being poor and sick, by being a suffering presence in the Christian community. They did in fact provide a new spiritual center for the Christian community of Verona. Bishop Tebaldus in 1141 decreed that every year on the anniversary of the consecration of Santa Croce or within its octave "all Christian men and women should peacefully and devoutly come [to the church of Santa Croce] to pray and to ask forgiveness for their infirmities and they should offer something of their goods to the charity of the brothers and the poor and sick."[136]

The bishop's invitation to all Christians draws attention to another important aspect of the new spirituality Santa Croce represents: it was radically inclusive. By equating holiness with weakness and poverty, rather than with ascetic virtuosity and learning, it offered all Christians an opportunity to achieve spiritual perfection. This was a notable departure from the exclusivity that characterized religious institutions and theories of spiritual perfection in the early Middle Ages. Ratherius of Verona, in his *Praeloquia*, was one of the earliest theologians to envision, at least theoretically, forms of spiritual perfection lay persons could attain.[137] Two cen-

---

not until 1199 did a priest act "on account and in the name of" (*vice et nomine*) Santa Croce. ASVR, Istituto Esposti, nos. 23 and 32.

132. *ASVR*, Ospitale Civico, no. 75.

133. *ASVR*, Istituto Esposti, no. 1 app.

134. *ASVR*, Istituto Esposti, nos. 7, 9, 12, 17.

135. The term appears for the first time in a document dated 2 November 1199, *ASVR*, Istituto Esposti, no. 32.

136. *ASVR*, S. Silvestro, no. 9 app.

137. Ilarino da Milano, "La spiritualità dei laici nei *Praeloquia* di Raterio di Verona," *Raterio da Verona* (Todi, 1973), pp. 35–93, especially p. 75 et seq.

turies later, with the emergence of institutions like Santa Croce, the pursuit
of holiness became more than just a theoretical possibility for all Christians.

⌐⌐ The institutions of the religious life, and the ideals to which they
⌐⌐ were devoted, changed in Verona over the eleventh and early twelfth
centuries. Before 1000 Benedictine monasticism, its life of prayer and
learning, was the religious life. By 1150 traditional Benedictine monasticism had company in Verona. There were new congregations of Benedictines like the Vallombrosians, who championed a stricter interpretation of
the Benedictine Rule and had both spiritual and political ties outside the
diocese. There were those like the regular canons of San Giorgio who
abandoned the rule altogether. They sought greater freedom to move in
the world and to comfort its poor. They accomplished reform. There were
also new hospitals for the wretched, for poor and sick lepers. These stood
as pitiful reminders of every Christian's infirmities and called fellow Christians to charity. In 1150 there was a greater diversity in both the structures
and visions of the religious life.

These religious houses, we must recall, still constituted only a small
percentage of the institutions which comprised the Veronese Church. But
the influence of the spirituality that informed the new institutions, and of
the new houses themselves, is evident in the Veronese Church as a whole.

The prestige accorded the leaders of these new interpretations of the
religious life is one measure of this influence. When arbiters were needed
to sit in judgment upon the religious lives of others, the prior of the regular
canons at San Giorgio in Braida and the abbot of the Vallombrosian monastery of Santissima Trinità were often chosen.[138] In a rancorous contest of
more than five years (1179–1184) between the monastery of Santa Maria in
Organo and the clergy of two of her subject urban churches, Santa Maria
Antica and Santa Margarita, the prior of San Giorgio was called upon to
mediate the dispute.[139] Both the prior of San Giorgio and the abbot of

138. Both San Giorgio in Braida and Santissima Trinità were under papal protection, but by 1175
so too were eight other institutions, and by the end of the century these were joined by seven
others. Something more than their connection to the Holy See is behind their choice as
arbiters.

139. Kehr, IP 7.1: 253–55. This controversy not only raged for five years but resulted in
accusations of book stealing! In dispute was the right of the clergy of both these churches to
elect other priests and clerics to their number. The prior and the Holy See ultimately upheld

Santissima Trinità, in another example, were sent by Pope Celestine III to adjudicate a dispute in 1191 between the cathedral canons of Padua and the abbot of Santa Maria di Praglia.[140] Common people as well as popes also seemed to see the leaders of these two institutions as particularly holy and wise. In 1149, Isachinus left his goods to his three sons, but instructed his wife Nigra that if his sons should die without heirs, she should offer these things for the good of his soul "with the counsel of the abbot of Santissima Trinità and the prior of San Giorgio."[141]

The naming of churches throughout the Veronese diocese also attests to the wide influence of the new spirituality. Churches continued to be consecrated to monastic saints. Saint Martin of Tours became even more popular than he had been in the early Middle Ages, and churches were also dedicated to Saint Anthony, Saint Benedict, and Saint John Cassian. Moreover, several foundations were consecrated to specifically eremitic saints. Before 1021 a church was dedicated to Saint Leonard, a sixth-century hermit who became extremely popular throughout Europe in the eleventh century. Most of the lives written of him date from this period.[142] Another Veronese church was consecrated in the twelfth century to Saint Giles, a hermit who became associated with the Camaldoli movement.[143] Probably most revealing, however, is the interest shown in the twelfth century in an early Veronese bishop, Mauro. Bishop of Verona from 610 to 622, Mauro renounced the see to become a hermit in the mountains. Not until the twelfth century was a church built in his honor, and in the same period his name was added to the liturgical calendar of the cathedral.[144] Bishop Mauro had more appeal to the twelfth century than to his own times. Although Verona was not one of the leading centers of the eremitical movements of the eleventh and twelfth centuries, the ideals of these movements clearly inspired the Veronese.

The naming of churches in the diocese in the eleventh and twelfth centuries also reveals a new compassion for the weak, the sick, and the suffering. Most early medieval churches were named after martyrs, apos-

---

the clergy's right to elect and the abbot of Santa Maria in Organo's right to confirm their choices.

140. Kehr, IP 7.1: 170–71.

141. ASV, Fondo Veneto, no. 7026.

142. David Hugh Farmer, The Oxford Dictionary of Saints (Oxford, 1987), p. 264.

143. Annales Camaldulenses 1: 181–82.

144. Antonio Spagnolo, "Tre calendarii medioevali veronesi," AMAV 90 (1913–14): 177, 213; Meersseman, L'orazionale, pp. 20, 128–29.

tles, or bishops. While such saints remained popular protectors, the Blessed Virgin became the most favored patron of eleventh and twelfth century foundations.[145] Mary was the great intercessor, special protectress of the weak and powerless.[146] Two churches in this period were also named for Lazarus, patron of the poor and sick.[147] The dedications of several new churches—notably Santa Croce and San Sepolcro—also reveal a new feeling for the suffering of Christ.[148]

By the mid-twelfth century, the Veronese Church had new spiritual leaders and a new spirituality. Both the institutional structures and the ideals of religious life were more varied than before. Benedictine monasticism continued to play an important and respected role in the diocese, while new institutions emerged that were more concerned with charity than with liturgy. These new visions of the religious life and the more flexible institutional forms they developed set important precedents and patterns for the development of the religious life in the thirteenth century. The arrival of Francis of Assisi outside the Porta San Fermo in 1220 astonished few in Verona, for poverty had been an important element in religious life for close to a century.[149]

145. Nearly half (48%) of the titled churches founded before the millennium were named for martyrs or apostles. From 1000 to 1150, dedications of churches to the Virgin were the most numerous, accounting for close to a quarter (23%) of all foundations in the period.

146. Jean Leclercq et al., A History of Christian Spirituality (London, 1968), pp. 250–54.

147. Many medieval leper hospitals were named for Lazarus, but for the fictitious Lazarus of the parable of Dives and Lazarus (Luke 16: 19–31) rather than Lazarus of Bethany, brother of Martha and Mary. Farmer, Dictionary, pp. 259–60.

148. Étienne Delaruelle, "Le crucifix dans la piété populaire et dans l'art, du VIe au Xe siècle," and "La vie commune des clercs et la spiritualité populaire au XIe siècle," in La piété populaire au moyen âge (Turin, 1975), pp. 27–42, 89–91. The cross was also a highly significant symbol in the Milanese radical reform movement called the pataria. See Cinzio Violante, "I laici nel movimento patarino," in I laici nella «societas Christiana» dei secoli XI e XII (Milan, 1968), p. 661.

149. Herbert Grundmann in his classic study of medieval religious movements emphasized the importance of "Christ-like poverty" in the twelfth century, and increasingly scholars have been forced to reassess the novelty of the thirteenth-century mendicant orders. Lester K. Little's recent study of confraternities in Bergamo, for example, highlights continuities between the twelfth and thirteenth centuries: "From the point of view of Pope Innocent III, the appearance at the papal court in 1210 of Francis of Assisi with eleven companions seeking approval of their way of life was not startling or even particularly innovative." Lester K. Little, Liberty, Charity, Fraternity (Northampton, Mass., and Bergamo, 1988), pp. 39, 57; Herbert Grundmann, Religiöse Bewegungen im Mittelalter (Berlin, 1935), pp. 13–50. The different approaches taken to the reevaluation of thirteenth century mendicancy in light of twelfth-century spirituality are well represented in La povertà del secolo XII e Francesco d'Assisi (citation above, note 112).

The forces behind the manifold changes in religious life were complex. The increased affluence of Veronese society made the foundation of new institutions possible and freed more individuals to dedicate themselves to God. This same affluence probably contributed to the changed character of Veronese Christianity. When so many found themselves prosperous, poverty surely seemed less an enduring fact of life and more a lack of fortune to be pitied. Like the spirituality it spawned, this awareness of change only intensified: a massive wheel of fortune came to dominate the facade of San Zeno in the late twelfth century. But who was most deeply moved by the discomfort or anxiety that change brought? Who used their affluence to found or support new religious institutions?

# 4 THE SUPPORT OF ECCLESIASTICAL INSTITUTIONS

**T**HUS far, the needs and desires of lay persons have remained a muted presence just below the surface of our narrative.[1] Lay people built those many new churches that our graphs, tables, and maps too dispassionately record. Their concerns and complaints surely prompted reforms, even if their discontent lacked the violent drama of Milan's *pataria* movement, in which lay people and the lower clergy boycotted and even forcibly removed simoniacal and concubinary priests. Lay people gave gifts of land and money to churches and, by the early twelfth century at places like Santa Croce, they undertook bold new charitable initiatives. The relationship between the laity and the evolution of the Veronese Church merits closer scrutiny. To what extent did the actions and ideas of lay persons promote or influence ecclesiastical change in the eleventh and early twelfth centuries? Before attempting to answer this question, we must consider several methodological problems.

First, in the period under consideration, lay persons and clerics never constituted clearly demarcated social groups; and what distinguished one from the other changed over the eleventh and early twelfth centuries. All clerics began their lives as lay persons and most retained ties with their families after ordination. At the beginning of our period, most clerics had their own families (wives and children); they lived with lay persons. Edu-

---

1. Lay persons are those who are not specially consecrated or vowed to the service of God. This definition, which will be used here, emerged over the central Middle Ages in relation to the developing concept of "cleric." In this period, "cleric" was used in two primary senses. In a strict sense, it denoted someone who had received minor orders (a secular cleric). It was used in a much broader fashion regarding the privileges clerical status conferred, and in this sense included all religious (and often pilgrims, penitents, crusaders, and students). Here, I will use the terms "cleric," "clergy," and "clerical" in this broad sense to indicate all those who through vows or consecration specially devoted themselves to the service of God. DDC 3: 828–30; 6: 328. On the emergence of the categories "clergy" and "laity," see also I. S. Robinson, "Gregory VII and the Soldiers of Christ," *History* 58 (1973): 169–92.

cation, the adoption of the communal life, and new expectations of clerical behavior slowly made the secular clergy more distinct from the laity over the eleventh and early twelfth centuries. At the same time, however, the boundary between the religious and the laity was becoming much more permeable than it had been in the early Middle Ages, when to be religious was to be a monk or nun. The new regular canons were very active in the world. The status of both the lepers and those who cared for them at Santa Croce was particularly indeterminate: the bishop clearly considered them a religious group, but it is unclear if the brothers and sisters actually took solemn vows. One must keep in mind, therefore, that the concerns of clergy and laity were not always different, and that the amount of contact between clergy and laity facilitated constant exchanges of views and values.

Given the nebulous boundaries between these groups, a focus on institutions helps clarify our analysis. By examining the relations of lay persons with ecclesiastical institutions we can perhaps gain some insight into both their religiosity and their influence on the Church. These relations, of course, were of many different kinds. The most important relations, sacramental and devotional encounters, rarely left traces in the documentary record. Nor were relations of a more individual or personal nature recorded: the charismatic attraction of a particular preacher, the veneration accorded a long life of piety, or the animosity provoked by an arrogant or domineering priest. Almost all of the surviving documentation describes economic relations: sales, rentals, and exchanges of real property. But there is one type of economic transaction in which the relations between lay persons and ecclesiastical institutions included a spiritual dimension: the material support of churches through donations.[2]

Donations were public acts transferring property, but the language with which they were transacted indicates spiritual or religious motivation. Donors asserted that they were moved by concern for the well-being of their souls and those of their relatives. Certainly, worldly motivations also played a role. Social, economic, and political concerns were often advanced through gifts to ecclesiastical institutions.[3] But the existence, even

2. I include in "donations" transfers of wealth effected both through charters of donation and through testamentary bequests.

3. Cinzio Violante, "Nobiltà e chiese in Pisa durante i secoli XI e XII: Il monastero di S. Matteo (Prime ricerche)," in *Adel und Kirche*, ed. Josef Fleckenstein and Karl Schmid (Fribourg, 1968), pp. 259–79; Barbara H. Rosenwein, *To Be the Neighbor of Saint Peter* (Ithaca, N.Y., 1989), especially pp. 49–77.

The distribution of donations varies across time, but these changes do not indicate changes

importance, of other motivating factors should not lead us to discount the spiritual concerns voiced in these documents. The 241 surviving donations to Veronese ecclesiastical institutions and by Veronese donors from the late eighth to the mid-twelfth century provide precious information about lay religiosity and ecclesiastical change.

They also allow us to examine an entire community and the distribution of its donations among all ecclesiastical institutions. Most studies of benefactions concentrate on one foundation or order.[4] This approach illuminates lay generosity as seen from the point of view of the recipient. It obscures the charitable activities that the same donors directed toward other foundations, and those of the institution's neighbors who were not its patrons. The study of pious gifts has also tended to focus on religious (regular) institutions: Benedictine monasteries, houses of regular canons, the mendicant orders. Donations to institutions of the secular clergy have received scant attention.[5] By looking at all ecclesiastical institutions, secular and religious, and the choices of an entire community of donors, it is possible to illuminate broad changes in ecclesiastical donations over a long period of time.

Taking such an approach also provides us a new angle on a recurrent historiographical issue. Most studies of donations to ecclesiastical institutions have been concerned with the relationship between social change and religious innovation. Many scholars, for example, have suggested that

---

in the strength of religiosity. Changes in the number of donations correlate strongly with the survival of documents in general (the more documents, the more donations). The correlation coefficient is .7 for the number of surviving donations compared with the total number of surviving documents by quarter century. Donations constitute only 13% of all surviving Veronese documents before 1150, a much lower percentage than one might find in French cartularies. The difference is explained by the large number of leases, exchanges, and sales generally found in Italian archival collections of charters.

4. Good examples of this approach are Barbara H. Rosenwein, *Rhinoceros Bound: Cluny in the Tenth Century* (Philadelphia, 1982); Penelope Johnson, *Prayer, Patronage, and Power: The Abbey of la Trinité, Vendôme, 1032–1187* (New York, 1981); and Bennett D. Hill, *English Cistercian Monasteries and Their Patrons in the Twelfth Century* (Urbana, 1968).

5. While one of the great virtues of Constance Bouchard's recent book is its focus on an entire region rather than on a single house, her main interest is still monasteries: Constance Brittain Bouchard, *Sword, Miter, and Cloister: Nobility and the Church in Burgundy, 980–1198* (Ithaca, N.Y., 1987). Canonries of secular clergy have received some general attention, but their patrons have not been much studied. M. Giusti, "Le canoniche della città e diocesi di Lucca al tempo della riforma gregoriana," *Studi gregoriani* 3 (1948): 321–67; *La vita comune del clero nei secoli XI e XII* (Milan, 1962).

the new urban classes (merchants, notaries) and noble families that emerged in the central Middle Ages were responsible for the success of new religious orders such as the Augustinian canons and the mendicants. The urban ministries of these orders and their world-embracing visions of the Christian life supposedly appealed to the nouveaux riches.[6] Verona did experience both social diversification and the emergence of new religious foundations, but the patterns of relationships between Veronese donors and the ecclesiastical institutions they supported suggest a revision of this thesis.[7] Close scrutiny of Veronese donors and their charitable choices reveals no clear connection between new social groups and new religious houses. It does, however, indicate that new economic practices were crucial to religious innovation. Furthermore, the most significant shift in donations was not in favor of new religious houses but in favor of the secular clergy.

Two of the most obvious changes from the early Middle Ages to the mid-twelfth century are increased social diversity among donors and more complex patterns of bequests. In early medieval Verona those wealthy enough to act as donors were few, and they fall into four distinct

6. I mention only a few notable examples. R. W. Southern has argued that "new families of modest means" were behind the success of the Augustinian canons: *Western Society and the Church in the Middle Ages* (Harmondsworth, 1970), pp. 245–50. Lester K. Little has also suggested a connection between the new social groups of the central Middle Ages and the new forms of religious life born in this period: *Religious Poverty and the Profit Economy in Medieval Europe* (Ithaca, N.Y., 1978), pp. 132–33, 205. Daniel R. Lesnick links the urban *popolo grasso* and *popolo* of Florence to the Dominican and Franciscan orders: *Preaching in Medieval Florence: The Social World of Franciscan and Dominican Spirituality* (Athens, Ga., 1989). John B. Freed similarly posits a connection between new social groups—the new lower or ministerial nobility and urban patricians—and the friars in Germany: *The Friars and German Society in the Thirteenth Century* (Cambridge, Mass., 1977), pp. 109–34. Usually the support of these new social groups for new religious institutions is measured through the social character of an institution's membership and its benefactors. Southern, in the case of Augustinian canons, gauges support through benefactions. Lesnick uses both membership and testamentary bequests, as well as the location of mendicant foundations and confraternity affiliations. Southern, *Western Society*, pp. 245–48; Lesnick, *Preaching*, pp. 46–62.

7. Most studies linking social and economic change to religious change have focused upon the thirteenth century. The documentation available to scholars from this period is certainly more abundant than the materials surviving for the eleventh and twelfth centuries. If, however, there is a connection between social and economic change and religious change in medieval Europe, it seems important to scrutinize the period when intense social and economic change began.

groups: kings and emperors, the titled Frankish nobility, wealthy Lombard and Roman families, and clerics.[8] Furthermore, each of these groups had well-circumscribed spheres of generosity.

Kings and emperors were significant donors making large gifts: churches with all their possessions, entire manors, and fiscal rights. While several major Veronese ecclesiastical institutions received imperial donations,[9] imperial generosity was focused in a special way on the church and monastery of the city's patron saint, San Zeno. Charlemagne and his son Pippin rebuilt and reendowed the church and monastery in the early ninth century; their successors confirmed and increased San Zeno's patrimony.[10] Until the crisis of the *regnum* in the early tenth century, the emperors were the monastery's only patrons.[11] San Zeno was clearly the emperor's church.

Verona's titled Frankish nobility at first endowed monasteries outside the Veronese diocese, such as the abbey of San Silvestro at Nonantola and the monastery of San Zaccaria in Venice,[12] but in the late tenth century they began to support the city's cathedral chapter.[13] The city's wealthy Lombard and Roman families tended to make their donations to the Veronese Benedictine monastery of Santa Maria in Organo. Their gifts were generally smaller than those made by the Frankish nobility and of scattered lands rather than whole manors. A certain Illasus, for example, gave Santa Maria

---

8. A Frankish nobility formed in Verona as Carolingian rule was established in the late eighth century. They were the vassals of the emperor and came to control vast expanses of land through this association. They are identifiable by their profession of Salic law. This relatively new nobility superseded an older aristocracy of Lombard and Roman origin (professing these laws). For the ethnic mixture in northern Italy during this period, see Chris Wickham, *Early Medieval Italy* (Totowa, N.J., 1981), pp. 64–79.

9. The Benedictine monasteries of Santa Maria in Organo and San Fermo received imperial donations, as did the cathedral canons. *CDV* 1 nos. 122, 228; 2 nos. 11, 15, 17, 73, 202, 250; G. B. Biancolini, *Chiese*, 1: 329.

10. Charlemagne and Pippin: *CDV* 1 nos. 76, 77, 78, 80, 81, 84, 92, 93; Louis the Pious, *CDV* 1 no. 117; Lothar I, *CDV* 1 nos. 142, 157, 160, 162; Louis II, *CDV* 1 nos. 190, 209, 242; Carloman, *CDV* 1 no. 266.

11. Only after the decline of Carolingian rule in the early tenth century did the monastery begin to receive gifts from local nobles: *CDV* 2 nos. 53, 107, 108, 206.

12. Count Anselm made several large donations to Nonantola in the early tenth century, *CDV* 2 nos. 98, 106; Count Ingelfredus and the Marquis Milo supported San Zaccaria, *CDV* 2 nos. 126, 255.

13. *ACV*, II–4–1r (AC 68 m2 n5), III–5–6r (BC 36 m3 n4); *ASVR*, uncatalogued MSS, Dionisi Piomarta, August 987.

in Organo half-fields (his brother Gauspert held the other halves) in four different communities in the northern mountainous region of the diocese.[14]

Clerics as a group also followed distinctive patterns of giving, founding scole for clerics and xenodochia for the poor. Archdeacon Pacificus in 844, Bishop Billongus in 846, Bishop Notker in 921, Bishop John of Pavia in 922, and the vicedominus Dagibert in 931 instituted xenodochia in the city of Verona "for the relief of Christ's poor."[15] A scola emerged at a church built by Bishop Audo in Sezano (just north of the city). Other clerical donations supported scole at the suburban churches of San Pietro in Castello and Santo Stefano.[16]

Several patterns emerge in the charitable choices made by these groups in the early Middle Ages. All donors explicitly stated that their gifts were made for the good of their own souls and those of their relatives. When they made a donation, they expected to be commemorated with prayers and largess to the poor, and donors were serious about getting what they paid for. Several stipulated that if their property was misused and their pious wishes unfulfilled, the gift should either be returned to the heirs or transferred to another religious authority.[17] Most donors narrowly focused their gifts on one or two institutions, donating land and other immobiles (houses, mills).

While concern to have prayers and good works offered for the donor's soul lay behind all benefactions, lay and clerical patrons in Verona sought to achieve these ends through different means. Lay donors showed an overwhelming preference for Benedictine monasteries. They either made donations to established monasteries or founded their own.[18] In the eyes of the laity, these institutions were the best places to ask for prayers and to have largess distributed. The clergy, however, tended to establish their own institutions—xenodochia and scole—for the same purposes. One could see in this an attempted vindication of their own status in a society that saw monks as living the most perfect Christian life. Or, perhaps they simply felt more confident that their fellow secular clerics would remember them

14. CDV 1 no. 144. Other similar donations: CDV 1 nos. 114 and 145; ASVR, S. Maria in Organo, no. 14.
15. CDV 1 nos. 176, 182; 2 nos. 177, 186, 214.
16. CDV 1 nos. 196, 197, 200, 201, 208, 217; CDV 2 nos. 223, 247; ASVR, S. Stefano, no. 2.
17. CDV 2 nos. 199, 214; ACV, II–4–6r (BC 45 mp n10).
18. CDV 1 no. 72; 2 no. 256.

with prayers. In either case, while the early medieval clergy may have been much like the laity in their everyday lives, their bequests reveal different strategies for securing eternal life.

After 1000, these clear and fairly simple early patterns of patronage broke down, as both the Veronese Church and Veronese society became more complex and finely articulated. The ecclesiastical landscape became more varied, with the foundation of numerous new churches and religious houses. At the same time, many new groups emerged in Veronese society: merchants, urban functionaries, artisans, castellans, and affluent members of rural communities. A close scrutiny of donations after 1000 from two different vantage points shows no clear connection between these new groups and new visions of the religious life. Let us first look at the social character of donations to innovative ecclesiastical institutions and then at the charitable choices made by these new donors.

Verona's most innovative new religious institution in this period was the church and leper hospital of Santa Croce, which was founded in the third decade of the twelfth century. Santa Croce appears to have gotten its start through small cash bequests and alms, and it would not be unreasonable to think that some of these nameless petty donors were from the lower social orders. But Santa Croce also received donations from the old comital nobility and from leading imperial vassals (*capitanei*, or captains). Count Riprand of the Gandolfingi da Palazzo made a sizable donation and even became a *conversus* of Santa Croce in 1164.[19] His father, Vibert, was among the leading citizens present at the consecration of Santa Croce in 1141. In addition to the count, two captains were present: Albert Tenca of the Erzoni (later rector of the commune) and Tebaldus Musio of the Turrisendi. Crescenzius de Bonzeno of the mercantile Crescenzi family attended, as did the knights Godo of the Avvocati family and Porcetus.[20] Another of the captains of the city, Odelricus Saketus, made his will and died among the lepers at Santa Croce in 1156. He left them several pieces of land. Odelricus had become lord of Zevio as a vassal of Duke Henry of Bavaria in 1139 and was a consul of the Veronese commune in 1140.[21] Santa Croce's supporters were drawn from all levels of Veronese society, from

19. *ASVR*, Istituto Esposti, no. 9.
20. *ASVR*, S. Silvestro, no. 5 app.
21. *ASVR*, S. Silvestro, no. 9 app.; Andrea Castagnetti, *La società veronese nel medioevo II: Ceti e famiglie dominanti nella prima età comunale* (Verona, 1987), p. 17.

counts and captains to members of mercantile families and nameless almsgivers.

This diversity in the social status of donors is also evident in another new ecclesiastical institution, the regular canonry of San Giorgio in Braida. Many of the city's elite supported the house. Alberic da Lendinari and Gerard da Nogarole, both captains with close ties to the powerful d'Este family, and Basafolia, a member of the Turrisendi family, witnessed Bishop Bernard's decree establishing the canonry.[22] San Giorgio also received a large bequest in the will of Isachinus, a relative by marriage to the comital family of the Gandolfingi da Palazzo.[23] In addition to these elites, castellans of Vigasio and Sabbion made donations to San Giorgio, as did even lesser men who made their gifts with the consent of their lord.[24] The class of urban judicial functionaries is also well represented among the canons' supporters. Benenatus *prudens iuris* made a donation of land in 1131 and served as a witness to other transactions of the house.[25] Milo *iudex de Verona* also left a bequest to San Giorgio.[26] Moreover, the regular canons attracted bequests from many of the blacksmiths (*ferrarii*) who populated the neighborhood around the church. In 1148 Algo son of Aldo the blacksmith and his son Henry made a donation of several pieces of land and two cows to San Giorgio. They made the gift for their souls and for another (unnamed) son of Algo who was a canon of San Giorgio.[27]

Verona's most novel religious institutions drew support from all levels of Veronese society; their appeal was broader than any one social group. At the same time, if we look at the individual donations made by members of new social groups, such as merchants and judicial functionaries, no affinity for religious novelty is evident. The city's wealthiest merchant, John Monticoli, chose to enrich the old Benedictine foundation of Nonantola as well as the newer Benedictine monastery of San Nazaro.[28] Judges and urban functionaries also reveal conservative tastes in their donations. Aldegerius

22. *ASV*, Fondo Veneto, no. 6886.

23. *ASV*, Fondo Veneto, no. 7026. The will was redacted in the "palacio" of Count Riprand of the Gandolfingi da Palazzo. The count's wife Garsenda was the sister of Isachinus.

24. *ASV*, Fondo Veneto, nos. 6888, 6891, 6912, and no. 6928, wherein Vivianus and Albiza of Illasi made a donation "with assent from our lord Niticherus" ("per consensum Nitichero seniore nostro").

25. *ASV*, Fondo Veneto, nos. 6899, 6903.

26. *ASV*, Fondo Veneto, no. 7035.

27. *ASV*, Fondo Veneto, no. 6970; no. 7000 records another gift from a blacksmith, Crescentio *ferrario*, in 1155.

28. *ASVR*, S. Silvestro, no. 189 app*, doc. 2; SS. Nazaro e Celso, no. 817.

*vicedominus* and his sons donated land to San Nazaro, as did the *iudex* Sentichus and his brother.[29] Even if one considers exchanges of land, which by law had to be favorable to ecclesiastical institutions, Verona's notaries and judges appear in relations with Benedictine houses.[30]

Clearly, then, the new social groups that came to prominence through economic change and urban growth were very conservative as ecclesiastical donors. Here, an essential but often neglected aspect of ecclesiastical donations deserves emphasis. Traditionally great nobles, the early medieval rich and famous, acted as patrons. The new families of the eleventh and twelfth centuries, those who amassed fortunes through trade or rural lordships, aspired to nobility. Ecclesiastical donations were a traditional means of asserting social prominence and displaying wealth. It is then not entirely surprising that "new men" made donations to well-established Benedictine houses. The highest nobility traditionally favored these institutions, and those hoping to join these elites mimicked them. Those with grand social aspirations were not big supporters of innovation.

Those a notch lower on the social pyramid—artisans, poor knights, and the wealthier residents of outlying communities—acted differently as donors, but they too showed no marked preference for novel religious institutions. Artisans gravitated toward churches in their neighborhoods. Eghinus *faber*, for example, made a donation to the chapel of San Giorgio in Salsis, his local church.[31] The blacksmiths outside the Porta Santo Stefano supported either San Giorgio in Braida or Santo Stefano.[32]

Those who did not even identify themselves with a patronymic (most likely an indication of low status) usually made donations either to a church in their community or to a monastery that held lands and exerted seigneurial authority in the area.[33] This pattern is particularly strong for the

---

29. *ASVR*, SS. Nazaro e Celso, no. 806 and no. 27.

30. *ASVR*, Ospitale Civico, no. 57; SS. Nazaro e Celso, no. 544.

31. *ACV*, I–5–2r (BC 39 m2 n8).

32. *ASV*, Fondo Veneto, nos. 6970, 7000; *ASVR*, S. Giovanni in Valle, no. 1.

33. Urban residents to urban institutions: *ASVR*, S. Maria in Organo, nos. 28 and 52; S. Stefano, no. 25; *ACV*, I–5–6v (AC 57 m5 n115). In 1051 a couple identifying themselves only as Ingelbert, called Curto, and Bona made a gift to San Zeno. They were inhabitants of San Vito, where the monastery held seigneurial rights and much land. The couple retained usufruct for life. *ASVR*, Ospitale Civico, no. 41. An inhabitant of Colognola identified only as Iso made a donation to San Nazaro, one of the most prominent landholders in the area. *ASVR*, SS. Nazaro e Celso, no. 315.

monastery of San Nazaro. Many of its donors who were not members of leading families were residents in the neighborhood around the monastery or in one of its rural communities.[34] Often residents of these rural communities made their donations to the local church, which was under the authority of the abbot of San Nazaro. In 1146, for example, five brothers (Lugnus, Vivianus, John, Tedolfus, and Boniface), inhabitants of Soave, made a donation to the church of Santa Maria in Soave, which was governed by San Nazaro.[35]

Other evidence indicates that local churches were in fact becoming focal points for a more active lay piety. A document of 1131 reveals the first lay confraternity in Verona, the *convivium* of the urban church of Santa Felicita. Its *gastaldus* was a tailor; another one of the "brothers" of the *convivium* was a rope maker. They acted with the consent of their brothers and "for the honor and aid of the church of Santa Felicita."[36]

This suggests that geographical proximity to a church or monastery, perhaps contact with its clergy, was an important factor directing both the piety and the gifts of less wealthy donors. The very wealthy, especially the highest nobility, often endowed institutions distant from their family seats. For these, the type of institution may have been a decisive factor, and Benedictine monasteries remained popular with the high nobility. Lesser donors seem to have stayed closer to home. They endowed institutions they knew well, those whose clerics offered them the sacraments or whose monks frequented their communities on the abbot's business. The pres-

34. Lanfranc and Emeltruda "living outside Porta Organo" made a donation in 1082. *ASVR*, SS. Nazaro e Celso, no. 628. The monastery also seems to have drawn many of its recruits from the neighborhood just outside the Porta Organo. Gisla, who identified herself as the sister of Ardicius, a monk of San Nazaro, donated twelve pieces of land to the monastery in 1147. She lived "in the aforesaid [neighborhood of] Porta Organo" ("in suprascripta porta [Organi]"). *ASVR*, SS. Nazaro e Celso, no. 641. In 1158 Vivianus, brother of Mark, "from the same [neighborhood of] Porta Santa Maria," donated "myself to God and to the aforesaid monastery [San Nazaro] with all that I have." *ASVR*, SS. Nazaro e Celso, no. 2232.

35. *ASVR*, SS. Nazaro e Celso, no. 1215; another example, no. 630 to San Briccio in Lavagno.

36. *ASV*, Fondo Veneto, no. 6896; Gerolamo Biscaro, "Attraverso le carte di S. Giorgio in Braida di Verona esistenti nell'Archivio Vaticano," *Atti del Reale istituto veneto di scienze, lettere, ed arti* 92 (1932–33), 990–95; on lay confraternities generally see Lester K. Little, *Liberty, Charity, Fraternity* (Northampton, Mass., and Bergamo, 1988), and André Vauchez, *Les laïcs au moyen âge* (Paris, 1987), pp. 93–122. Donations also suggest that collegially organized *plebes* in the diocese of Lucca were becoming "new foci of piety" in the eleventh century: see Duane J. Osheim, *An Italian Lordship* (Berkeley and Los Angeles, 1977), p. 22.

ence exerted by an institution, the impression it made within a community, seems to have prompted those with lesser means to donate.

As Veronese society became more affluent in the eleventh and twelfth centuries, even those who were not aristocrats had the resources to make donations. These new donors' gifts reveal a limited field of vision. Perhaps this was because of circumscribed mobility. An artisan or petty knight had little reason to roam, whereas merchants, notaries, and judges traveled widely in the practice of their professions. Perhaps, too, these lesser donors had more locally based aspirations. Rather than choosing a prestigious monastery where counts and captains made their gifts, they chose a church where their donation would bring them the respect of their immediate neighbors.

Although the new social groups of the central Middle Ages showed no preference for novel institutions, many of their economic practices were essential to religious innovation. The development of a much more sophisticated monetary economy aided the emergence of new ecclesiastical institutions and their new visions of the religious life.

The impact of the development of a monetary economy upon the financial support of ecclesiastical institutions is most evident in changing testamentary practices. In Verona, the early medieval pattern of leaving land to one or two ecclesiastical institutions gave way by the early twelfth century to that of leaving cash sums to many churches.[37] The 1147 will of

37. This change is not a mere artifact of shifts in notarial practice. In early medieval Veronese documents, individuals distributed their goods through an *ordinatio*, or *pagina ordinationis*. This form was used to leave real property as well as personal possessions and household goods. For example, Bishop Billongus's *ordinatio* (846) distributed lands and houses in "Gussenagia" and movables: gold, silver, money, a brass basin, a purse, linens, wools, silks, his carriages, horses (broken and unbroken), yoke-broken oxen, cows, pigs, sheep, grain, and wine. This documentary form endured through the eleventh century. In the early twelfth century, slight changes in formulary appear. The language used to convey the testator's wishes remained more or less the same, but notaries began redacting the document in the form of a *brevis*, or brief (a versatile form used for several purposes). More substantial changes occurred in the second half of the twelfth century, when these acts were first called *testamenta*. A Veronese notary in 1155 called one such document a "charter of testament and last will" ("cartula testamenti ultimeque voluntatis"). The testator no longer "ordered his goods" (*ordinavit bona sua*); from the mid-twelfth century he "made a testament" (*fecit testamentum*). The testament, like its predecessors the *ordinatio* and *brevis*, was used to convey both movable and immovable goods. *CDV* 1 no. 182; *ASV*, Fondo Veneto, nos. 6999, 7000.

Bacialertus, son of the ecclesiastical advocate (*causidicus*) Teuzo and an inhabitant of the city of Verona, is typical. He instructed that his shield and his silver cup should be sold and that the price should be offered for the good of his soul: ten pounds to the regular canonry of San Giorgio in Braida; five to the cathedral building fund, five to the urban church of San Salvar da Forgnano; three pounds each to the Benedictine monasteries of San Zeno, San Fermo, and Santissima Trinità; and three pounds apiece to two hospitals. Bacialertus left the rest of his goods to his son.[38]

The institutions designated were usually a mixture of old, new, secular, and religious. Ambroxius de Clavega (Chiavica) in 1145 left all lands and one hundred pounds to the monastery of San Nazaro. He instructed the abbot to distribute sums to four other Benedictine monasteries: twenty solidi (one pound) each to the old Benedictine houses of San Zeno and San Fermo, ten solidi to Santa Maria in Organo, and twenty to the new Vallombrosian monastery of Santissima Trinità. Ambroxius also favored the secular clergy and urban churches. He left one hundred solidi (five pounds) and land in Quinzano to the city's Congregation of secular clerics. He also left sums to the churches of Santa Maria alla Chiavica, Santa Margarita, San Pietro in Castello, San Giovanni in Valle, the church of the Holy Sepulcher, and San Michele. Finally, he asked that three pounds be given to the leper hospital at Santa Croce.[39] This mixture of Benedictine monasteries, urban churches, and hospitals was common.[40]

A number of things are significant about the change in the way the Veronese drew up their wills. First, the trend toward leaving donations to a wide variety of institutions suggests a certain ambivalence in the face of religious change. Donors reacted to the emergence of a great variety of new ecclesiastical institutions by spreading out their resources. The mixture of institutions patronized suggests an attempt to hedge one's bets, or amortize one's risk, by giving a little to every type of institution.

Second, this new testamentary pattern of scattering small donations in

38. *ASV*, Fondo Veneto, no. 6955.

39. *ASVR*, Clero Intrinseco, registro 12 (Ist. Ant. Reg. II), fol. 140. The value of the sums distributed here is modest. In the twelfth century, prices for a strip of arable land ranged from five to ten pounds; for a vineyard, from five to twenty-five pounds. The sums Ambroxius left were, for the most part, insufficient to purchase a piece of land.

40. Duane Osheim has found the same pattern at Lucca. He gives the example of the testament of Sassolino del fu Gherardo Sassi (1185) which left fifty-eight bequests, most between one and three pounds, "to nearly every church within the city, as well as to twelve monasteries and eight hospitals." Duane J. Osheim, *A Tuscan Monastery and Its Social World* (Rome, 1989), pp. 155–56.

cash reproduces the act of almsgiving. The will, more than being a final disposition of property, became a final dispersion of alms. Such use of the testamentary instrument as a formalized final almsgiving suggests the deep impact of the new spirituality of the twelfth century. As religious sentiment expressed new concern for the poor and sick of this world, those passing to the next assumed the posture of almsgivers in their final legal documents.[41]

Third, this strategy was made possible by the expansion of a money economy. Some testators seemed to have had a certain amount of wealth in cash at the writing of the will. Others left instructions as to what property should be converted to cash through sale. Bacialertus directed that his shield and cup should be sold; Bonus de Diraniola instructed that all his property should be sold after the death of his wife.[42] Not only did this practice stimulate the land market, but such gifts in cash also had distinct advantages for ecclesiastical institutions. A gift of property, to be of value, required a certain amount of administration on the part of the receiving institution, and properties far removed from the church or monastery's main holdings could be more trouble than they were worth. A gift of cash could be applied to a variety of needs, including the purchase of property to consolidate holdings.

Cash gifts, in fact, seem to have been crucial to the emergence of Verona's most novel religious institution of the twelfth century, Santa Croce. No patrimony was organized and donated to the church and hospital at its

41. Samuel K. Cohn, Jr., *Death and Property in Siena, 1205–1800* (Baltimore, 1988), discusses the disappearance of this testamentary practice of making numerous small bequests in cash. His thirteenth- and fourteenth-century Sienese evidence reveals even more highly fragmented bequests than those discussed here. Whereas twelfth-century Veronese wills left bequests to about a dozen institutions, thirteenth- and fourteenth-century Sienese wills left sums to between thirty and fifty institutions. Cohn shows how this "mendicant" pattern of scattering one's earthly goods across the ecclesiastical landscape in a myriad of testamentary bequests gave way to a "humanistic" approach. After the plague of 1363, the Sienese left larger sums to a few churches and chose to support ongoing institutions for social charity, such as dowry funds, rather than scatter alms indiscriminately to thousands of paupers. Cohn shows how this new pattern evinced concern to preserve the earthly memory of the individual, contrasting sharply with the "mendicant" obliteration of the self in the dissolution and distribution of one's goods at death. The Veronese evidence presented here demonstrates that this "mendicant" pattern appeared before the mendicants. Although it is related to the spirituality which reached its fullest development in the Franciscans, it is also related to the new variety of religious institutions and to greater economic sophistication.

42. *ASV*, Fondo Veneto, nos. 6955, 6999.

foundation, as was the case with traditional religious houses. The surviving documentation, for example, indicates no donations of land to Santa Croce in its first three decades.[43] Nearly all the documents of the hospital record cash purchases of land: representatives of the hospital bought property for the lepers in Montorio, Zevio, and Castelrotto.[44] Where did these representatives get the money to purchase a patrimony for the hospital? The hospital was receiving donations in cash from those Christian men and women Bishop Tebaldus had called upon to support the lepers' "holy charity" when he consecrated their church in 1141. We know that the *malsani* were remembered with sums in several wills: Ambroxius de Clavega, for example, left them three pounds, as did Zintilisia, wife of Tobaldus de Ara.[45] A purchase was made by the *gastaldus* of the hospital in 1161 with twenty-two pounds of denarii, "which Roland de Bussolengo and his wife Beatrix paid from their own denarii for the redemption of their souls." Roland and his wife were witnesses to this purchase made with the money they donated to Santa Croce.[46]

Cash was not the only aspect of the new mercantile economy that contributed to the development of Santa Croce. The house also entered into new kinds of property agreements. In 1154 Santa Croce's treasurer received a pledge of land to secure a risky purchase, and in 1167 a charter reveals the house involved in a collective ownership and rental arrangement with two other institutions.[47]

It is perhaps not surprising that a religious institution so novel in its interpretation of religious life and its mission as Santa Croce should also prove financially innovative. But the fact that a determined group of people who attracted alms and small cash gifts could progressively accumulate enough to buy a patrimony suggests that a monetary economy was conducive to the emergence of innovative religious institutions. Santa Croce emerged without being "founded" or endowed by a wealthy patron; the denarii of lesser donors were sufficient.

43. The first evidence of the hospital's existence comes in 1136, but it did not receive a donation of land until the will of Odelricus Saketus in 1156. *ASVR*, S. Silvestro, no. 9 app.

44. *ASVR*, S. Silvestro, no. 2 (1136); Istituto Esposti, no. 1 (1136); Ospitale Civico, no. 75 (1141); Istituto Esposti, no. 1 app. (1149), no. 5 (1153).

45. *ASVR*, Clero Intrinseco, registro 12 (Ist. Ant. Reg. II), fol. 140; *ASV*, Fondo Veneto, no. 7043.

46. *ASVR*, Istituto Esposti, no. 7.

47. *ASVR*, Istituto Esposti, no. 6; *ASV*, Fondo Veneto, no. 7121.

Before 1000, the ecclesiastical institutions receiving the largest number of donations were those favored by the laity, Benedictine monasteries. San Zeno and Santa Maria in Organo were Verona's most favored institutions. After the year 1000, with the emergence of a new variety of institutions for the religious life, these two venerable monasteries suffered a real decline in donations. Which institutions supplanted San Zeno and Santa Maria in Organo? New foundations for the religious life drew the support of wealthy donors, but the most significant shift in donations was toward the secular clergy and their institutions. This shift began in the last quarter of the eleventh century, the most intense period of the Gregorian reform movement, and became well established in the early twelfth century.

The impact of the investiture crisis on ecclesiastical donations is clearest in the chronology of benefactions to the emperor's church, San Zeno. The monastery received donations until 1068,[48] but then received no gifts or bequests for more than four decades. Small donations resumed in the second decade of the twelfth century, but San Zeno never recovered its earlier popularity.[49]

Not all Benedictine monasteries, however, suffered such a precipitous decline. The monastery of San Nazaro, founded in the early eleventh century and strongly supported by Verona's bishops, was increasingly favored by local donors. It consistently received gifts and bequests through the eleventh and twelfth centuries.[50] So too did several reformed institutions within the city: the regular canonry of San Giorgio in Braida and the Vallombrosian monastery of Santissima Trinità.[51] Several reformed monas-

---

48. *ASVR*, Ospitale Civico, nos. 19 (1004), 24 (1020), 36 (1040), 41 (1051); Orfanotrofio Femminile, no. 20 (1054); Ospitale Civico, nos. 42 (1056), 48 (1061), 49 (1062), 52 (1067), 51 (1068, to the "ospicium").

49. *ASVR*, Ospitale Civico, no. 66. The monastery received only small cash testamentary bequests in the twelfth century: these donations were mainly to support the rebuilding of the church after an earthquake in 1117, and none of these wills made San Zeno their major beneficiary. *ASVR*, S. Stefano, no. 33; *Regestro Mantovano*, ed. Pietro Torelli (Rome, 1914), no. 229; *ASVR*, Clero Intrinseco, registro 12 (Ist. Ant. Reg. II), fol. 140; *ASV*, Fondo Veneto, nos. 6955, 6979, and 7043.

50. *ASVR*, SS. Nazaro e Celso, nos. 1534 (1034), 434 (1036), 313 (1062), 914 (1075); BC, MSS Lodovico Perini, busta 26 (1075); *ASVR*, SS. Nazaro e Celso, nos. 627 (1081), 628 (1082), 27 (1090), 1206 (1094), 314 (1099), 629 (1100), 630 (1102), 806 (1118), 967 (1129), 1 (1146), 641 (1147), 2232 (1158).

51. San Giorgio in Braida: *ASV*, Fondo Veneto, nos. 6881 (1123), 6888 (1128), 6899 (1131), 6903 (1133), 6891 (1134), 6893 (1134), 6912 (1136), 6923 (1142), 6937 (1143), 6970 (1148). Santissima

teries outside the diocese also attracted Veronese donations. Cluny received one donation,[52] and two eleventh-century foundations just beyond the borders of the diocese of Verona received several.[53]

But the most dramatic shift in donations following the investiture crisis was not from old institutions for the religious life to new or reformed ones. It was from the regular to the secular clergy. Before 1000 the secular clergy supported their own: as donors they founded and made donations to institutions for secular clerics.[54] By the early twelfth century lay donors too were making gifts to the institutions of the secular clergy.

Lay donations to the city's *scole* and *xenodochia* became frequent from the late eleventh century. Santo Stefano, which had both a *scola* and a *xenodochium*, was particularly well endowed. It received numerous donations over the eleventh and twelfth centuries, all from lay donors.[55] The cathedral canons too, and the *xenodochia* they administered, received several lay

---

Trinità: Biancolini, *Chiese* 4: 755; Paolo Sambin, *Nuovi documenti padovani dei secoli XI–XII* (Venice, 1955), pp. 13–14 (no. 9); a twelfth-century poem names Vivianus "Bibensacqua" (Bevilacqua) as one of the chief patrons of the monastery: Paolo Guerrini, "Un cardinale gregoriano a Brescia: Il vescovo Arimanno," *Studi gregoriani* 2 (1947): 374; the monastery's necrology records other Veronese donors: *Annales Sanctae Trinitatis, MGH SS* 19: 2.

52. Auguste Bernard and Alexandre Bruel, *Recueil des chartes de l'abbay de Cluny* (Paris, 1876–1903) 5: 86–87 (no. 3736).

53. The monastery of San Benedetto was erected in 1007 on an island created by the confluence of the Po and one of its branches, the Lirone. It acquired the aura of sanctity from a hermit named Simeon, who came to live there shortly after its founding and died in 1016. San Benedetto subsequently became affiliated with Cluny, and its monks were known for their rigorous observance of the Benedictine Rule. Gina Fasoli, "Monasteri Padani," in *Monasteri in alta Italia dopo le invasioni saracene e magiare (sec. X–XII)* (Turin, 1966), pp. 189–91. Veronese donations: *Regesto Mantovano*, nos. 200, 206, 207, 229. Another nearby monastery noted for reform, Santa Maria della Vangadizza, was also the home of a saintly hermit in the eleventh century. By the early twelfth it was affiliated with the Camaldoli, and it too attracted Veronese donations. *ASVR*, S. Salvar Corte Regia, Repertorio 1725 (1055); *ACV*, I–5–4v (AC 47 m3 n7) (1065); Mittarelli-Costadoni, *Annales Camaldulenses* 2: no. 143 (1073) and 3: no. 45 (1085); *ACV*, III–8–3v (AC 15 m3 n3) (1157). On the early history of this house, see Egidio Rossini, "Ugo 'gratia Dei gloriosissimus dux et marchio' e il monastero della Vangadizza," *Atti e memorie del Sodalizio vangadiciense* 2 (1982), 3–25.

54. This shift in donations toward the secular clergy is not a by-product of the greater number of surviving charters after the millennium. Thanks to Verona's capitular archive, good documentation for the secular clergy exists from the early Middle Ages. See Giuseppe Zivelonghi, "Strumenti e spunti di ricerca nei documenti dell'Archivio Capitolare di Verona," in *Verona dalla caduta dei Carolingi al libero comune* (Verona, 1987), pp. 117–76, especially pp. 117–22.

55. *ASVR*, S. Stefano, nos. 3 (1057), 17 (1086); *ACV*, II–5–8v (sec. XI); *ASVR*, S. Stefano, nos. 23 (1109), 25 (1111), 37 (1122), 39 (1124), 43 (1128), 52 (1141).

donations.[56] Lay patrons supported the new city-wide congregation for the secular clergy as well as individual urban churches.[57]

What does this shift in donations toward the secular clergy mean? First, to a certain degree it gives evidence of the "monasticization" of the secular clergy. The Gregorian reform, by demanding celibacy and the communal life of the secular clergy, brought their way of life closer to that of religious. It seems that *scole* of the secular clergy came to be perceived as reservoirs of prayers, not unlike monasteries. Donors made their gifts to these institutions of the secular clergy for the good of their souls. Several of these donations gave specific directions as to what should be done on the anniversary of the donor's death. In 1122 a widow named Walda made a donation to Santo Stefano for her soul, instructing that on the anniversary of her death each priest should receive a denarius and a candle (the standard payment for a mass).[58] A husband and wife, Girard and Berta, gave the same instructions in a donation to the urban church of Santa Maria alla Chiavica in 1153.[59] This suggests that these urban churches with communities of secular clerics were keeping necrologies—calendars indicating the anniversaries of patrons and members—just as monasteries did.

But not all of the new attraction of donors to the secular clergy can be attributed to their more "monastic" organization. That lay persons began for the first time to make donations beyond tithes to their local or parish church suggests a new valuation of the sacramental and cultic functions of the clergy.[60] An artisan named Eghinus made a donation to his local church, the chapel of San Giorgio in Salsis, as early as 1028.[61] The husband

56. Canons: *ACV*, I–5–6v (AC 57 m5 n15) (1100), II–6–6r (AC 25 m5 n12) (1123), I–6–5v (BC 13 m4 n3, doc. 1) (1147). *Xenodochia: ACV*, I–6–1r (1047); *ASVR*, S. Maria in Organo, no. 52; S. Michele in Compagna, no. 4 app.

57. On congregations of secular clergy in this region, see Antonio Rigon, *Clero e città* (Padua, 1988), and, in Verona, above (Chapter 2). Donations to the congregation: *ASVR*, Clero Intrinseco, registro 13 (Ist. Ant. Reg. I), fol. 107 (1102); registro 12 (Ist. Ant. Reg. II), fol. 140 (1145). Donations to other urban churches: BC, MSS Lodovico Perini, busta 22, "Padri Dominicani" (1082); *ASVR*, S. Maria in Organo, no. 28 (1055); Clero Intrinseco, registro 15 (Ist. Ant. Reg. III), fol. 79 (1109); S. Anastasia, no. 22 (1153).

58. *ASVR*, S. Stefano, no. 37.

59. *ASVR*, S. Anastasia, no. 22.

60. A strong concern about the sacraments and their efficacy animated lay participation in the Milanese *pataria*. See Cinzio Violante, "I laici nel movimento patarino," pp. 597–687 in *I laici nella «societas christiana» dei secoli XI e XII* (Milan, 1968), p. 686.

61. San Giorgio in Salsis was a chapel dependent upon the *plebs* of San Andrea de Sandrà. The

and wife Amizo and Veronica, "living next to the church of San Iacopo," made a donation to that church in 1109.[62] In making a gift to Santo Stefano, a widow named Tota identified herself as "living near that church" ("abitatrix prope ipsam ecclesiam").[63] Lay donors were giving gifts to the church nearest them, where they most likely received the sacraments, prayed, and venerated the saints.

This shift toward the secular clergy was also rooted in the emergence of a new lower social tier of donors. As discussed above, artisans, petty knights, and the wealthier residents of outlying communities began to appear as donors after 1000, and they usually made their gifts to local churches. Many of these local churches were parishes or dependent chapels administered by secular clerics.

The Veronese evidence is too limited to do more than suggest these factors. But clearly, for whatever reason, in the wake of the Gregorian Reform lay donors were as likely to support the secular clergy as religious houses. If nothing else, this demonstrates some greater esteem for the secular clergy. They were now serious competitors for donors' gifts; their institutions no longer relied on "alumni" giving.

These patterns of donations reveal much about what lay people wanted from the Church. First and foremost, they wanted prayers to be said for the good of their souls. Over the entire period, from the eighth to the mid-twelfth century, lay persons gave gifts to those institutions which would offer prayers. This is surely a major factor explaining the persistent popularity of Benedictine monasteries. These institutions, and the religious life they cultivated, were uniquely focused on prayer. It is worth noting that at least in Verona, the closing of Benedictine monasteries did not coincide with the heroic era of Saint Francis and Saint Dominic; their demise occurred during the second mendicant generation, when both the Franciscan and the Dominican orders had adopted most of the conventional arrangements of other religious institutions.[64]

---

donor identified himself as "from the village of Assiona" ("de vico Assiona"). Assiona, now Sona, is three kilometers from San Giorgio in Salsis. ACV, I–5–2r (BC 39 m2 n8).

62. ASVR, Clero Intrinseco, registro 15 (Ist. Ant. Reg. III), fol. 79.

63. ASVR, S. Stefano, no. 43.

64. The Benedictine monastery of San Fermo was ceded to the Franciscans in 1261; in the 1290s

Against this backdrop of the constant desire for prayers, new lay inter-ests did emerge in eleventh- and twelfth-century donations. Support of institutions to train the secular clergy (*scole*) and of the churches these secular clerics served evinces a new lay concern with pastoral care. This may indicate a growing recognition that the soul's well-being is affected as much by the ministrations of the clergy during one's life as by prayers said after one's death.[65] It surely indicates the highly localized piety of the new tier of less well-to-do donors. Lay people seem to have wanted churches staffed by competent priests to offer them the sacraments in their commu-nities. Some also wanted a more intense involvement in that local church and formed *convivia*.

Did lay people want novelty? Did they support religious innovation? The answer to these questions is both affirmative and negative. Clearly, new religious experiments like the regular canonry of San Giorgio and the leper hospital of Santa Croce received support from lay people of all social ranks. No one segment of Veronese society can be credited with the success of these new endeavors. Santa Croce was the creation of lay people, who found the means to innovate in the availability of money and new property arrangements. The economic tools developed by merchants were more important in facilitating religious innovation than the merchants them-selves. Social and economic change after the millennium empowered those inspired by new religious visions to promote them through the foundation of lasting institutions.

The testamentary practices of lay persons, however, reveal some ambiv-alence about the proliferation of new kinds of ecclesiastical institutions. When drawing up their wills, lay persons spread their resources among a

---

several abbeys were left deserted. It was in this second half of the thirteenth century that both the Dominicans and the Franciscans gave up itinerancy, established fixed convents and churches, and acquired property for their support. By the end of the century, both orders had much in common with their Benedictine forbears. Significantly, their more settled character allowed them to offer those services most desired by the laity: the "Libro dei Morti" of the Dominican church of Santa Maria Novella in Florence—a list of deceased lay persons who were to be remembered with prayers on the anniversaries of their deaths—commences in 1290. *Santa Maria Novella, un convento nella città* (Pistoia, 1980) 2: 29, 73. On the changes within the mendicant orders, see Ralph Francis Bennett, *The Early Dominicans* (Cambridge, 1937), pp. 145–56; John Moorman, *A History of the Franciscan Order* (Oxford, 1968), pp. 118–22; Malcolm D. Lambert, *Franciscan Poverty* (London, 1961), pp. 161–65.

65. Examples of donations to secular institutions that did not ask for prayers after death: *ACV*, I–5–6v (AC 57 m5 n15) and II–6–6r (AC 25 m5 n12); *ASVR*, S. Stefano, no. 43.

wide variety of ecclesiastical institutions. In this, the attitudes of the laity were not very different from those of the clergy. An air of discomfiture informs even the writings of clerical authors defending the new diversity. The anonymous author of a mid-twelfth-century tract on the proliferation of religious groups assumed that the many differences apparent among them constituted a problem requiring explanation: this diversity in callings had to be proven to be pleasing to God.[66] In the meantime, Veronese testators took no chances.

The similarities, rather than the differences, between laity and clergy seem most important in offering an answer to the question posed at the beginning of this chapter. To what extent did the actions and ideas of lay persons promote or influence ecclesiastical change in the eleventh and early twelfth centuries? The laity definitely played a crucial role. They sometimes initiated new religious endeavors, and their support was critical to all ecclesiastical institutions. But the clergy was just as likely to innovate.[67] The new institutions and reforms of the secular clergy were the work of bishops and clerics. Bishops founded new monasteries like San Nazaro and Calavena; it was Bishop Bernard who established regular canons at San Giorgio. One can not characterize the eleventh- and twelfth-century Church as a stodgy institution that reformed and improved only at the vigorous prompting of the laity. Bishops and clerics usually took the initiative, and lay people supported their efforts. And when lay persons took the initiative—as at Santa Croce—they were supported not only by other lay persons, but also by the bishop and his clergy.

The new spirituality that emerged in the eleventh and twelfth centuries was the work of both lay people and clerics. Its creation was a cooperative venture. But after the mid-twelfth century, this highly creative spirit of cooperation broke down. A council held in Verona in 1184 condemned

66. "Since different servants of God have arisen from the beginning of the early church, and many kinds of callings have come into being, and particularly in our day, institutions of monks and canons differing in habit and worship are increasing, it is necessary to show, with God's help, how such servants of God differ and what the purposes of the different forms of callings are. So I undertake to show that these differences among the callings please God." *Libellus de diversis ordinibus et professionibus qui sunt in aecclesia*, ed. and trans. G. Constable and B. Smith (Oxford, 1972), pp. 2–3.

67. Violante reminds us that even the *pataria*, a movement often cited as evidence of new lay activism, was initiated and led by clerics. There was only one lay person, the knight Erlembald, among the leaders. Violante, "I laici," pp. 600–602, 605, 614.

several new lay initiatives as heretical; a century later in the city's amphi-theater 166 heretics were executed in a powerful, fiery display of clerical authority.[68] How and why did the mutuality that informed relations within the Veronese Church during the eleventh and early twelfth centuries dete-riorate? Our answer lies in the organization of authority within the Church and its development over these crucial centuries.

68. Carlo Cipolla, *La storia politica di Verona* (Verona, 1899; rpt. Verona, 1954), pp. 107–8, 127–28.

# 5  ECCLESIASTICAL ORGANIZATION

**T**HE structure of the Veronese diocese and the very nature of the ties that bound its many ecclesiastical institutions into a Church changed profoundly over the eleventh and early twelfth centuries. In the turbulent early Middle Ages, small institutions had sought the protection of larger ones, creating several competing networks of dependencies within the diocese. Ecclesiastical authority, as a result, was highly fragmented. Over the eleventh and early twelfth centuries, the bishops of Verona progressively established their dominion over the diocese. They brought new churches under their authority, turning to their advantage the tremendous growth transforming the diocese. The bonds between ecclesiastical institutions grew more sophisticated as custom was modified by new ideas about authority and small institutions sought confraternal, rather than subordinate, relationships. By the mid-twelfth century, the organizational structures that were to characterize the high medieval Church had emerged.

The most common relationship between Veronese ecclesiastical institutions in the early Middle Ages was the "subjection" of a smaller institution to a larger one. Usually this relationship was established when the founder of a church or monastery gave the institution to a larger house. The sisters Autconda and Natalia, for example, when they founded their monastery of Santa Maria in Solaro in 745, placed it under the monastery of Santa Maria in Organo.[1] Bishop Audo also placed the church and *xenodochium* he had built in Sezano under the tutelage of Santa Maria.[2] Dagibert,

---

1. *CDV* 1 no. 33.
2. *CDV* 1 no. 219. Other examples: In 910 Count Anselm left a chapel and oratory on his manor "at the two oaks" to the monastery of S. Silvestro di Nonantola, *CDV* 2 no. 98; Count Milo in 929 bestowed the church of Santa Maria at Ronco upon the cathedral chapter, *CDV* 2 no. 205.

archdeacon of the cathedral chapter and the bishop's *vicedominus*, chose to place the church and *xenodochium* he had built on his own property under the power of the cathedral canons.[3] Ecclesiastical institutions also received subject churches and monasteries through pious gifts. Charlemagne donated the monastery of San Pietro in Moratica, and the churches of San Lorenzo in Ostiglia and Santi Fermo e Rustico, to the monastery of San Zeno.[4] Pippin later added the churches of Sant'Andrea Incaffi and San Zeno in Bardolino to this grant.[5] Bishops too could subject churches or chapels to other ecclesiastical institutions. In 811 Bishop Ratoldus placed the chapel of San Bartolomeo under the nearby church of San Pietro in Castello.[6]

What was given to the institution was the physical structure of the church or monastery, the lands or goods attached to it, and control over its clergy or religious. Throughout Western Europe in the early Middle Ages, proprietary rights were thought to yield ecclesiastical jurisdiction.[7] Objections were sometimes raised when lay persons exercised control over churches, but not when other ecclesiastical personages or institutions did so. The will drawn up by Bishop Notker of Verona in 927 illustrates these ideas in action. The bishop had among his possessions a chapel dedicated to the Blessed Virgin on a manor he owned near Trent. The manor and its church were first ceded to Bishop Bernard of Trent. After Bernard's death, Notker's vassal Odelbert was to have usufruct of the manor for life. The will specifically stipulated that Odelbert should appoint (*ordinet*) the priest who would serve in the manor's chapel. After Odelbert's death, the manor and this chapel devolved to the cathedral chapter of Verona.[8] Notice that Notker did not feel a need to specify that Bishop Bernard, during his life, or the canons, after Odelbert's death, should appoint the chapel's priest. Odelbert only seems to have merited this specific stipulation because he, unlike the other two beneficiaries, was a lay person. Clearly, Notker assumed that those reading his will would not question the bishop of Trent's or the Veronese cathedral chapter's right to appoint the chapel's priest.

Although many churches, like Notker's chapel, became the dependen-

3. *CDV* 2 no. 214.
4. *CDV* 1 nos. 76 and 117.
5. *CDV* 1 no. 84. San Zeno acquired a monastery in Treviso (San Teonisto, called "monasterium novum") from the Emperor Lothar in 840 and had gained the church of Santa Maria and San Tommaso in Sacco by 853. *CDV* 1 nos. 160, 162.
6. *CDV* 1 no. 95.
7. Catherine E. Boyd, *Tithes and Parishes in Medieval Italy* (Ithaca, N.Y., 1952), pp. 55–74, 252–54.
8. *CDV* 2 no. 199.

cies of other ecclesiastical institutions because they were located on a piece of donated property, others were subjected for more specifically pious reasons. The sisters Autconda and Natalia, for example, stated explicitly that they placed their monastery under the control of Santa Maria in Organo in order to preserve and foster the religious life: "We want the monastery of Santa Maria outside the gate to have the defense and admonition of [our] holy monastery . . . on condition that if some discord should have arisen among the sisters which we are not able to eradicate, then the abbot (himself or through some God fearing person) ought to cut off that [cause] of the evil, expelling and correcting it . . ."[9] Bishop Ratoldus, invoking his role as watchful shepherd of the Church, explained that he placed the church of San Bartolomeo under the control of San Pietro in Castello in order that its "present and future priests might serve God more freely."[10]

Founders placing their churches or monasteries under the authority of another institution hoped by doing so to protect them from the depredations of the powerful. The archdeacon and *vicedominus* Dagibert, when placing his church and *xenodochium* under the cathedral chapter, revealed a whole series of threats he hoped the association would ward off. He did not want powerful persons, lay or ecclesiastical, to destroy or diminish the arrangements he had made for the *xenodochium*. He did not want these powerful persons to get control of the institution for themselves or their friends. He particularly feared that some powerful person might alienate the *xenodochium* to another.[11] If the cathedral chapter could not protect his foundation from all these possible threats, Dagibert wanted the bishop of Trent to take control of it.[12]

The subjugation of one ecclesiastical institution to another, then, was

9. "Defensionem uero uel admonicionem sancti monasterii uolumus abere ad monasterium sancte Marie foris porta . . . cum condictione ut si aliquid discordia inter sorores fuerit exorta quam non possimus per nos euellere, tunc abba per semetipsum au Deo timentem personam ipsum mali debeat mouendum et corrigendum amputare . . ." *CDV* 1 no. 33.

10. ". . . quatenus illius aecclesie presentes scilicet et futuri sacerdotes liberius deo seruiant . . ." *CDV* 1 no. 95.

11. Such fears were well founded in the tenth century. Lay appropriation of Church property—through the giving of benefices (*beneficia*) or long term leases (*livelli*)—steadily increased from the mid-ninth century. Lucchese documentation offers extraordinarily detailed evidence of this trend, but the problem was quite widespread. Boyd, *Tithes and Parishes*, pp. 87–102; Cinzio Violante, "Pievi e parrocchie nell'Italia centro-settentrionale durante i secoli XI e XII," in *Le istituzioni ecclesiastiche della «societas christiana» dei secoli XI–XII: Diocesi, pievi e parrocchie* (Milan, 1977), pp. 657–83.

12. *CDV* 2 no. 214.

intended to guard against corruption in the religious life and to protect the institution from powerful persons. Small churches or monasteries in the early Middle Ages were obviously seen as especially vulnerable to both these evils. If this perceived vulnerability was the original motive for subjecting one institution to another, how in reality did this relationship function? What did it entail for both parties? Early medieval Veronese charters offer us some glimpses of these relationships in progress.

The subject institution usually owed an annual fee to its "mother" house. The church of Mazagata owed the bishop a pound of wax and a pound of incense every year on the feast of San Zeno.[13] Dagibert's *xenodoch-ium* paid sixty pounds of oil to the cathedral every year, "so that the candle which hangs before the door may brightly shine both day and night" and five pounds of wax, so that the scriptures could be read at night.[14] The heads of subject institutions also took an oath of obedience. A charter of 854 records such an oath taken by Eufrasia, the abbess of Santa Maria in Solaro, along with her sisters. The abbess professed to have been appointed and consecrated by the patriarch of Aquileia (to whom Santa Maria in Organo owed obedience) and promised to obey the abbot of Santa Maria.[15]

In return, the controlling institution administered and defended the property of the subject church. The abbot of Santa Maria in Organo, for example, acquired, exchanged, and rented lands on behalf of its subject church of San Lorenzo in Sezano.[16] Bishop Ratherius arranged exchanges of lands on behalf of San Pietro in Castello and San Pietro in Monastero.[17] The mediation of a powerful figure such as the bishop of Verona or the abbot of Santa Maria in Organo certainly facilitated land exchanges benefiting smaller institutions. Vestiges of other aid given to subject institutions

13. *ACV*, II–6–7v (BC 17 m4 n7).

14. The document also provided for the payment of those who maintained these candles. ". . . singulis annis sexaginta libras olei in Eclesia Matricularis dentur, ut cicendelum quod ante portam pendet die noctuque ardere splendeat et custodes ipsius Eclesie pro fatigio cicendeli quod habuerint unum modium anone e unum modium vini de xenedochio meo singuulis annis recipiant, et exinde quinque libras cerarum in Eclesiam Matricularis ad legendas per noctem Deo lectiones donentur. Et qui cereum custodierit unum modium anone et unum modium vini de iamdicto xenedochio recipiat." *CDV* 2 no. 214.

15. *CDV* 1 no. 192.

16. *CDV* 2 nos. 220, 234, 239, 252, 253, 257, 262.

17. *CDV* 2 no. 236 and Ratherius, "Urkunden," pp. 35–38.

survive in inscriptions. Three ninth-century inscriptions record that Audibert, abbot of Santa Maria in Organo, aided in the rebuilding of Santa Sofia in the Valpolicella, San Donato di Moroni in the Valpantena, and Santa Maria in Gazzo. All three were dependent churches of the monastery.[18]

A certain mutuality informed these relationships of subordination and dependence in the early Middle Ages. Surely large institutions gained prestige and some economic benefit from their networks of dependent churches. These advantages, however, seem balanced in the documentary record by charitable acts and by numerous, seemingly sincere, protestations of concern. Undoubtedly, many small churches and monasteries would not have survived the turbulent tenth century if not for the protection and aid supplied by their "mother" houses.

But these ties of subordination and dependence, however beneficial, were determined by the wishes of founders and the needs of the house without reference to any clear system of diocesan organization. They reveal, in fact, little or no distinction between churches exercising care of souls, on the one hand, and monastic churches or private chapels on the other. It is indeed difficult to discern a pastoral "system" in the early medieval diocese. There were *plebes*, but they were very few.[19] They seem not to have had well-defined territories, and nearby chapels appear not to have been dependent upon them.[20] Most of the churches that appear in our early medieval documents were manorial churches, and the relationship, if any, between these and the *plebes* is unclear. This lack of discrimination between different kinds of churches meant that ties of dependence linked various types of ecclesiastical institutions to one another, creating several rather heterogeneous organizational groupings.

---

18. Luigi Simeoni, "Iscrizioni medievali di monumenti veronesi," *AMAV* 85 (1908–9): 69; Alessandro da Lisca, "La chiesa di S. Maria Maggiore al Gazzo Veronese," *AMAV* 119 (1940–41): 144–46.

19. Fewer than 20% of the churches before the millennium are identified as *plebes*; that percentage doubles by the mid-twelfth century.

20. The baptismal church of San Pietro in Tillida, meticulously described by Andrea Castagnetti using a tenth-century inventory, had only a quite loosely defined territory. The inventory lists eleven nearby "vici" where the church held property; seven of these *vici* owed the church tithes. Within the geographical zone of those owing tithes, however, are several other *vici* that seem to have had no relation with the *plebs*. Several other churches within this zone were directly dependent upon the bishop. Andrea Castagnetti, *La pieve rurale nell'Italia padana* (Rome, 1976), pp. 17, 49.

The development of these relationships of dependence among ecclesiastical institutions also created several competing hierarchies within the Veronese diocese. Religious authority in the city was, as a result, highly fragmented. Four major institutions had networks of dependencies: the bishop, the cathedral chapter, the monastery of San Zeno, and the monastery of Santa Maria in Organo. From the late eighth century, the bishop and San Zeno were closely allied with one another and with the emperors. Santa Maria in Organo, however, claimed exemption from the bishop's authority through its direct dependence upon the patriarch of Aquileia. The cathedral chapter, which later also claimed dependence upon Aquileia, became increasingly independent of the bishop over the early Middle Ages. All of these important alignments had their origins in the transition from Lombard to Carolingian rule.

Probably as early as the fifth century, and certainly by the late sixth, the Veronese see had recognized the patriarch of Aquileia as its metropolitan. In 590, Verona's bishop Junior and many other Aquileian suffragans signed a letter supporting the patriarch's position in the long Schism of the Three Chapters.[21] The monastery of Santa Maria in Organo, however, clearly developed a more intense relationship with Aquileia, probably during the Lombard era. Both this Veronese monastery and the patriarchate had strong Lombard connections. King Liutprand had supported Santa Maria in Organo and its dependencies,[22] and long after the end of Lombard hegemony those who professed Lombard law continued to favor the abbey.[23] Aquileia's ties with the Lombards stemmed from its politically important location on the frontier of Byzantine territory.[24] The see's con-

---

21. *CDV* 1 nos. 12–17; *VerST* 2: 29; The schism began in 544 when the Emperor Justinian condemned some of the teachings of Theodore of Mopsuestia, Theodoret of Cyr, and Ibas of Edessa. All three purportedly upheld Nestorian interpretations of the human and divine natures in Christ. The court at Constantinople was able, through rather brutally direct tactics, to silence papal opposition, but much of the western Church refused to accept Justinian's edict. The see of Aquileia and its suffragans were among those who resisted, and they remained unreconciled for a century and a half. It was during this long schism that the bishop of Aquileia adopted the title of "patriarch," to compete with a rival "patriarch" who had emerged at Grado (supported by the Byzantines). Pio Paschini, *San Paolino patriarca e la chiesa aquileise alla fine del secolo VIII* (Udine, 1906; rpt. Udine, 1977), pp. 4–11.

22. He made donations to both Santa Maria in Organo and its subject monastery Santa Maria in Gazzo. *CDV* 1 nos. 25, 30.

23. See above, Chapter 4, section I.

24. Nearby Cividale was an important fortified Lombard outpost, seat of the duke of Friuli. The

nections became even more pronounced during the schism, when its patriarch was supported by the Lombards and his rival in Grado was supported by the Byzantines. Although it is impossible to pinpoint when Santa Maria in Organo became directly dependent upon the patriarch, the monastery was clearly claiming dependence by the late eighth century.[25] There is convincing evidence by the tenth century that this dependence had been established.[26]

The ties between Verona's bishop and the monastery of San Zeno were also well developed by the advent of Carolingian rule. The importance of the city's patron saint is obvious in this intimate relationship. The successors of Verona's first bishop had their earliest seat at San Procolo, next to the monastery built over Zeno's remains. Even after the bishops moved into the walled city, they attempted to share the aura of the patron saint. From the eighth century, the bishops referred to their see as the *domus sancti zenonis* or the *pars sancti zenonis*, making it barely distinguishable at times from the monastery or church of San Zeno.[27] The bishop received part of the alms given to the saint on his feast day and controlled the annual market held at San Zeno.[28]

It was therefore natural that when Carolingian rule was established, Charlemagne both provided a new bishop and began patronizing the church and monastery of San Zeno.[29] Together, the bishop and the monastery of San Zeno formed the *pars imperii* in the city: the bishop was ap-

patriarch Calixtus (726–34) moved the see to Cividale after Aquileia suffered repeated Byzantine incursions. Paschini, *San Paolino*, pp. 3, 11.

25. A clearly false document dated 585 claiming the monastery's dependence on the patriarch was quoted in a diploma of Charlemagne confirming the patrimony of the patriarchate in 792. *CDV* 1 no. 59; Pio Paschini, "Le vicende politiche e religiose del Friuli nei secoli nono e decimo," *Nuovo archivio veneto* n.s. 21 (1911): 428.

26. Ibid., pp. 430–32.

27. *CDV* 1 no. 71. Saint Zeno, in his early association with the see, was what hagiographers characterize as a "traditional type" of saintly episcopal patron. Usually, as was the case in Modena and Reggio Emilia, the patron's close association with the see resulted in the translation of his relics when the see moved. Zeno's relics probably remained at the monastery outside the walls because of the wealth and power of the monastic community there. See Paolo Golinelli, *«Indiscreta sanctitas.» Studi sui rapporti tra culti, poteri, e società nel pieno medioevo* (Rome, 1988), pp. 56, 58–61 (especially note 20, p. 59), 65–66; Paolo Golinelli, *Culto dei santi e vita cittadina a Reggio Emilia (secoli IX–XII)* (Modena, 1980), pp. 107–14.

28. *CDV* 1 nos. 96 and 117.

29. Ederle, *Dizionario*, p. 26; *CDV* 1 nos. 53, 76, 78, 81. See also above, Chapter 4, section I.

pointed by the emperor to represent him in the city, and San Zeno was the emperor's church. By 833 Emperor Lothar had formalized this already close relationship by committing the monastery and church of San Zeno to the care of the bishop.[30]

It was in this same period that the Veronese cathedral chapter first emerged as a significant institution. During the heyday of Carolingian rule, the chapter and the city's Frankish bishops worked harmoniously together. Particularly noteworthy was the period when Pacificus (776–844) was archdeacon of the chapter. Born just after the Carolingian conquest, this local cleric was sent to the monastery of Reichenau for his education. Upon his return, he took charge of the chapter's school and scriptorium; under his direction the chapter experienced its own Carolingian renaissance. Pacificus himself composed numerous liturgical texts and copied many others. He also corresponded with other clerics within the empire, exchanging copies of texts.[31] During the long absence of Bishop Ratoldus at the imperial court from 834 to 840, it was Pacificus who administered the diocese.[32]

But as the Carolingian empire disintegrated, the chapter took on a more intensely local character. It began receiving donations from local elites and adopted a more independent posture in relations with the city's imperial bishops.[33] Episcopal absences like Ratoldus's surely contributed to this development.[34] A quarrel between the canons and the abbot of San Zeno resolved in 866 reveals this more aggressive stance. Louis the Pious had decreed that a portion (20 mancusos or 50 solidi) of the alms given at San Zeno's tomb on his feast day should go to "the bishop of the city and his

---

30. *CDV* 1 no. 143.

31. *CDV* 1 nos. 167, 168.

32. Pacificus's epitaph credits him with 218 books! His liturgical compositions are considered his most innovative work, but he also composed a mnemonic verse and several scriptural glosses. He inherited the administration of the diocese when Ratoldus was appointed the Empress Judith's advocate. Meersseman, *L'orazionale*, pp. 3–5.

33. A similar development is evident in Pistoia. The cathedral chapter began receiving significant gifts from local donors in the late tenth century and became increasingly independent of the bishop over the eleventh century. Natale Rauty, *Storia di Pistoia I* (Florence, 1988), pp. 227, 304–11.

34. Ratoldus's successor, Nottingus, only held the see four years before being transferred to Brescia, and there is some doubt as to whether he was ever present in Verona. Bishop Agino had a similarly short tenure (844–47) and spent at least part of it with the imperial entourage at Rome for Louis II's coronation. Ederle, *Dizionario*, pp. 27–28; *CDV* 1 no. 173.

clergy."[35] A half century later, however, the canons were claiming the right to this portion. The dispute became so heated (the notary called it a "grandis altercatio") that the bishop had to admonish both sides to keep the peace. He ceded half the alms to the canons and half to the monks to end the dispute.[36] Under some earlier bishop, the chapter had probably become accustomed to receiving the alms and, over time, came to perceive this gift as a right. Nevertheless, the chapter's quiet appropriation of an episcopal revenue and its contentious defense of this gain is striking. It ominously foreshadows later relations between the chapter and the bishop.

The sum effect of all these alignments on the structure of the diocese was to fracture authority. By the tenth century many churches looked to the bishop and San Zeno as their ecclesiastical authorities. Many others, however, looked to Santa Maria in Organo, which claimed exemption from the bishop's authority. Still others looked to the cathedral chapter, which increasingly resisted the bishop's control. These divided allegiances within the diocese maintained a seemingly untroubled equilibrium until the mid-tenth century. The balance of power was first upset by the desire for reform. Bishop Ratherius fought continually with the chapter and, as we have seen, viewed the canons as the major impediment to the reform of the clergy. Although Ratherius was unsuccessful in his attempts to diminish the chapter's power, his stormy episcopate seems to have hardened the divide between the episcopal faction and those institutions asserting independence. The relationship of these institutions to episcopal authority became an issue under his successors.

In 995, at a synod held in Verona with the patriarch presiding, Otbertus challenged the exemption of the clergy of two churches dependent upon Santa Maria in Organo. The bishop complained that the priests of Santa Maria Antica and Santa Margarita refused to obey him. Specifically, they refused to attend his synods and refused to participate in processions with the other churches of the city or to attend public masses for special feasts. The patriarch answered that this was an "ancient custom." Otbertus, however, was supported by the other bishops present from Vicenza, Treviso, and Trent. The council agreed that the clergy of these two churches should

35. ". . . ut in festiuitate ipsius sancti Zenonis annis singulis, aut mancusos uiginti aut quinquaginta solidos argenti accipere debeat pontifex ipsius ciuitatis cum suis clericis ab ipsis monachis ibidem deseruientibus . . ." *CDV* 1 no. 117.
36. *CDV* 1 no. 233.

attend the bishop's synods, processions, and masses. But it also specified that the bishop did not have the power to correct or punish these clerics in his court; he must resolve any difficulties with their "advocate," the abbot of Santa Maria in Organo.[37]

This was only the beginning of a long process that would define the limits of these exemptions and ultimately reorganize the diocese more clearly under the authority of the bishop. Calls for reform in the tenth century first revealed the inadequacies of the early medieval organization of the diocese. As the demand for reform became more strident, and as the diocese grew, this early medieval balance of power was dismantled.

Several influences shaped the reorganization of the Veronese diocese after the millennium. Reform ideology, imperial politics, demographic expansion, the rise of lordship and of law, all contributed to the new order. Above all, the pressing need both to provide and improve pastoral care resulted in an increased recognition of the importance of the episcopate and a very different structure of authority within the Veronese Church.

The major change in the organization of the diocese by the mid-twelfth century was that the bishop was much more clearly controlling it. Churches exercising care of souls came to form a distinct system and were recognized as the bishop's special concern. Even where the physical structure and goods of such churches remained beyond his jurisdiction, their clergy and spiritual functions came under the bishop's authority. Other hierarchies of dependencies and exempt institutions still existed in the mid-twelfth century, but the bishop's hierarchy of institutions and jurisdictions came to overshadow all others.

Several twelfth-century papal bulls reveal this new episcopal dominance. The growth in dependencies of those institutions claiming independence from episcopal authority—Santa Maria in Organo and the cathedral chapter—did not keep pace with the expansion of the bishop's jurisdiction after the millennium. A bull of 1177 reveals that the monastery of Santa Maria in Organo had gained only three new dependent churches after the millennium.[38] The canons, however, had expanded both their patrimony and their network of dependent institutions. They were the

37. Mansi 19, cols. 197–98.
38. PL 200: 1126–27.

bishop's chief competitors.[39] At the millennium, the chapter controlled several urban *xenodochia* and seven churches: San Giorgio, San Giovanni Battista, Santa Cecilia, San Giovanni in Valle, San Pietro in Carnario, San Giovanni Battista in Quinzano, and San Michele in Campagna.[40] By the mid-twelfth century they had added at least fourteen churches to their network of dependencies as well as several manorial chapels. A bull of 1177 confirmed to the chapter all of the churches above, plus San Clemente, San Faustino, San Fermo in Cortalta, San Paolo in Prun, Ognissanti in Novara, Santa Maria in Turano, San Cassiano and Ognissanti in Marzana, San Pancrazio, San Giorgio in Salsis, San Michele in Calmasino, San Faustino in Mondragone, and San Prosdocimo.[41]

Yet however much the canons' network of dependencies had expanded, the extent of the bishop's jurisdictions within the diocese far exceeded all his competitors' by the mid-twelfth century. Pope Eugene III's bull confirming the see's possessions in 1145 lists seven monasteries, the churches of the city, fifty-four baptismal churches with their dependent chapels, and at least fourteen other churches. Although there are several inconsistencies between this bull and other documentation, this papal confirmation is too important a source to be discounted.[42]

39. It was not uncommon for cathedral chapters to have control of baptismal churches, but most bishops struggled with monasteries to get control of the *plebes* in their dioceses. Boyd, *Tithes and Parishes*, pp. 84–85; Emilio Cristiani, "Le origini della vita canonica nella diocesi di Volterra (secc. X–XII)," in *La vita comune del clero nei secoli XI e XII* (Milan, 1962) 2: 241; Uta-Renate Blumenthal, *The Investiture Controversy* (Philadelphia, 1988), pp. 69–70.

40. Ratoldus's foundation charter of 813 (*CDV* 1 nos. 101, 102) granted the canons San Michele "in Flexio" (in Campagna) and San Giovanni in Valle. The canons also controlled their own church of San Giorgio, built by archdeacon Pacificus. San Giovanni in Quinzano, also built by Pacificus, was subjected to the canons in his will of 844 (*CDV* 1 no. 176). Santa Cecilia, first mentioned in a document of 973 [ACV, II–4–5r (AC 61 mp n6)], appears as one of the chapter's churches in the eleventh-century liturgical document known as the *Carpsum* [L'orazionale, pp. 117–18.] San Pietro in Carnario was built sometime before 955 by Count Milo and, although ordained in his will to come under the authority of San Zaccaria in Venice (*CDV* 2 no. 255), seems to have come into the hands of the canons instead.

41. The bull (*PL* 200: 1110–11) also included chapels at Pradelle (within the Veronese diocese) and at the manor of Badabiones (in Trent). I have not included in this count the church of San Ambrogio de Casale Alto. It is listed in this 1177 confirmation to the canons, but also appears in Eugene III's earlier bull confirming the bishop's possessions. The same is the case for the churches of Lusia. Perhaps, as we know was the case from San Giorgio in Salsis, the canons owned the property of these churches but the bishop reserved care of souls.

42. Veronese historians have used the bull to outline the contours of the diocese in the mid-twelfth century but have done so only with hesitancy, maintaining that the list of *plebes* seems

First, although the bull is by no means a complete picture of all the churches in the Veronese diocese, it is a nearly complete portrait of its baptismal churches in the mid-twelfth century. A systematic study of all Veronese documents through the mid-twelfth century reveals only seven churches identified as *plebes* that are not included in the bull: San Fermo in Nono,[43] San Giovanni Battista in Quinzano,[44] Santa Maria in Garda,[45] San Lorenzo in Ostiglia,[46] Santa Maria in Sorgà,[47] Sant'Andrea (north of Calavena),[48] and the *plebs* of Mondragone.[49] There are reasons why each of these churches is absent from the bull. San Fermo in Nono probably no longer existed by the time the bull was compiled. Neither the church nor the place name, Nono, is mentioned after 1127, and movements of the Adige in this region make it highly likely that the settlement was abandoned and the territory of the *plebs* divided up among Zevio, Ronco, and Tombazosana.[50] San Giovanni Battista in Quinzano and San Faustino in Mondragone were directly dependent upon the cathedral chapter and Santa Maria in Sorgà upon Santa Maria in Organo,[51] and thus do not appear in the bull. San Lorenzo in Ostiglia was dependent upon San Zeno,[52] as probably was Santa Maria in Garda.[53] Sant'Andrea was dependent upon the

---

very incomplete. Egidio Rossini, "Insediamenti, chiese e monasteri nel territorio di Verona," *Chiese-terr.*, p. 84.

43. First identified as a *plebs* in 860, CDV 1 no. 217; mentioned again in 959, CDV 2 no. 263, and for the last time in 1127, ASVR, S. Stefano, no. 41.

44. CDV 1 nos. 174, 176.

45. Probably ancient, but definitely called *plebs* as of 1056, ASVR, Ospitale Civico, no. 42.

46. In existence from at least the ninth century, San Lorenzo was definitely a *plebs* by the mid-twelfth century. ASVR, Ospitale Civico, no. 1 app.

47. Called simply *ecclesia* in a document of 939, in which this church was given to Santa Maria in Organo, it is called a *plebs* by 1011. CDV 2 no. 222; ASVR, Famiglia Maggio, no. 3.

48. This church appears as a *plebs* in a document of 1115, ASVR, SS. Nazaro e Celso, no. 803.

49. ASVR, SS. Apostoli, no. 7, dated 1146.

50. Castagnetti, *La pieve*, pp. 54–64.

51. PL 200: 1100–11, 1126–28.

52. The mid-twelfth-century litigation concerning Ostiglia verifies San Lorenzo's dependence upon the monastery of San Zeno. A witness testified that he saw the abbot of San Zeno answer for the church of San Lorenzo in the diocesan synod, and other witnesses testified to the presence of the monastery's abbots and monks at the church. ASVR, Ospitale Civico, no. 1 app.

53. The evidence for Santa Maria's dependence upon San Zeno is more indirect. The only mention of this *plebs* occurs in a document of 1056 concerning the monastery of San Zeno (ASVR, Ospitale Civico, no. 42). In it, the priest of the *plebs* is identified as "abitator in Bardolino," where the monastery was the major proprietor and definitely controlled the chapel of San

monastery of Santi Nazaro e Celso.[54] Both these monasteries already appear on the bull as subject to the authority of the bishop.[55]

Thus, Pope Eugene's bull shows that the bishop of Verona by 1145 had established his jurisdiction over fifty-seven of the sixty documented baptismal churches in the diocese. It is important to remember here, lest such episcopal dominance seem normal, that it was not a natural or necessary development from the organization of the Veronese Church at the millennium. The immense power and prestige of the cathedral chapter had bested Bishop Ratherius in the tenth century. How then had Verona's bishops established their jurisdiction over so much of their diocese by the mid-twelfth century? How had their hierarchy of dependencies come to overshadow all others?

First, as the Veronese Church expanded over the eleventh and early twelfth centuries, control over churches was usually established through proprietary or seigneurial rights.[56] The churches gained by the cathedral chapter follow this pattern: the canons held castles or estates (villis) at Prun, Marzana, and Calmasino and exercised seigneurial rights in them.[57] Thus, they came to control the churches of San Paolo in Prun, Ognissanti in Marzana, and San Michele in Calmasino.[58] Although the chapter's temporal holdings within the diocese had expanded greatly after the millennium, the bishop's had expanded even more rapidly. By the mid-twelfth century, the chapter held significant property and seigneurial rights in

Zeno. There is also some evidence that the monastery controlled another church in Garda, San Vigilio. Massimo Ragnolini, *Garda* (Verona, 1972), p. 49.

54. In the only document (1115) mentioning this *plebs*, the abbot of San Nazaro was exchanging all his lands within the castle and *plebs* of San Andrea for lands in the village of "Mundonus," *ASVR*, SS. Nazaro e Celso, no. 803.

55. Giancarlo Andenna discovered similar lacunae using a bull of Innocent II (1133), confirming the possessions of the bishop of Novara, to study the baptismal churches of that diocese. Several known *plebes* were missing from the bull because they were dependent either upon the cathedral chapter of Novara or upon other ecclesiastical institutions. Giancarlo Andenna, "Le pievi della diocesi di Novara," in *Le istituzioni . . . Diocesi, pievi, e parrocchie*, pp. 496–98.

56. This was true in other regions as well. In the diocese of Asti in Piedmont, the baptismal churches under the bishop's "rule and authority" (*regimine et potestate*) were on lands controlled by the see. Lucio Casto, "Il fondamento patrimoniale della potenza vescovile di Asti," *Bollettino storico–bibliografico subalpino* 73 (1975): 34–35.

57. *MGH DD* 4: 134–38 (no. 96) dated 1027; the diploma granted the canons the regalian rights of requisitioning fodder (*fodrum*) and hearing pleas (*placita*) in their castles and on their estates.

58. *PL* 200: 1110.

twenty-six communities within the diocese, the bishop in at least forty.[59] The bishop's manors in communities such as Ponti, Peschiera, Legnago, Minerbe, Bovolone, Isola Rizza, Colognola, Montorio, and Negrar led to his control of their new *plebes* in the eleventh century.

This connection between secular and ecclesiastical jurisdiction meant that the imperial allegiance of Verona's bishops aided the same cause championed by papal advocates of reform. The gains of Verona's bishops as temporal lords increased their ecclesiastical authority by bringing more churches, especially in new communities, under their jurisdiction. Temporal authority, however, was closely controlled in the region because of Verona's strategic importance to the empire, and it was only through the bishop's close relationship with imperial power that the see's temporal lordship was expanded.[60]

Some of the *plebes* in the bull, however, were in communities where the bishop held no known property or seigneurial rights. Many of these— Avio, Brentonico, Caprino, Lazise, Sirmione—were in the area between Lake Garda and the Adige, where imperial possessions and authority were still very significant. Others were on the plain, and here we find examples of *plebes* controlled by the bishop even where seigneurial authority was held by the cathedral chapter. Pope Eugene's bull confirms the baptismal churches of Cerea, Angiari, and Ronco to the bishop. The castles at Cerea and Angiari, however, were controlled by the canons; charters even reveal that the chapter received the churches of Angiari and Ronco in the tenth

---

59. Based on a comparison of two diplomata of Frederick Barbarossa confirming the possessions of the chapter and the see, both issued in 1154: MGH DD 10.1: 141–47 (nos. 87 and 88). For the state of each institution's holdings at the millennium see, for the bishop, MGH DD 2 (Otto III): 607–8 (no. 199) dated 996 and for the chapter, MGH DD 2 (Otto II): 361–62 (no. 305) dated 983.

60. Ecclesiastical institutions were the main beneficiaries when seigneurial rights were ceded; the emperors preferred them over lay lords, even over the Veronese counts. The bishop, the cathedral chapter, the monastery of San Zeno, and other institutions in the city became the brokers of such rights, subinfeudating them to knightly families. Andrea Castagnetti, *La Marca Veronese-Trevigiana* (Turin, 1986), pp. 8–36. For another example of reform established through episcopal lordship and property, see Karlotto Bogumil, *Das Bistum Halberstadt im 12. Jahrhundert* (Cologne, 1972), pp. 159–66. A contrary development can be seen in the diocese of Asti. There, the bishops renounced their traditional alliance with imperial power and espoused the papal cause. Expansion of the episcopal patrimony, which had been strong from the mid-tenth century, halted with this renunciation of imperial support. Lucio Casto, "Il fondamento patrimoniale," pp. 65–66.

century from lay donors.[61] How did the bishop get control of these baptismal churches? Unfortunately, our documentation offers no direct answers. It does, however, offer hints.

Litigation was clearly one means by which the bishop gained control of churches. Moreover, several twelfth-century cases underscore how closely associated were temporal authority and ecclesiastical jurisdiction. Bishop Tebaldus of Verona pursued long litigations with the canons claiming temporal jurisdiction of Porcile, Cerea, and Angiari in the 1140s.[62] He was not successful in his bid for temporal authority but, as the bull of 1145 reveals, he did gain ecclesiastical authority over the churches of these communities. Other cases reveal how ecclesiastical authority was finally extricated from temporal lordship in the mid-twelfth century.

The first and best documented litigation concerns the baptismal church of Nogara.[63] Once part of the royal manor "at the Two Oaks" (*ad Duos Robores*), the area that became the territory of Nogara was parcelled out to various loyal followers by Emperor Berengar I in the early tenth century. He granted the royal chapel of San Pietro to a deacon of the Veronese Church, Audibert, in 905 and in the next year conceded to this deacon the right to build a castle there "on account of the incursion of the pagans."[64] He also granted Audibert the right to hold a market, to collect tolls, and to exercise at Nogara all the seigneurial rights usually reserved to the crown. By 908 Audibert had built his castle and ceded half of it to the count of Verona.[65] This half of the castle came to the abbot of the monastery of San

---

61. Count Milo donated the church of Santa Maria in Ronco, which became the *plebs*, to the canons in 929, *CDV* 2 no. 205; Countess Ermengarda donated the castle and chapel of Angiari to the canons in 995, *ACV*, III–5–6r (BC 36 m3 n4).

62. From his elevation to the see in 1135 until 1138, Bishop Tebaldus challenged the canons' claim to the *districtus* of Porcile. Pope Innocent II settled the case in favor of the chapter, *ACV*, II–7–1r (AC 53 m2 n1). During the 1140s the bishop, again unsuccessfully, claimed jurisdiction over the castle of Cerea. The case resulted in extensive and interesting documentation, all preserved in the archive of the cathedral chapter. The 1146 decision of the papal legate in favor of the canons is *ACV*, II–7–3v (BC 45 mp n4). Some of the documentation indicates that the castle of Angiari was also in question. In 1137 the canons petitioned Empress Richenza to confirm their claim to the castles of Cerea *and* Angiari, *MGH DD* 8 (Richenza): 232–34 (no. 4).

63. All of the documentation for this case is published in Girolamo Tiraboschi, *Storia dell'augusta badia di S. Silvestro di Nonantola* (Modena, 1784–85). The case is discussed in great detail by Gabriella Rossetti, "Formazione e caratteri delle signorie di castello e dei poteri territoriali dei vescovi sulle città nella langobardia del secolo X," *Aevum* 49 (1975): 241–309.

64. Also published in *CDV* 2 nos. 66 and 76.

65. The donation is revealed in a judgment rendered by Emperor Berengar I in favor of San

Silvestro di Nonantola through the will of Count Anselm two years later.[66] By 1017 Nonantola had received the other half of the castle, in addition to much land in the area, in donations from the Marquis Boniface and his wife, Richilda.[67]

Thus the abbot of Nonantola became lord of this new seigneurial and territorial unit, the castle and *fundus* of Nogara. In the tenth century there were at least two chapels in the area: San Pietro, given to the deacon Audibert in 905, and San Zeno in Rovescello. The Marquis Boniface and his wife had built a chapel within the castle, dedicated to San Silvestro, and this they donated to the abbot along with the right to ordain its clergy. Boniface and Richilda also promised the abbot in 1017 to build a new church in Rovescello within three years. Of these four churches, it is clear that by the twelfth century the old royal chapel of San Pietro had become the baptismal church.[68] In 1139, the bishop of Verona began a long series of litigations claiming possession of this *plebs* at Nogara.

Pope Innocent II commended the dispute to the bishops of Vicenza and Mantua in April 1139. When Bishop Tebaldus of Verona did not present himself in Nogara that June to receive the judgment of these legates, they affirmed the abbot of Nonantola's right to the church. The case reopened in 1144, and another papal legate, the Cardinal priest Peter, again confirmed Nonantola's possession of the church.[69] Finally in 1145 a definitive agreement ended the quarrel. The bishop of Verona was granted the "ius parochiale" of San Pietro in Nogara. The letter is very clear about what this *ius* entailed. It gave the bishop of Verona the right to approve the archpriest elected by the clergy of the *plebs*, to invest that archpriest with the care of souls in his church, and to receive an oath of obedience from him. The bishop could perform ordinations of clergy there and had the right to discipline the clergy. He had the right to consecrate the church, and any of its altars and dependent chapels. The clergy of the *plebs* had to accept his visitations and offer the bishop hospitality. The abbot of Nonantola still had control over the property of the church, the "ius fundi." He retained the

---

Silvestro in 913. A certain Gariberga (a relative of Audibert?) was challenging the monastery's possession of the castle. *CDV* 2 no. 120.

66. *CDV* 2 no. 98.
67. Rossetti, "Formazione," pp. 278–79.
68. Ibid., pp. 278, 282–83.
69. Ibid., p. 283.

right to approve the archpriest elected by the clergy of the *plebs* and could invest him with the temporal goods of the church.[70]

This separation of ecclesiastical jurisdiction from temporal lordship was an important development. In 1122 it had helped resolve the investiture crisis: bishops henceforward received their spiritual authority from the pope and the temporal goods of their churches from their sovereign. By the mid-twelfth century, the application of this principle to ecclesiastical jurisdiction within the diocese decisively aided the bishop's quest for authority. It allowed him to secure ecclesiastical control without temporal jurisdiction.[71]

Another case from the mid-twelfth century reveals the bishop of Verona actually using this concept to extend his authority at the expense of the cathedral chapter. The canons claimed control of the church of San Giorgio in Salsis, a chapel dependent upon the baptismal church of Sant' Andrea di Sandrà. As in the case of Nogara, the claim was committed to papal legates. They judged spiritual authority over San Giorgio to belong to its *plebs* (already controlled by the bishop); the canons retained temporal authority.[72]

The reform movement and the investiture crisis contributed a valuable distinction between temporal and spiritual rights that aided the clarification and unification of authority within the Veronese diocese. The reform movement also propagated the idea that the bishop should rule his diocese, since it was through bishops that reform would be implemented.[73] Although Verona's bishops remained loyal to the emperor, it seems likely

70. Tiraboschi, *Storia* 2: 259–60 (no. 277). Similar kinds of cases occupied the canonists in the late twelfth century and early thirteenth. See Kenneth Pennington, *Pope and Bishops* (Philadelphia, 1984), pp. 154–86.

71. Augusto Vasina has briefly chronicled the emergence of a recognized ecclesiastical jurisdiction separate from patrimonial authority in Ravenna; he too sees this accomplished in the twelfth century. Augusto Vasina, "Le pievi dell'area Ravennate prima e dopo il Mille," in *Le istituzioni . . . Diocesi, pievi, e parrocchie*, pp. 607–27.

72. ACV, II–7–4v (AC 13 mp n4); I–6–6r (BC 27 m4 n1); Kehr, IP 7.1: 240.

73. The reformers' recognition of the importance of the episcopate is obvious in the centrality of the issue of episcopal investiture. Fliche, *La réforme* 2: 235–39. The saintly reforming bishop, in fact, became the hero of the reform movement. Pierre Toubert, *Les structures du Latium médiéval* (Rome, 1973) 2: 807–29. The canons of the Council of Melfi in 1089 demonstrate the importance of episcopal authority in the implementation of reform. Cinzio Violante, "Il monachesimo cluniacense di fronte al mondo politico ed ecclesiastico: Secoli X e XI" in *Studi sulla cristianità medioevale*, ed. Piero Zerbi (Milan, 1972), pp. 40–56.

that the general dispersion of this idea aided them in their efforts to establish their office as undisputed head of the diocese. As we have already seen, reform ideas greatly influenced the secular clergy. They increasingly looked to the bishop for leadership.

The bishop's influence with the clergy, indeed, was another means by which he increased his authority over areas where he held no temporal lordship.[74] While in the early Middle Ages the chapter trained most of the diocese's clergy, over the eleventh century many other *scole* had emerged to provide clergy for an expanding Church. As we have seen, the bishops of Verona and institutions under their authority were extremely prominent in the development of these *scole*. The Congregations of secular clergy—which came to represent the majority of clerics exercising care of souls in the diocese—appear allied with the bishop against the cathedral chapter by the mid-twelfth century. In a judicial proceeding in which Bishop Tebaldus presided, the archpriest of the urban Congregation and many of its clerics supported the bishop's judgment against the canons' claim to the church of Sant'Alessandro.[75]

The bishop had not only gained increased influence over the secular clergy during the eleventh and early twelfth centuries, but he had also increased his control over religious institutions. Whereas other bishops in this period struggled with monasteries for control of *plebes*, in Verona the bishop's consistent adversaries were the canons. Bishop Tebaldus's litigation with the abbot of Nonantola was the only episcopal dispute with a monastic institution. Why? Because by the twelfth century the see had already forged alliances with most of the monastic institutions in the diocese. The 1145 bull lists seven monasteries directly under the authority of the bishop. In addition to San Zeno, the bishop controlled two of the most successful and respected new monasteries of the eleventh century: San Nazaro and San Pietro in Calavena. Even when the bishop did not have direct authority over an institution, the see had cultivated strong ties. The monastery of San Giorgio in Braida, for example, does not appear on the 1145 bull as directly subject to the bishop; its founder had placed limits

---

74. Gabriella Rossetti has also noted the importance of the spread of the communal life in increasing the bishop's control over the secular clergy and the parochial system. The image, in fact, of the bishop changed radically over this period from that of a great noble defending the church to that of a paternal collaborator with the clergy in the pastoral care of the diocese. Gabriella Rossetti, "Origine sociale e formazione dei vescovi del «regnum italiae» nei secoli XI e XII" in *Le istituzioni . . . Diocesi, pievi, e parrocchie*, pp. 59, 66–75, 83.

75. ASVR, S. Martino d'Avesa, no. 1.

upon the bishop's authority over the house.[76] Yet San Giorgio was founded with the assistance of Bishop Walther and maintained close ties with the see. Thus Bishop Bernard was able to step in and reform the house in the early twelfth century without opposition. The leper hospital at Santa Croce provides another example. Although not listed in Eugene's bull as under the authority of the bishop, the house had received the early support of Bishop Tebaldus and looked to him for guidance. When a disagreement arose at Santa Croce, the dispute was submitted to the bishop's judgment.[77] Fostering new religious institutions increased the bishop's de facto authority within the diocese.

This last example suggests a vitally important means used by the bishop to expand his dominion: his pastoral presence. Through the fulfillment of sacred functions and the exercise of spiritual leadership the bishop established an authority that was at first charismatic, then juridical. A long scroll of testimony concerning the church of San Lorenzo at Ostiglia offers ample evidence of such spiritual presence yielding jurisdiction. When the bishop of Mantua tried to claim San Lorenzo in the mid-twelfth century, numerous witnesses recounted in detail how they knew that the church belonged to the diocese of Verona. Girard, the *gastaldus* of Ostiglia, recalled, "I saw Bishop Bernard received in Ostiglia with the ringing of bells, and lodged there; [I saw him] anoint the children of Ostiglia. Before that [sic], I saw Bishop Tebaldus who similarly came to Ostiglia, was lodged, and confirmed children. Another time he came and similarly anointed the children."[78] The recurrent visits of Veronese bishops to confirm youths with sacred chrism established their authority over the community. Considering that Ostiglia is only 35 kilometers from Mantua and more than 45 from Verona, sacramental presence was a much stronger force for jurisdiction than geography. How energetic a bishop was in administering the sacraments and consecrating churches could determine the extent of his jurisdiction.

76. Cadalus specified that the bishop had no authority to alienate any of the goods of the monastery; nor could he interfere in the election of the abbot. The bishop was, however, to consecrate the abbot elected by the monks and to "defend and govern" the monastery. *ASV*, Fondo Veneto, no. 6793.
77. *ASVR*, Istituto Esposti, no. 4".
78. "Episcopum Bernardum vidi susceptum in ostilia sonantibus campanis et ospitatum et [cri]smare pueros ostilie. Priusquam vidi episcopum Tebaldum qui prius venit ostiliam similiter susceptum et ospitatum et pueros confirmare. Alia vice venit et similiter pueros crismavit." *ASVR*, Ospitale Civico, no. 223.

Episcopal dominance within the organization of the Veronese Church was achieved through the expansion of the bishop's temporal lordship, through the development of a concept of ecclesiastical authority distinct from temporal jurisdiction, through the bishop's willingness to foster new institutions for the secular clergy as well as for the religious life, and through his work as pastor. Both the imperial ties of Verona's bishops and the reform movement contributed to this expansion of episcopal authority. The expansion of the Veronese Church was also intimately a part of this development. The great multiplication of churches within the diocese in the eleventh and early twelfth centuries both brought questions of organization to the fore and provided new opportunities to assert authority. It seems no coincidence that the period of the most rapid increase in the emergence of new churches—the second quarter of the twelfth century— was also the era of the most clamorous battles over jurisdictions. Uncontrolled growth meant unclear organization; lack of clarity forced clarification. Lack of clarity also offered numerous opportunities for the bishop to step in and assert leadership, to build his hierarchy of jurisdictions and ultimately to order his diocese under his authority. That Verona's bishops successfully met the challenge of growth seems clear from Eugene III's bull.

What was the structure over which the bishop presided by the mid-twelfth century? At the core of diocesan organization was the system of pastoral care. In the city, it consisted of an urban *plebs*, the cathedral, with many *tituli* or parishes dependent upon it.[79] This subdivision of the urban *plebs*, or devolution of pastoral care to neighborhood churches, probably occurred in the late eleventh century, definitely by the mid-twelfth. Pastoral care in the countryside was also organized around baptismal churches and their dependent chapels. Pope Eugene's bull is mainly a list of *plebes cum capellis*. These formed the main organizational framework of the diocese. It should be noted here that the Veronese diocese was not conceived of as an aggregate of encastled churches, as were the dioceses of Lazio by the mid-twelfth century.[80] Encastlement occurred unevenly

79. Jurisdiction over these churches exercising care of souls within the city was probably what Pope Eugene III meant to confirm to the bishop in the phrase "churches of this city" ("ecclesias ipsius civitatis"). We know, of course, that he did not have direct authority over the canons' church of San Giorgio and their other urban churches. This is one of the inconsistencies in the bull that have left it suspect.
80. Toubert, *Les structures* 2: 797–98, 860–67.

within the Veronese diocese—more on the open plain than in the hills, and very little in areas where imperial and comital authority remained strong[81]—and its impact on ecclesiastical organization was also very uneven. Some new *plebes* were in castles, some were not. Most early medieval *plebes* were not superseded by encastled churches. Overall, the diocese as it appears in the 1145 bull was a collection of baptismal churches and their dependent chapels, encastled or not. What is different from the early Middle Ages is that baptismal churches were more numerous and by the twelfth century had networks of dependent chapels and discrete territories. This much more highly articulated hierarchy of churches with care of souls was also more clearly delineated from other kinds of ecclesiastical institutions.[82]

There do seem to have been interstices in this network of *plebes cum capellis*. The 1145 bull lists fourteen *ecclesiae* under the bishop's authority.[83] They are not identified as *plebes*, but most of them, like the baptismal churches in the bull, are described only by a place name: the church "of Terrazzo," "of Bonferraro," "of Casaleone," or "of Salizzole."[84] That they are identified by a place name, rather than a title (Santa Maria, San Pietro, etc.), suggests that these were the only churches in these communities. Several later became baptismal churches or chapels dependent upon a *plebs*: Terrazzo and Salizzole were *plebes* by 1295; Casaleone was a baptismal

81. Andrea Castagnetti, "La pianura veronese nel medioevo. La conquista del suolo e la regolamentazione delle acque," in *Una città e il suo fiume: Verona e l'Adige*, ed. Giorgio Borelli (Verona, 1977) 1: 50–54; Andrea Castagnetti, *La Valpolicella dall'alto medioevo all'età comunale* (Verona, 1984), pp. 34–42.

82. This separation of the pastoral system from religious, especially monastic, institutions became a strong theme in the reform movement. In the ninth and tenth centuries, the acquisition of baptismal churches by monasteries was considered a means of getting these churches out of the hands of lay persons. But increased exemptions of monasteries from diocesan jurisdiction (Cluny being a prime example) led to recognition of the need for episcopal control of the pastoral system. From late in Gregory VII's pontificate, and especially under his successor Urban II, monasteries were increasingly prohibited from acquiring parochial institutions. Violante, "Pievi," p. 691 et seq.; Violante, "Il monachesimo," pp. 38–49; Toubert, *Les structures* 2: 898–924.

83. Andenna also discovered such *ecclesiae* in the 1133 Novarese bull. He suggested that these churches were in areas not yet organized into plebanal territories, or in areas being reorganized. Andenna, "Le pievi," pp. 493–94.

84. Of the fourteen, only three are identified by their titles: the church of San Pietro in Tartaro, the church of San Lazaro [no place name given], and the church of San Ambrogio de Casale Alto. The rest, like the baptismal churches on the list, are identified only by place name.

church and Bonferraro a dependent chapel by the end of the Middle Ages.[85] Could these churches have been claimed by the bishop because they were in new communities likely to merit a baptismal church? A document of 1135 reveals Bishop Bernard granting tithes to the church of Mazagata "in order that the priests of this church may administer baptism there" ("ut sacerdotes ipsius ecclesie ibi baptismum faciant"). The bishop made the church dependent upon the see: it was to pay no tribute to anyone, except its annual fee to the bishop, paid on the feast of San Zeno.[86] These other *ecclesiae* listed in the bull were all, like Mazagata, in areas where lands were being cleared and drained. It seems likely that these churches were considered incipient *plebes*; that the bishop in 1145 had already claimed them as part of his hierarchy suggests foresight and an aggressive effort to incorporate new churches into the system of pastoral care.

In addition to the structure of churches exercising care of souls, there were religious institutions and their dependencies. These hierarchies, dominant in the early Middle Ages, were now dwarfed by the pastoral system. Most of the religious institutions of the diocese, as we have seen, were already subject to the bishop's authority or strongly allied with the see. In the overall structure of the Veronese diocese, the cathedral chapter resembles a religious institution despite being composed of secular clerics. Because of its independent status and often difficult relations with the bishop, it had been increasingly excluded and isolated from the system of pastoral care over the eleventh and twelfth centuries.

Relationships of dependency formed in the early Middle Ages were maintained after the millennium and new ones established. The tenor of these relationships, however, changed. Whereas a definite mutuality informed these ties in the early Middle Ages, by the twelfth century these relationships were chiefly concerned with control.

In the 1180s, for example, two urban churches dependent upon the monastery of Santa Maria in Organo waged long legal battles against its

85. Terrazzo and Salizzole appear on the list of member churches of the rural Congregation sending delegates to the election of Bishop Bonincontro in 1295 (the document is published in Antonio Spagnolo, "Il clero veronese nella elezione del vescovo, 1080–1338," *AMAV* 84 (1907–8): 100–105). These two, plus Casaleone and Bonferraro, were among the baptismal churches and chapels visited by Bishop Giberti in the early sixteenth century. Rossini, "Insediamenti," pp. 88–89, and p. 85 on these *ecclesiae*.
86. ACV, II–6–7v (BC 17 m4 n7).

abbot. The cases resulted in several papal letters over seven years. At issue was whether the clergy of Santa Maria Antica and Santa Margarita had the right to elect other clerics to their churches. The abbot of Santa Maria claimed the right to assign priests and clerics to these churches. A letter of Pope Lucius III in 1184 judged the clergy of Santa Maria Antica to have the right to elect other clerics to the church. Once elected, however, the cleric had to present himself to the abbot to be confirmed and tonsured. The church still, the letter reminded, had to pay its annual fee to Santa Maria in Organo. If, however, the abbot "maliciously" delayed confirming the elected cleric, the cleric could present himself to either the bishop of Verona or the patriarch of Aquileia for confirmation and tonsure.[87] A letter outlining the same solution resolved Santa Margarita's case in 1185/1186.[88]

These two subject institutions were obviously chafing under the control of the abbot; they wanted more independence and more freedom to arrange their own affairs. Essentially, the early medieval conditions that had created a need for these relationships of subordination were much less pressing in the twelfth century. In a less turbulent environment, Santa Margarita and Santa Maria Antica no longer needed or wanted the abbot's administration and intercession. The abbot, however, insisted on a certain degree of control and the traditional annual fee paid by the dependent church.[89]

A similar emphasis on authority and control pervades the settlement concerning the *plebs* of Nogara. The emphasis in Pope Eugene III's letter settling the dispute was on the bishop's authority: his right to approve and invest the archpriest, his right to consecrate the church and its dependencies, his right to ordain and correct its clergy. It also stressed what the clergy of Nogara owed the bishop: an oath of obedience from the archpriest, hospitality when the bishop visited, certain sums when he had to go to

87. Kehr, IP 7.1: 254.
88. Ibid., p. 255.
89. Another good example of a dependent institution trying to extricate itself from this subordinate relationship is provided by the monastery of San Michele in Campagna in the late twelfth century. This female Benedictine house had been dependent upon the cathedral chapter since the tenth century, but having grown tremendously in wealth and prestige in the eleventh and twelfth centuries, it tried to challenge the control of the canons. Valeria Monese Recchia, "Aspetti sociali ed economici nella vita di un monastero benedettino femminile: S. Michele in Campagna di Verona dal secolo XI al periodo ezzeliniano," *Archivio veneto*, ser. 5, 98 (1973): 19–25. This phenomenon was not unique to Verona. For examples from southern Italy in the second half of the twelfth century, see G. A. Loud, *Church and Society in the Norman Principality of Capua*, 1058–1197 (Oxford, 1985), p. 218.

Rome. By the mid-twelfth century there is little evidence that subject institutions received anything in return for their dependence.

At the same time that small institutions were finding relationships of dependence much more oppressive, they began to forge new, more equal, relationships with other churches. The Congregation of urban clergy was essentially a confraternal, guild-like association of urban churches. The member churches participated as equals in the Congregation. The relationship was formed for mutual benefit, not control. These horizontal relations between churches were also aimed at power, but power achieved and shared collectively. That ecclesiastical institutions should begin to form such horizontal ties in the twelfth century is not surprising: the development of urban and rural communes, *consorterie*, tower societies, and guilds distinguished this era.

Generally, by the twelfth century all relationships between ecclesiastical institutions, vertical or horizontal, were increasingly defined by law. This was the great age of the renewed study of Roman law and the codification of canon law. The "ancient custom" a tenth-century patriarch could invoke in a dispute was being slowly refined, reconsidered, and brought into accordance with general principles. Relationships between ecclesiastical institutions were, as a result, much more sophisticated. Rights of jurisdiction were separated from property; notions and procedures of consent and election were developed.

The Veronese Church in the year 1150 was certainly in some ways more hierarchical than before. It was more clearly organized under the authority of its bishop. Yet one should not leap from "more hierarchical" to a vision of a "more feudal" Church.[90] Ecclesiastical institutions, of course, still had vassals. The Church's relations with the lay world were informed by feudal customs and practices. But relations between ecclesiastical institutions

---

90. Veronese evidence here supports the objections of both J. F. Larmarignier and Cinzio Violante to the broadly disseminated notion of the "feudal Church." Relations of dependence between ecclesiastical institutions were not "feudal" in any sense other than the vertical nature of the relationship. [J. F. Lamarignier, "Hiérarchie monastique et hiérarchie féodale," *Revue historique de droit français et étranger*, ser. 4, 31 (1953): 171–74.] Violante is right to point out a certain feudal tendency in ecclesiastical organization when ecclesiastical authority was still tied to proprietary and seigneurial rights. But this tendency, as he says, was but a "moment" in the development of ecclesiastical structures; by the late eleventh century, an organization based on a hierarchy of offices was superseding the earlier, vaguely feudal line of development. Violante, "Il monachesimo," pp. 14, 34 et seq.; see especially the long discursive footnote on the "feudal Church," n. 59, pp. 34–36.

were by the mid-twelfth century less personal and more institutionalized; they were defined more by law and less by turbulence and necessity.

Increased organizational sophistication and stability, however, had a negative side. By the second half of the twelfth century, the desire to establish order began to limit and restrict innovation. Churches could not be built without permission. New religious movements were perceived as threats to a hard-won and fragile order rather than as opportunities for expanding authority and strengthening the Church. By the end of the century, even to other churchmen the urge to control seemed oppressive and stifling. In 1199 Pope Innocent III reprimanded the bishop of Verona for his zeal, "lest the wheat be eradicated with the chaff, or the vineyard be ruined in driving out the worm."[91] He cautioned the prelate to use discretion, and ordered him to reconsider his excommunication of certain pious lay persons called Humiliati.[92]

Both these negative and positive characteristics seem highly significant because the institutional arrangements the Veronese Church developed in the eleventh and twelfth centuries would prove remarkably durable. The basic structure of authority within the diocese in 1150—the bishop controlling the network of baptismal churches and dependent chapels that constituted the core of the diocese, as well as most of its religious institutions—endures today. The distinctions developed by the twelfth century to separate temporal from spiritual jurisdiction, and to apportion rights within relationships between institutions, provided the basic organizational patterns of the medieval Church. These organizational structures, moreover, created tensions not only for innovative evangelical lay movements. The tensions they produced affected even those at the very apex of these structures: the bishops.

91. "Licet in agro patris familias evangelici zizania saepe pullulent inter messes, et vineam Domini Sabaoth interdum nitatur tinea demoliri; sic tamen prudens agricola vinitorque discretus salubre debet remedium invenire, ne vel triticum evellatur inter zizania, vel in dejectione tineae vinea corrumpatur." *PL* 214: 788.

92. *PL* 214: 789. On the Humiliati, see Lester Little, *Religious Poverty and the Profit Economy in Medieval Europe* (Ithaca, N.Y., 1978), pp. 113–20; on the background to Innocent III's letter, see Brenda Bolton, "Innocent III's Treatment of the Humiliati," *Studies in Church History* 8 (1972): 73–82.

# 6  THE BISHOPS AND THEIR SEE

**T**HERE were two critical turning points in the formation of the medieval Veronese episcopate. The first was in the late eighth century. From the origins of the see to 780, Veronese bishops led a missionary and oppressed Church from outside the city walls. After the conversion of the Lombards and the Carolingian conquest, the bishops were allied with political authority and came to rule a dominant and empowered Church from the heart of the city. From the late eighth to the early twelfth century, the bishops were foreigners appointed by the emperor both to uphold his authority and to oversee Christian life in the diocese. A second turning point in the early twelfth century came when the Concordat of Worms in 1122 ended direct imperial investiture of bishops; local Veronese clerics elected by the cathedral chapter came to hold the see. These bishops were still political figures, but their politics were more local: they and their supporters were an important constituent element in the free commune that had emerged in Verona. With the retreat of the see's traditional imperial allies, Verona's bishops increasingly turned to Rome and to the successors of Saint Peter for support. At the same time that the see was struggling to adjust to these revolutionary political and ecclesiological changes, it still faced enormous spiritual and institutional challenges within the diocese. In the early twelfth century, the diocese was more populous, in souls and in institutions. Its organization was more complex, and it was animated with new religious expectations. In its earliest centuries, saintly bishops abounded in the see. By the mid-twelfth century, the desire for saints was no less, but the episcopal office had become a difficult milieu for the holy.

From the third century to the late eighth, the two most striking characteristics of the Veronese episcopate are the overwhelming reputation for sanctity enjoyed by the bishops and the scarcity of solid documentation concerning their careers.[1] Thirty-six of the 43 bishops who held the see before 780 (84 percent) are venerated as saints. Although very little survives to illumine the lives of these early saintly bishops, some of the conditions that shaped their episcopates can be identified.

In this early period, Verona's bishops were leaders of a persecuted Church huddled on the city's periphery. As in other Roman cities, Christianity had its earliest havens in the cemeteries on Verona's outskirts. The early Christians' reverence for and attachment to those whom Peter Brown has called "the very special dead"—martyrs and other exemplary Christians whose powers were believed to emanate from their graves—resulted in the foundation of Christian churches on burial sites; always, by Roman funerary custom, outside the city.[2] Verona's first church lay in one such cemetery off the Via Postumia southwest of the city. Dating from the third century, this church eventually took the name of Verona's fourth bishop, the martyr Proculus (260–301).[3] This church was also the first resting place of the town's patron, Bishop Zeno, "who through his preaching led Verona to baptism."[4]

In the fifth century, however, Verona's bishops for unknown reasons moved their see to the church of Santo Stefano. This church had been built on a burial site just beyond the walls of the *castrum* along the Via Claudia Augusta, where the remains of forty Veronese martyrs were interred. These local martyrs had been executed during the persecutions of the Emperor Diocletian; perhaps it was a desire to associate the see with their veneration that prompted the move.[5] Both of these early episcopal churches—Santo Stefano and San Procolo—were located on the city's periphery and built on ground sanctified by martyrs' blood. Both their location and their patrons celebrate the marginalized position of the see.

1. The series of early bishops has been pieced together from several sources. Chief among them are the *Versus de Verona* (lines 40 to 54 enumerate several early bishops) and the "Velo di Classe," a woven and embroidered cloth decorated with images of early bishops. Several martyrologies, conciliar *acta*, inscriptions, and a few early charters provide references to the early leaders of the Veronese Church. See Ederle, *Dizionario; Versus de Verona. Versum de Mediolano civitate,* ed. G. B. Pighi (Bologna, 1960); Carlo Cipolla, "Il Velo di Classe," *Le gallerie nazionali italiane* 3 (1897): 194–249.

2. Peter Brown, *The Cult of the Saints* (Chicago, 1981), chap. 1, especially pp. vii, 3, 8–9.

3. *San Proculo* (Verona, 1988); Luigi Simeoni, "Le sedi della cattedrale a Verona prima dell'attuale," *Studi storici veronesi* 4 (1953): 13–16.

4. ". . . qui Veronam predicando deduxit ad baptismo." *Versus de Verona,* p. 153, line 46.

5. Simeoni, "Le sedi," p. 16 et seq.; Alessandro Da Lisca, "La basilica di S. Stefano in Verona," *AMAV* 114 (1935–36): 45–52.

Clearly the early bishops of Verona were without political power and often on bad terms with the city's rulers. The Goths who ruled Verona in the fifth and sixth centuries were Arian Christians and seem not to have developed any particular liking for the local Catholic bishop. The Gothic king Theodoric earned the special odium of local Christians in the late fifth century by ordering the destruction of Santo Stefano. Despite, or to spite, the Arian king's hostility, the church was rebuilt, and Verona's bishops continued to reside there until the late eighth century.[6] Succeeding the Goths as rulers of the city in the late sixth century were the Lombards, another Arian Christian people. The Lombard kings eventually accepted Catholic Christianity, but only under Kings Desiderius and Liutprand in the eighth century could Catholics claim dominance in the city. The new position of the Church after the conversion of the Lombards was aptly symbolized by the transfer of the bishop's *cathedra* to a location within the walls of the city for the first time.[7]

This transfer marked the beginning of a new era. From the third to the late eighth century, Verona's bishops had presided over a Church purified and steeled by the blood of recent martyrs. The oppression suffered by this early Christian community created ideal conditions for the cultivation of episcopal holiness, and most of these bishops are remembered as having met this challenge. Most of the conditions that yielded saintly bishops, however, seem to have vanished with the conversion of Verona's Lombard rulers. Although Lombard hegemony did not long outlast this conversion, Verona's new Carolingian overlords solidified and deepened the see's rapprochement with secular political authority.

From the coming of the Carolingians to the end of the investiture conflict, Verona's bishops were imperially appointed foreigners. They came from far north of the Alps, from places like Reichenau, Corvey, Liège, Ulm, and Hildesheim.[8] The early Carolingian appointees came from

---

6. *VerST* 2: 9–10. On the question of where the bishops presided during the rebuilding, see Simeoni, "Le sedi," pp. 18–23. Da Lisca, on the basis of archaeological evidence, contends that the church was only partially destroyed.

7. The earliest Lombard donations to the Church date from this period: *CDV* 1 nos. 25, 30, 39, 53; Biancolini, *Chiese* 2: 474. On the movement of the cathedral to Santa Maria Matricolare, see *VerST* 2: 44.

8. German prelates were common in the sees of northeastern Italy and in Piedmont. See Romuald Bauerreiss, "Vescovi bavaresi nell'Italia settentrionale tra la fine del X secolo e l'inizio

imperial monasteries. Both Egino (780–803) and his successor, probably his nephew, Ratoldus (803–840) were monks of Reichenau.[9] Another route to the see was through the imperial court chapel. Walther, bishop from 1037 to 1055, began his career this way.[10] Walbrunn (1094–1100) also came out of the chapel; he was chancellor to Henry IV.[11] Still others came to the see through their kin: Bishop Hilduin (928–931) was a relative of Hugh of Provence, who claimed the iron crown of Italy in 926.[12] By his own account, John (1015–1037) became bishop because his father enjoyed the favor of Emperor Henry II.[13] At the same time that John was raised to the see, his father was made count of Garda and his brother count of Verona.[14]

One should not assume from these routes to the Veronese *cathedra* that the see was a dumping ground for court toadies and annoying relatives. Imperial investiture brought some rather extraordinary men to Verona. Bishop Egino (780–803) was the architect of St. Peter's basilica in Re-

---

dell'XI," in *Vescovi e diocesi in Italia nel medioevo (sec. IX–XIII)* (Padua, 1964), pp. 157–60; G. Biscaro, "Le temporalità del vescovo di Treviso dal secolo IX al XIII," *Archivio veneto*, ser. 5, 18 (1936): 32–33; Giorgio Cracco, "Religione, Chiesa, pietà," in *Storia di Vicenza II* (Vicenza, 1988), pp. 368, 385–86; Angelo Tafi, *La chiesa aretina dalle origini al 1032* (Arezzo, 1972), p. 267; Fedele Savio, *Gli antichi vescovi d'Italia, La Lombardia*, 2 vols. (Florence, 1913; Bergamo, 1932) 2: 43–44, 257–61; Fedele Savio, *Gli antichi vescovi d'Italia: Il Piemonte* (Turin, 1898) pp. 87, 127–28, 340–43, 387, 443, 445–46, 451–52, 463, 466–67, 475. See also Hans Pahncke, *Geschichte der Bischöfe Italiens deutscher Nation von 951–1264, I. Teil, Einleitende Periode 951–1004* (Berlin, 1913), pp. 72–105.

9. Meersseman, *L'orazionale*, p. 4.

10. Josef Fleckenstein, *Die Hofkapelle der deutschen Könige, II: Die Hofkapelle im Rahmen der Ottonisch-Salischen Reichskirche* (Stuttgart, 1966). On the court chapel as a route to prominent sees, see Timothy Reuter, "The 'Imperial Church System' of the Ottonian and Salian Rulers: A Reconsideration," *Journal of Ecclesiastical History* 33 (1982): 352–53.

11. MGH DD 6: 599 (no. 444), 602 (no. 446). The role, influence, and composition of the chapel did change under Henry IV, especially during the regency of Anno of Cologne and Adalbert of Bremen. From 1077, however, the emperor was appointing most of his bishops from the chapel. See Josef Fleckenstein, "Hofkapelle und Reichsepiskopat unter Heinrich IV," *Investiturstreit und Reichsverfassung*, ed. Josef Fleckenstein (Munich, 1973), pp. 117–40.

12. Ederle, *Dizionario*, p. 29.

13. ACV, I–5–2r (BC 46 m3 n4); also published in Biancolini, *Chiese* 2: 470–72.

14. Vittorio Cavallari, "Il conte di Verona fra il X e l'XI secolo," *AMAV* 142 (1965–66): 94–100. All of these routes to the see are typical for their periods. Monastic bishops were common in the Carolingian and early Ottonian era, but members of cathedral chapters came to dominate in the eleventh century, and in the late Salian period the court chapel achieved its greatest importance as preparation for the episcopate. See Herbert Zielinski, *Der Reichsepiskopat in spätottonischer und salischer Zeit (1002–1125)* (Stuttgart, 1984), pp. 243–44.

ichenau before he was sent to oversee the diocese.[15] Nottingus (840–844) was a friend of Hincmar of Reims, a correspondent of Rabanus Maurus, and a theologian in his own right.[16] Bishop Adelard (876–915) was a poet as well as a diplomat.[17] Ratherius (932–935, 946–947, 961–968) was one of the few intellectual luminaries the tenth century produced,[18] and Bruno (1072–1080) was master of the cathedral school of Hildesheim before being raised to the see.[19]

The outstanding qualities of many of these leaders, however, were only intermittently enjoyed by local believers. Imperial bishops were government functionaries as well as pastors.[20] The entire characterization and

15. Georg Kaspar Nagler, *Neues allgemeines Künstlerlexikon* (Munich, 1835–52) 4: 87.

16. *CDV* 1 no. 161; Ederle, *Dizionario,* pp. 27–28.

17. *Carmen de Adalhardo episcopo Veronensi, MGH, Poetae Latini aevi Carolini* 3: 693–95; Ederle, *Dizionario,* p. 29.

18. After Ratherius had lost the Veronese see for the second time, he was called to the court of Otto I by the emperor's brother Bruno, who (a contemporary chronicler assures us) "valued the many arguments of the philosophers. Ratherius is summoned and held to be first among the palace philosophers" ("multiplicibus philosophorum pollebat argumentis. Advocatur Ratherius; et habetur inter palatinos philosophos primus"). *Folcuini Gesta Abbatum Lobiensium, MGH SS* 4: 64.

19. *Chronicon Hildesheimense, MGH SS* 7: 848.

20. The secular power of bishops has been an important topic in both German and Italian scholarship. The essays in *I poteri temporali dei vescovi in Italia e in Germania nel medioevo,* ed. Carlo Guido Mor, Heinrich Schmidinger (Bologna, 1979) well illustrate the shared interests in this topic. Its importance in the German tradition stems from the prominent role played by territorial states, many of them ecclesiastical, in modern German history. Günter Glaeske's *Die Erzbischöfe von Hamburg-Bremen als Reichsfürsten* (937–1258) (Hildesheim, 1962) and Gabriele Meier's more recent *Die Bischöfe von Paderborn und ihr Bistum im Hochmittelalter* (Paderborn, 1987) are good examples of this emphasis. Because of the importance of the rise of the free communes in the Italian historiographical tradition, the public authority exercised by bishops has also preoccupied Italian scholars. Bishops did act as conduits of public authority, receiving rights and privileges from emperors that they later ceded to emerging communal governments. This emphasis, however, yields a rather passive view of episcopal relations with imperial authority, portraying bishops as mere recipients of imperial largesse rather than as active participants in imperial government. The modern history of Italy has, obviously, shaped this marked reluctance to acknowledge the involvement of Italian sees in German imperial domination of the medieval kingdom of Italy and has produced a noticeable ambivalence about prelates wielding secular authority. Gioacchino Volpe, for example, in a study of the Lunigiana published just after World War I, characterized the bishop's administration of justice, leadership of an army, and entourage of ministers and vassals as the transplantation of "rude German episcopal courts" to "cultured and already bourgeois Tuscany" ("...richiama l'immagine delle rudi corti vescovili germaniche o di Trento o di Aquileia, traspiante ai confini della culta ed ormai

definition of the imperial Church, or Reichskirchensystem, has been reevaluated in recent years,[21] but it is still abundantly clear that imperial bishops performed many important services for their monarchs.[22] The emperor's justice was often administered by prelates. In 820 Bishop Ratoldus, acting as missus domini imperatoris, decided a case between the count of Verona and the monastery of Nonantola.[23] Similarly, Bishop Adelard decided a dispute over lands in 880 as missus of Charles the Fat.[24]

Although many such duties could be accomplished in the see, many could not. The counsel that bishops owed their monarch often necessitated their presence at synods or in the imperial entourage. Bishop Otbertus, a confidant of the young Otto III, was frequently on the road with the emperor. He was with Otto in Ravenna in 996, with him in Pavia and Ravenna in 1001, and with Henry II in Regensburg the following year.[25] Bishop Bruno in January of 1076 attended a synod at Worms and was among those who signed a letter to Pope Gregory VII renouncing obedience to him.[26] His successor, Bishop Segebonus, signed the decree of the Synod of Brixen (25 June 1080) declaring Pope Gregory deposed.[27] The

---

borghese Toscana."). Gioacchino Volpe, Toscana medievale (Florence, 1964), p. 316; see also Volpe's discussion of the development of episcopal authority in Volterra, reprinted in the same volume, pp. 149–57 and Eugenio Dupré Theseider, "Vescovi e città nell'Italia precomunale," in Vescovi e diocesi, pp. 71–84. Luigi Simeoni's interpretation of Verona's Bishop Tebaldus (discussed below) stands firmly within this tradition. Cinzio Violante's work, exceptional in many ways, is particularly notable for surmounting these tendencies; see La società milanese nell'età precomunale (Rome, 1953; rpt. Rome, 1974), pp. 184–85, 216–17.

21. On the definition of the Reichskirchensystem see Josef Fleckenstein, "Zum Begriff der Ottonisch-Salischen Reichskirche," Geschichte, Wirtschaft, Gesellschaft, ed. Erich Hassinger et al. (Berlin, 1974), pp. 61–71 and, more recently, Josef Fleckenstein, "Problematik und Gestalt der Ottonisch-Salischen Reichskirche," Reich und Kirche vor dem Investiturstreit, ed. Karl Schmid (Munich, 1985), pp. 83–98; on its functioning, see Reuter, "'Imperial Church System'," pp. 347–48, 373–74.

22. A good overview is Zielinski, Der Reichsepiskopat, pp. 199–242.

23. CDV 1 no. 121.

24. CDV 1 no. 273.

25. MGH DD 2: 602 (no. 192), 827–29 (no. 396), 844 (no. 411), and 3: 27 (no. 24). Bishop Notker drew up his will in 921 in Mantua, "where the most glorious emperor lord Berengar was presiding" ("ubi domnus Berengarius gloriosisimus imperator preerat"). CDV 2 no. 177. Bishop Wolftrigel was with Henry IV in Padua in 1096, and Bishop Hezilo attended him in Kaiserworth in 1101. MGH DD 6: 611 (no. 452), 641 (no. 471).

26. MGH Const. 1: 106–8 (no. 58).

27. Ibid., pp. 117–20 (nos. 69–70).

slow pace of travel and the considerable distances the bishop often had to cover meant that he could be absent from his see for months at a time.[28]

The chief results of this aspect of the episcopal alliance with power were the strengthening of the cathedral chapter and the development of the office of *vicedominus*. As has already been discussed, from the ninth century the cathedral chapter became not only the guardian of local ecclesiastical culture but also increasingly independent, wealthy, and powerful. The involvement of the bishop in matters outside the diocese and his occasional absences encouraged this development. The delegation of some administrative duties to a subordinate was also a natural result of these exigencies. The office of *vicedominus* emerged shortly after the installation of imperial bishops began. The first evidence of this functionary comes from a judicial case of 806 in which the *vicedominus* Paul, at the command of Bishop Ratoldus, presented the see's claim to possession of a forest against that of Count Ademar.[29] In 866 the deacon Adelbert, *vicedominus* of Bishop Aistulf, enacted an exchange of lands.[30] These officials continue to appear in charters of the tenth and eleventh centuries. Some were clerics, all of these deacons: the abovementioned Adelbert; the deacon Dagibert, who transacted episcopal business as *vicedominus* in 931; and the famous Cadalus, who as a deacon served as Bishop Walther's *vicedominus*.[31] Ratoldus's *vicedominus* Paul was not identified as a cleric, and the early twelfth-century *vicedominus* Aldegerius was most definitely a lay person. He is identified as an episcopal vassal as well as *vicedominus* in a document of 1100 and appears in a donation to the monastery of San Nazaro with his two sons, Penzo and William.[32]

---

28. Bishop Ratoldus was absent from the see for six years on imperial business (see above, Chapter 5, note 32). This was probably abnormal, but it is admittedly difficult to chart the duration of episcopal absences. One should also note that episcopal absenteeism did not end when direct imperial investiture was curtailed with the Synod of Worms in 1122. Papal and provincial councils in the late twelfth and thirteenth centuries pulled bishops out of their sees nearly as frequently as had imperial business. The appeal of disputed elections to the Holy See, and later the system of papal provisions itself, often resulted in vacancies of months if not years. Absence from one's see, however, did not necessarily mean neglect of its concerns. Bishop Benno II of Osnabrück used his time and influence at the imperial court to restore to his see tithes held by two powerful monasteries for centuries. Edgar N. Johnson, "Bishop Benno II of Osnabrück," *Speculum* 16 (1941): 402–3.

29. CDV 1 no. 71.

30. CDV 1 no. 234.

31. CDV 2 nos. 211, 214; ASVR, S. Anastasia, no. 5; ASV, Fondo Veneto, nos. 6781, 6795, 6796.

32. Biancolini, *Chiese* 3: 295–96; ASVR, SS. Nazaro e Celso, no. 806. In other cities, lay members of

The purpose of having a *vicedominus* was clearly to provide for the administration of the episcopal patrimony on a continuous basis. All of the documents in which these functionaries appear deal with the disposition or defense of episcopal lands and rights. There are also hints of a fuller administrative apparatus. Louis II in 873 granted the bishop of Verona the right to appoint "advocates and defenders" if the see or the monastery of San Zeno was involved in litigation. This was a right the bishop definitely exercised: at a judicial session before Henry II in 1021 the abbot of San Zeno appeared "with the judge Amelgausus, advocate of the bishop of [the see] of Saint Zeno and of this monastery."[33] In the early twelfth century a man named Jordan, "advocate of this church, Santa Maria Matricolare," appears several times.[34] Louis also conceded that the see "may have notaries and chancellors to write documents." These notaries did not have to pay fees to imperial authorities and were entirely under ecclesiastical control.[35]

The great size and complexity of the episcopal patrimony certainly kept this administrative corps busy. The see had several kinds of resources; extensive real property was the most basic. Louis II in 860 granted the manor of Riva on Lake Garda to the see, and we know from a fragmentary inventory that the bishops also held manors at Legnago and "Massincago" before the millennium.[36] The same inventory also indicates lands in Sabbion, Vangadizza, Begosso, Porto Legnago, and Bonavigo (all southeast of the city on the plain).[37] By the early twelfth century the patrimony had swelled to include several more manors near Garda (at Malcesine, Cisano, Peschiera, Desenzano, San Lazaro and Balsemate on the Mincio), several in

---

local lineages served as episcopal *vicedomini* much earlier (in Treviso from the tenth century and in Florence from the early eleventh century). It seems to me significant that the appearance of a lay *vicedominus* in Verona coincides with the eclipse of imperial authority in the city during the investiture conflict. Biscaro, "Le temporalità," pp. 21–25; George W. Dameron, *Episcopal Power and Florentine Society, 1000–1320* (Cambridge, Mass., 1991), pp. 28–29.

33. Two years later he presented himself at another judicial proceeding, which took place at the bishop's house, with the notary and advocate. Manaresi, *Placiti* 2/2: 626–29 (no. 309), 661–63 (no. 320); ASVR, Ospitale Civico, no. 26.

34. ACV, I–6–4r (AC 12 mp n11, doc. 2); III–7–8v (AC 16 m7 n11); II–7–1r (AC 10 m4 n4).

35. CDV 1 no. 242.

36. CDV 1 no. 209; *Inventari altomedievali di terre, coloni, e redditi*, ed. Andrea Castagnetti et al. (Rome, 1979), pp. 101, 106. Castagnetti locates "Massincago" in the zone east of the Adige toward Vicenza, between Arcole, Lonigo, and Cologna Veneta.

37. *Inventari*, pp. 102, 104–6.

the diocese of Brescia, and others in the foothills and on the plain.[38] The see also held Cavalpone, Roverchiara, Angiari, Isola Rizza, Bovolone, Campalano, Grezzana, the entire Valle Longazeria, and at least nine castles.[39] The see's holdings were mostly concentrated around Lake Garda, in the Valle Longazeria, and along the Adige south and east of the city, particularly around Legnago.

In addition to real property, the see held significant fiscal rights related to commerce. The bishop controlled and collected dues at the city market in the forum (Piazza delle Erbe) as well as the market fairs held each year on the feast of the dedication of the basilica of San Zeno (8 December) and on Palm Sunday. The fees and tolls collected at the city's two busiest gates—the Porta San Zeno and the Porta San Fermo—also went to the see, as well as river tolls (*teloneum, ripaticum*) collected at the city and downstream at Porto Legnago.[40] The bishop also controlled the mint at Verona.[41] Until the mid-twelfth century, the Veronese mint was one of only three between the Alps and the Apennines (Pavia and Milan were the other two). Veronese *denarii* were the money of account not only in northeast Italy but also in southern Germany; they were not eclipsed until the revival of the Venetian mint in the late twelfth century.[42]

Finally, the bishop of Verona enjoyed immunity and seigneurial rights on all of his manors, in all of his castles, and in most of the other communities where he held considerable property. He was, in sum, a great lord. He held court, administered justice, and received all the services and payments normally reserved to the emperor. No duke, marquis, count, or viscount; no archbishop, or any other bishop; no imperial official great or

---

38. Caldiero, Arbizzano, Minerbe, and San Prosdocimo, plus half of the manors of Colognola, Illasi, Lavagno, Negrar, and San Giorgio di Valpolicella, MGH DD 10.1: 144–45 (no. 88).

39. Ibid.

40. *CDV* 1 no. 96; MGH DD 1: 474–75 (no. 348); Luigi Simeoni, "Dazii e tolonei medievali di diritto privato a Verona," *Studi storici veronesi* 8–9 (1957–58): 191–248. Cinzio Violante has discussed the important role bishops played in the development of a monetary economy through their control of such rights. Cinzio Violante, "I vescovi dell'Italia centro-settentrionale e lo sviluppo dell'economia monetaria," in *Vescovi e diocesi*, especially pp. 202–5, 210–11. See also Osheim, *An Italian Lordship*, pp. 89–90; Sabatino Ferrali, "Le temporalità del vescovado nei rapporti col comune a Pistoia nei secoli XII e XIII," in *Vescovi e diocesi*, p. 373; Biscaro, "Le temporalità," pp. 4–5, Volpe, *Toscana medievale*, p. 325.

41. MGH DD 10.1: 145 (no. 88).

42. Peter Spufford, *Handbook of Medieval Exchange* (London, 1986), p. 93; Peter Spufford, *Money and its Use in Medieval Europe* (Cambridge, 1988), pp. 189, 201, 227.

small could challenge, hinder, or limit his authority within his patrimony.[43] Bishop Bernard in the early twelfth century had a pillar erected in the middle of the village of Colognola to remind the inhabitants of his lordship.[44] There were, however, other less subtle reminders at the bishop's disposal: he had his own vassals. Often, as episcopal wills reveal, they were blood relatives. Bishop Billongus in 846 left property to Fulcernus and Gerard, "my vassals and kinsmen" ("uassis et parentibus meis"), and Bishop Audo's will of 860 left goods to a vassal and relative, his nephew Rimpert.[45] In addition to his vassals, the bishop could call upon the military services of the freemen known as "arimanni" and could requisition fodder for horses and food for his men.

This martial and lordly figure of a bishop may seem surprising or even appalling to modern eyes. It is difficult to know how his flock regarded him. The only description we have of a Veronese bishop appears in a delightful, yet factually suspect story of relic theft. The thief, Godeschalk, a monk of the abbey of Benediktbeuern in Bavaria, is sent by his abbot to seek famine relief from an old friend, Walther. Walther has become bishop of Verona and is described as "devoted to almsgiving, a distinguished

43. Otto I granted the see immunity in all its castles, and by the twelfth century this status had been extended to the bishop's other holdings: in Frederick I's diploma, immunity in all the properties named is confirmed as a preexisting privilege of the see. MGH DD 1: 474–75 (no. 348); MGH DD 10.1: 144–46 (no. 88). On episcopal immunities in general see Giuseppe Salvioli, *Storia delle immunità delle signorie e giustizie delle chiese in Italia* (Modena, 1889); for Verona, Andrea Castagnetti, "Aspetti politici, economici e sociali di chiese e monasteri" *Chiese-Ver.*, pp. 46–49.

The bishops of Verona, unlike many other bishops in northern Italian towns during the tenth and early eleventh centuries, were never granted full public authority in the city. It seems to have been an imperial policy to balance the power of those exercising public authority in the area so that no one local lord would become overmighty. In addition to the bishop, there was a count of Verona, and from the early eleventh century there was also a count of Garda. The duke of Bavaria kept a watchful eye on them all from 976, when the region was organized as a mark. See Andrea Castagnetti, *La Marca Veronese-Trevigiana* (Turin, 1986), especially pp. 3–44.

44. Giuseppe Sartori, *Colognola ai Colli* (Verona, 1959), p. 28.

45. *CDV* 1 nos. 182, 219. The bishop and his vassals were, of course, expected to aid the emperor in his campaigns. Bishops Oschisus of Pistoia and Gerard of Lucca contributed contingents for Louis II's expedition against the Saracens of Bari and Amantea (866–871). Meginhard of Fulda reports that two bishops were among the casualties of a battle with the Danes in 880, and the knights of Bishop Udalrich of Augsburg fought at the Battle of Lech. The Veronese who were summoned by Henry IV to lay siege to Nogara in 1095 were, most likely, the bishop's men. Natale Rauty, *Storia di Pistoia I* (Florence, 1988), pp. 177–83; Karl J. Leyser, *Medieval Germany and Its Neighbors 900–1250* (London, 1982), pp. 31, 56–63; Donizo, *Vita Mathildis* lib. 2: 779, MGH SS 22: 395.

preacher as well, and assiduous in other good works."[46] When Godeschalk arrives in Verona, he finds that the bishop is not in the city. He spends the night at the monastery of Santa Maria in Organo where, amid monkish postprandial chatter, he hears tales of one of the abbey's powerful patrons: Saint Anastasia. His interest piqued, Godeschalk nevertheless continues on his mission. He finds Bishop Walther in his castle at Peschiera and is kindly (benigne) received by him. He stays three days and nights with the bishop, telling him of the ten years of famine the Bavarian lands have suffered and of the great multitude still tortured by hunger, imploring the prelate for aid. Bishop Walther sends him away in peace, having given him a benefaction described as "not small" (non parvo).[47] His mission accomplished, Godeschalk retraces his steps to Santa Maria in Organo and steals the body of Saint Anastasia before returning to Benediktbeuern.

It is possible that Bishop Walther's fame for charity in this account owes more to exigencies of plot development than to veracity. But an important point remains: this eleventh-century author seemed sure that his audience would find it credible, if not normal, that an abbot would beseech the bishop of a wealthy see for relief and that the bishop would respond charitably. This reminds us that wealth and power need not always be equated with corruption and self-aggrandizement. From the late eighth century, Verona's bishops had become wealthy and powerful. But does that mean they were poor religious leaders?

Our bishops have left us few sources to assess their efforts, perhaps caring only for God's eternal judgment on their careers. They did not inspire individual episcopal biographies or collective gesta, but they did leave formal notarial charters recording the deeds they wished remembered. Their actions were also frequently preserved in imperial diplomata and in inscriptions scattered throughout the diocese. These sources suggest several ways in which the episcopal alliance with wealth and power redounded to the benefit of spiritual life in the diocese.

First, Verona's imperial bishops used their influence to gain protection and material support for ecclesiastical institutions in the diocese. In addition to numerous interventions on behalf of San Zeno,[48] Veronese bishops

---

46. "elemosinis deditus, egregius quidem praedicator et aliis bonis operibus deditus . . ." *Chronicon Benedictoburanum, MGH SS* 9: 226.

47. Ibid., pp. 226–7.

48. *CDV* 1 nos. 117, 160, 162, 190; *CDV* 2 no. 196; *MGH DD* 3: 387 (no. 309); 4: 132 (no. 95); 5: 264 (no. 203); 6: 483 (no. 363).

also used their proximity to the emperor to benefit the cathedral chapter and the monastery of San Nazaro. Bishops Ratoldus (820), Hildebrand (1014), and John (1027) each intervened with the emperor to secure confirmation of the chapter's patrimony.[49] In response to Bishop Walther's pleas, Conrad II agreed in 1038 to take the recently founded monastery of SS. Nazaro e Celso under his protection.[50] The bishops were effective local brokers of imperial patronage.

Second, they used their resources and connections to promote religious life and clerical ministries in the diocese. Remember that it was Bishop Ratoldus who organized and established the patrimony of the cathedral chapter in the early ninth century. Bishop Ratherius, as we have already seen, facilitated the development of *scole*, through donations and exchanges of property, to train secular clerics. His support of these new centers of clerical formation had long-term effects.[51] Bishop John's promotion of monastic life illustrates that even prelates whose backgrounds seem to hold little promise could turn out to be dynamic religious leaders. John received the see because his father had rendered loyal service to Henry II. But he seems not to have viewed his post as a sinecure: as bishop he aggressively fostered religious life. When a small religious community formed at the ancient church of San Nazaro, John helped piece together a patrimony for the fledgling monastery. He had obtained a third of the *curtis* of Corliano with its two chapels from Conrad II in 1031; and he bought another third of Corliano, plus Rivalta, Gaziolo, Villa, and Vigizolo from the brothers Otto and Bruno of Augsburg in 1036 for 800 pounds in silver and other goods.[52] He then donated these to San Nazaro.[53] Bishop John also restored the monastery of San Zeno at Malcesine, originally founded by two ninth-century Veronese hermits, Saints Benignus and Carus. The monastery had "been destroyed by neglect for a long while," but by the time of the bishop's charter in 1022 a new group of monks had sought out this deserted site on the shores of Lake Garda. The bishop confirmed the abbot there, noting that "for a long time we wisely observed how accomplished he was in the regular profession, how careful a procurator of his office he was, and how nobly he was honored by the fellowship of the rest of his

49. CDV 1 no. 122; MGH DD 3: 390 (no. 310); 4: 135 (no. 96).
50. MGH DD 4: 380 (no. 274).
51. See above, Chapter 2, p. 48 et seq.
52. ASVR, SS. Nazaro e Celso, nos. 39 and 433; MGH DD 4: 222–23 (no. 167).
53. ASVR, SS. Nazaro e Celso, no. 434.

brothers." John restored the patrimony of the house and decreed its freedom from outside interference, including his own and that of his successors.[54]

Moreover, many of these imperial bishops went well beyond their official responsibilities in their support of Veronese churches. Several episcopal wills and donations reveal that bishops gave their own property and goods to local ecclesiastical institutions. In 846 Bishop Billongus ordained in his will that after the decease of his relatives, a part of his property should go to the cathedral canons and another part to a church in Brescia. He also freed his slaves and left to several Veronese clerics "gold, silver, money, my bath, purse, linens, wools, silks, carriage teams . . . my horses, broken and unbroken, my broken oxen with yoke, cows, pigs, sheep and the rest of my animals, as well as grain and wine."[55] Bishop Notker in 921 willed that his house in the city of Verona be used as a *xenodochium* and endowed the institution with his lands (a manor and castle in the Valpantena, part of a forest, and several fields). He also left money to buy clothing for the monks of San Zeno.[56] Even the contentious Bishop Ratherius, whose experience with the Veronese could justifiably have left him bitter, willed a sum of money to the Veronese church of Santa Maria Consolatrice when he died at Namur in 974.[57]

Indeed, the role of liberal provider had a more charged aura in these centuries than we accord it today. The author of Notker's funerary inscription placed the bishop among the saints for his generosity:

> He was generous and pious. Indeed, as much as a benefactor was able to have, he bestowed upon his flock with a kindly and pure heart. For he ceded to the church estates, houses, and paternal rights to fields, retaining nothing for himself. Giving to all, filled with the light of charity, he goes entirely naked to all the ethers of the heavens. The Almighty warms the rejoicing [Notker] in his bosom and places him with his saints.[58]

---

54. The bishop ordered that all previous property of the house be restored, but also added the gift of a nearby spring with a mill built upon it and a piece of land. *ACV,* I–5–2r (BC 46 m3 n4), now badly water-damaged; see transcription in Biancolini, *Chiese* 2: 470–72.

55. *CDV* 1 no. 182.

56. *CDV* 2 nos. 177.

57. Ratherius, "Urkunden," p. 39.

58. The entire inscription reads:

   + PRAESVLIS HOC TVMVLO REQVIESCIT CORPVS HVMATVM

Amid the want of the early Middle Ages, providing well for one's diocese was a religious, not merely an administrative, task. The wealth at the bishop's disposal offered an opportunity for piety as well as a more worldly type of generosity to his flock.[59] The donations of property the bishops made, which might appear to us as simply evidence of good stewardship, seem to have struck contemporaries as divine dispensations and signs of holiness.

We cannot underestimate how much of the bishop's power was of this intangible religious sort, so discomfiting to the historian. His blessing could change the nature of things, creating holy ground from plain earth. These permanent transformations wrought by the bishop's consecration are commemorated in stone throughout the diocese: "In the year of our Lord 1060, 13th indiction, this church was consecrated on 17 August by Teutpald the bishop of Verona in honor of the Holy Cross, and Saint Michael, the holy martyrs Castor and Victor, and the holy Confessors

---

+ NOTKERII. LARGVS QVI FVIT ATQVAE PIVS.

+ NEMPE SVO QVICQVID POTVIT LARGITOR HABERE

+ CONTVLIT IPSE GREGI MENTE BENIGNE PVRA

+ PRAEDIA NAMQVE DOMOS CAMPORVM IVRA PATERNA

+ ECCLESIAE CESSIT NIL RETINENDO SIBI

+ OMNIBUS INPENDENS CARITATIS LVCE REPLETVS

+ OMNIA CAELORVM AETERA NVDVS ADIT

+ CONFOVET IN GREMIO GAVDENTEM SVMMA POTESTAS

+ ILLVM CVM SANCTIS COLLOCAT ATQVAE SVIS

+ VIRGO DEI GENETRIX CVIVS SE POSSE PVTAVIT

+ SALVARI PRECIBVS SVSCIPE VOTA SVI

+ OBIIT. IIII ID AUG ANNO DOMINICAE INCARNAT. DCCCC
XXVIII. INDIC. I.

Luisa Billo, "Le iscrizioni veronesi dell'alto medioevo," *Archivio veneto* 16 (1934): 70.

59. This image of the noble bishop using a substantial patrimony to provide generously for his people was common in northern Italy through the early eleventh century. See Gabriella Rossetti, "Origine sociale e formazione dei vescovi del 'Regnum Italiae' nei secoli XI e XII," *Le istituzioni ecclesiastiche della «societas christiana» dei secoli XI–XII: Diocesi, pievi, e parrocchie* (Milan, 1977), p. 59. The preservation of the patrimony, so that the bishop could be the *nutritor* of his people, also figures prominently among the virtues praised in episcopal *gesta*. See Michel Sot, "Historiographie épiscopale et modèle familial en occident au IXe siècle," *Annales: Économies, sociétés, civilisations* 33 (1978): 442–45. More than earthly expectations demanded such behavior: Anselm of Canterbury expressed anxiety about the reckoning he would have with the patron saint of his church if he failed to defend its rights. I. S. Robinson, *Authority and Resistance in the Investiture Contest* (Manchester and New York, 1978), p. 153.

Martin, Zeno, and Remigius."[60] The bishop also had a special relationship with the remains of the city's saintly guardians. When relics were moved, the bishop presided, and placed the holy remains in their new resting place. It was Bishop Anno who placed the relics of Saints Firmus and Rusticus in a lead coffer within the high altar of the church dedicated to their memory.[61] And although the holy hermits Benignus and Carus were called upon to carry the body of Saint Zeno into his newly rebuilt church, when King Pippin asked for some of the relics it was Bishop Ratoldus who was in control: "he [the king] finally with difficulty obtained from the bishop some particles of sinews, ashes, and clothing . . ."[62] The *Versus de Verona*, in celebrating the return from Istria in the late eighth century of the relics of Saints Firmus and Rusticus, clearly credited the bishop with the acquisition of more *custodes sanctissimi*, the holy patrons whose remains "Oh happy Verona . . . defend you and overcome even the most overpowering enemy."[63]

The bishop was also at the center of the liturgy. He alone could perform essential annual rites and, however widely he traveled, the bishop was supposed to be in the city from Palm Sunday to Pentecost, presiding over

60. The inscription is from San Michele in Mizzole: Billo, "Le iscrizioni," p. 106; another example is an inscription commemorating Bishop Otbertus's restoration of a church destroyed by the Magyars and his consecration of the new structure: Carlo Cipolla, "Di una iscrizione metrica riguardante Uberto vescovo di Verona," *Rendiconti della R. accademia dei Lincei; Classe di scienze morali, storiche, e filologiche* 5 (1896): 387. The rite of church consecration was an impressive liturgy. It was usually preceded by a procession, bringing the relics to be interred in the church to the site, and an all-night vigil, with hymns and festivities, keeping watch over the holy remains. The consecration ceremony began at dawn with the bishop and congregation processing three times around the church. After knocking on the door with his crozier three times, the bishop entered the church and inscribed the Greek and Latin alphabets in ashes strewn on the floor in the form of a cross. He purified the various parts of the edifice with holy water and, after the formal words of dedication, he consecrated the altar and walls with chrism. He sealed the relics in the altar using mortar mixed with holy water, salt, ashes, wine, and chrism. The consecration concluded with a mass. R. W. Muncey, *A History of the Consecration of Churches and Churchyards* (Cambridge, 1930), pp. 41–47; the Roman rite of consecration may be found in the *Liber sacramentorum* of Pope Gregory the Great, PL 78: 152–62.

61. "During the reign of Desiderius and Adelchis, on 27 March in the third indiction [765], the most holy bishop Anno placed the relics of Saints Fermus and Rusticus in this box" (REG D ET ADELCHE VI KAL APRILI / INDE TERTIA HANO SS EPESCOPO / RELQIA SS FERMI ET RVICI / CONLOCAVIT IN HAC CAPSA). Billo, "Le iscrizioni," pp. 28, 31.

62. "Tunc Rex reliquiarum aliquid postulavit, et vix tandem a Praesule obtinuit nervorum, cineris ac vestimentorum particulas . . ." *AASS* April 2: 75.

63. *Versus de Verona*, p. 154, lines 70–84; p. 153, lines 55–57.

the holiest rituals of the Christian year.[64] He consecrated the chrism used to baptize, confirm, anoint, and ordain. He blessed the branches carried on Palm Sunday. He was the focal point of the processions to stational churches that wound their way through the narrow streets of the city throughout Holy Week.[65] His ritual presence was always greeted with special acclamations or *laudes*, whether he was in the cathedral or visiting the many *plebes* scattered throughout the countryside.[66] The day of his ordination to the see was celebrated as a feast day: that of Bishop Otbertus, 25 October, was entered in the sacramentary in gold letters![67]

These liturgical glimpses of the bishop, even the self-conscious acts each left, are admittedly pale reflections or distant echoes of the men who held Saint Zeno's see. Only one of Verona's bishops in this period left sources capable of conveying a personality and a life story. In both, Bishop Ratherius offers us a vivid image of the imperial bishop. The very quantity of sources left by this bishop, and the intense personality they reveal, however, suggest that Ratherius was not an average bishop of Verona. Extremely well educated, he left a considerable body of works in a refined, if vexing, Latin style.[68] His ego was as vast as his learning; his intransigence and arrogance frequently resulted in disaster. Fiercely religious, he could also be harsh and disdainful toward those who did not share his monastic outlook. Although Ratherius can hardly be taken as a norm for the bishops of this period, he offers us a revealing caricature of the imperial episcopate. In the extremes of his language and actions the best and worst aspects of the *Reichskirchensystem* come into clear focus.

Ratherius's career began in the monastery of Lobbes in the diocese of Liège (in Lotharingia, now Belgium). As an oblate and then a monk there, he came to the attention of Abbot Hilduin, later bishop of Liège. When Hilduin was expelled from his see and went to Rome in search of another, he took Ratherius along as his secretary. From 928 to 931 Hilduin and Ratherius were with the imperial entourage of Hugh of Provence in Italy.

---

64. Most of Ratherius's surviving sermons were composed for these feasts. For 963 we have sermons from Lent, Easter, Ascension, and Pentecost; for 964, sermons for Lent and Holy Thursday; for 968, Easter, the Octave of Easter, one preached "post Pascha," and sermons for Ascension and Pentecost. Ratherius, *Op. Min.*, pp. 33–61, 65–89 and 97–105, 165–97.
65. Meersseman, *L'orazionale*, pp. 62, 111, 254–63.
66. Ibid., pp. 63–65.
67. Ibid., pp. 131–34, 73.
68. See Appendix A, section II, and the bibliography. Peter L. D. Reid has published a useful analysis of and guide to Ratherius's style: *Tenth-Century Latinity: Rather of Verona* (Malibu, 1981).

From this point on, Ratherius's career was inextricably caught up in imperial politics. Although not particularly well liked by Hugh, Ratherius had caught the eye of Pope John XI. Hugh's need for papal support won Ratherius the Veronese see in 931.[69]

Ratherius was more successful at gaining the see than at holding it. In 934, when Arnulf of Bavaria attempted to seize the Kingdom of Italy, Ratherius was caught wavering in his allegiance to Hugh; after Arnulf failed, Ratherius was incarcerated in a tower in Pavia for several years. After his successor in the see, Manasses of Arles, was similarly found disloyal to the emperor in 946, Ratherius managed to regain the see. He found its patrimony dispersed into the hands of laymen, and the clergy in a deplorable state. His attempts to restore the see and reform the clergy, however, only earned him the odium of the townspeople. In 948, on the orders of Hugh, Ratherius was forced to abandon the see again to Manasses (who, according to Ratherius, then sold the see to Milo, the nephew of the count of Verona). After Hugh's death, Ratherius allied himself with Otto I and was granted the see of Liège. But the political maneuvering of the bishops of Trier and Utrecht with the connivance of the local clergy ousted Ratherius within a year. Still in Otto's favor, he was able to regain the Veronese see in 961, when the emperor successfully intervened in Italy. This last stint in the see was Ratherius's longest, but it was no less turbulent than the previous two. With most of the populace and clergy arrayed against him, he lost the see for the last time in 968 and died four years later in Namur.[70]

Even this brief sketch of Ratherius's career reveals the difficulties political appointment of bishops could raise. The emperor's concern about the loyalty of his prelates or their ability to maintain the city's allegiance, especially during periods of grave political disturbance, could result in the removal of bishops from their sees. The intermittent character of Ratherius's episcopate in Verona was largely the result of such concerns. He lost the see in 934 because the emperor could not count on his loyalty and in 948 because he had hopelessly compromised his own position in the city by alienating local elites. The crisis afflicting the Italian kingdom in the first half of the tenth century, when several contenders fought for the iron crown amid Magyar and Saracen incursions, certainly made bishops like Ratherius more vulnerable to imperial suspicions.

---

69. Vittorio Cavallari, *Raterio e Verona* (Verona, 1967), pp. 7–8, 26 note 1.

70. Ibid., pp. 8–25. The best rendition in English of Ratherius's career is Reid's introduction to *Tenth-Century Latinity*, pp. 1–6.

The political instability accompanying the investiture controversy had a similar effect on the Veronese episcopate in the late eleventh and early twelfth centuries.[71] The bishops who held the see during this period did so but briefly. Even the dates of their pontificates are uncertain. Bishop Bruno was appointed to the see in 1072, but when Henry IV was beset by rebellion in Saxony the following year, Bruno accepted the *pallium* from Rome and a visit from the papacy's most aggressive ally, Countess Matilda of Canossa.[72] After Henry's penance at Canossa and his successful suppression of the Saxon revolt, however, Bruno appears firmly in the imperial camp: in January of 1076 he signed a letter castigating Gregory VII for sowing discord in the Church and renounced allegiance to the pontiff.[73] Another man, Segebonus, signed the decrees of the Synod of Brixen as bishop of Verona in 1080, although Bruno was still alive.[74] Segebonus had the longest tenure of any Veronese bishop during the investiture conflict, lasting fourteen years. The episcopates of his successors were more abbreviated: Walbrunn (1094–1100), Hezilo (1101), Wolftrigel (1102), Bertold (1102–1108?), Zufetus (1109–1111), Ubertus (1111?), Siginfred (1113–?),

71. The loyalty of Verona's bishops was essential to the imperial party during the investiture conflict. From 1092 to 1097, Italian support for the revolt of Henry IV's son Conrad and the opposition of south German dukes blocked the emperor's paths both south and north, effectively trapping him in the region around Verona, Padua, and Mantua. Salian reliance on Verona's bishops became even more intense when Verona's count, Albert of the San Bonifacio, became a vassal of Countess Matilda in 1106 in order to regain the fief of Cerea. Alfred Haverkamp, *Medieval Germany 1056–1273*, trans. Helga Braun and Richard Mortimer (Oxford, 1988), p. 121; Andrea Castagnetti, *La Marca*, p. 43.

72. IS 5: 767–68.

73. MGH *Const.* 1: 106–8 (no. 58). The bishop of Brescia wavered in a similar fashion. Cono showed enough openness to the Gregorian faction to be invited to the pontiff's Lenten synod in 1074, but with the failure of the Saxon rebellion he reaffirmed imperial loyalty and participated in the Synod of Brixen. Many imperial bishops were torn between duties to their sovereign, local sentiments, and fear of papal wrath. After Theoderic of Verdun renounced his obedience to Gregory VII at the Council of Mainz in 1080, his clergy and people would not allow him to enter the city until he sought pardon from the pope. Benno II of Osnabrück answered the emperor's summons to attend the Synod of Brixen in the same year, but not wanting to antagonize the pontiff he hid under the altar to avoid participating in the deposition of Gregory and the election of an anti-pope. Cinzio Violante, "La chiesa bresciana nel Medioevo," in *Storia di Brescia*, ed. Giovanni Treccani degli Alfieri, 5 vols. (Brescia, 1963–64) 1: 1037–38; Robinson, *Authority and Resistance*, pp. 153–60; Johnson, "Bishop Benno," pp. 400–401.

74. MGH *Const.* 1: 117–20 (nos. 69–70); Bruno lived until February of 1083 or 1084, when he was murdered by his chaplain: "Bruno magister scolarum Hildeneshem', postea Veronensis episcopus, a capellano suo occiditur. Obiit a. 1083 vel 1084 15 Kal. Mart." *Chronicon Hildesheimense*, MGH SS 7: 848.

Brimo (or Bruno? 1117–1122).[75] These very brief episcopates occurred during Henry V's successful rebellion against his father and the tumultuous early years of his reign.

The effects of this constant rotation of bishops through the see are difficult to gauge. The quality of religious life in the diocese seems vulnerable in these periods. Both of the documented interventions to reform abbeys—Ratherius's reform of Maguzzano in 966 and Bernard's of San Giorgio in Braida in 1123—immediately follow these periods of political turmoil and episcopal discontinuity.[76] Whether general instability or a lack of episcopal oversight (or some combination of the two) is to blame for the difficulties of these houses is, unfortunately, impossible to determine from the surviving documentation. Evidence on the state of the secular clergy is mixed. Despite upheavals and brief episcopates during the investiture crisis there is strong evidence of reform, particularly within the cathedral chapter.[77] Ratherius's attempts to reform the secular clergy were definitely impeded by imperial politics, but the brevity of his tenure in the see was not the chief problem.

Imperial priorities were what doomed this bishop's plans for reform. Ratherius had financed his new institution for training the lesser clergy by reallocating lands that had previously formed fiefs for several military retainers. While up to this point Otto I had shown support for Ratherius's reforms, he drew the line at the weakening of his own military resources. After the count of Verona, acting as imperial *missus*, placed the bishop on trial for various offenses, Ratherius's last sojourn in the see rapidly came to an end.[78] Clearly the military services imperial bishops owed their lord were, when push came to shove, considered more important than religious initiatives. This was the greatest weakness of the imperial Church system.

But if Ratherius's career highlights the political vulnerability of imperial bishops, it also suggests some of their strengths. The tensions in this bishop's relations with his clergy and people were extraordinarily high: Ratherius was demanding, uncompromising, and brutally forceful. After returning from the Council of Ravenna (967), for example, he held his own

75. Ederle, *Dizionario*, pp. 34–35; for Hezilo, *MGH DD* 6: 641 (no. 471).
76. Ratherius, "Urkunden," pp. 22–25; *ASV*, Fondo Veneto, no. 6886.
77. See above, Chapter 2, pp. 55–57.
78. Ratherius, *Briefe*, pp. 185–88; Fritz Weigle, "Il processo di Raterio di Verona," *Studi storici veronesi* 4 (1953): 29–44; Fritz Weigle, "Ratherius von Verona im Kampf um das Kirchengut 961–968," *Quellen und Forschungen aus italienischen Archiven und Bibliotheken* 28 (1937–38): 18–34.

diocesan synod to convey the council's reform decrees to his clergy. Many who opposed him refused to attend, and some of those who were present "with great insolence resolved that they would neither relinquish their excessive fondness for women, nor leave their offices." Ratherius's response was uncompromising. "I seized upon these and ordered them to be taken into custody until they complied."[79] He also tried to reform the laity: his ban against commerce on Sunday, and his order that the city's gates be barred to achieve this, provoked outrage.[80] Although some have questioned Ratherius's motives,[81] his repeated confrontations certainly

79. Both Otto I and Pope John XIII presided over the Council of Ravenna, where the archdiocese of Magdeburg was created to promote the Christianization of the Slavs and the archbishop of Salzburg was deposed and excommunicated. The decrees accomplishing these two actions survive, but no canons: Mansi 18A cols. 499–501. Ratherius's account of his attempts to carry out the legislation of the council appears in a 968 letter to Otto's chancellor in Italy, Bishop Ambrose of Bergamo: "Celebrata mediante Aprili universali synodo Ravennae reversus convocavi ex omnibus nostrae diocesis plebibus presbyteros et diaconos, relaturus ex praecepto serenissimi imperatoris quae inibi constituta sunt, ad concilium omnes. Cumque versutia mihi semper rebellium vitaeque meae insidiantium nostrae matris ecclesiae maiorum venire quidam sint dedignati illorum, ex his, qui convenerant, aliqui cum maxima deliberaverunt superbia, quod neque mulierositatem relinquerent neque ab officio cessarent. Quos comprehendi et custodiae mancipari usque ad satisfactionem praecepi." Ratherius, *Briefe*, pp. 183–84 (no. 33).

80. "Under pain of excommunication I ordered them to refrain from servile labor on the Lord's day. When I had not been able to prevail in the least, I ordered that the gates of the city be barred so that no carts could enter. They judged that this deed ought to be punished by either my death or expulsion" ("Cum excommunicatione interdixi, ut ab opere servili Dominica die cessarent. Id cum evincere nullo modo valuissem, portas obserari contra venientia plaustra praecepi. Hoc facinus aut morte aut expulsione mea debere iudicant expiari"). Ibid., p. 185 (no. 33).

81. Ratherius has, traditionally, been viewed as a "pregregorian" reformer. Fliche established this interpretation, and Cavallari did not abandon it. In a careful and thought-provoking contribution to a 1969 conference on Ratherius, however, Giovanni Miccoli challenged this view. He argued that Ratherius's exaltation of episcopal dignity, his battles against marriage and concubinage among the clergy, and his opposition to simony were instruments to affirm, sustain, consolidate, and defend his own personal power. Miccoli's critique of the "pregregorian" reformer interpretation is a salutary contribution to a more balanced understanding of this enigmatic figure. A close reading of Ratherius does reveal a good bit of self-interest at work. Miccoli's interpretation, however, rests on a sharp distinction between "political" and religious motivation, a distinction possible today but rather unlikely in the tenth century. Thus, for Miccoli, Ratherius's drive to control the clergy and ecclesiastical wealth of the diocese was dressed up in the veneer of reform but was substantially about politics and power: "they are battles painted in the hues of reform (the «mulierositas» or womanizing of the clergy, respect for canon law, the cultivation of pastoral care, all come into play), but their substance is political

made reform an issue. Such confrontations, moreover, would be improbable if the bishop were a local cleric elected to the see. The bishop's status as an outsider under the imperial system gave him certain advantages, particularly in achieving reform: he came to his see with a different perspective, one often informed by broader experience and better educational institutions than local ecclesiastical culture could provide, and with the charismatic and military authority of the emperor behind him. It was, one must remember, German clerics forced on the Holy See by Henry III who set the papacy on the path to reform in the mid-eleventh century.[82]

Ratherius's strong sense of episcopal dignity and authority also reflects the alliance with power that was fundamental to the *Reichskirchensystem*. The bishop's views on this subject have been amply discussed.[83] In the *Praeloquia* he says of bishops,

> They are Gods, Lords, Christs, heavens, angels, patriarchs, prophets, apostles, evangelists, martyrs; they are anointed, they are kings, they are princes, they are judges not only of men, but also of angels; they are the rams of the Lord's flock, shepherds of His sheep—not just any sheep, but those washed by the blood of Christ. They are teachers, heralds of the coming Judge; they are spies, the very pupils of the Lord's eyes. They are friends of the living God, sons of God, fathers, lights of the world, stars of the heavens, pillars of the Church. Doctors of souls, they are the door-keepers of paradise, they carry the keys to heaven, able to unlock or block entrance. They are the clouds upon

---

and about power. Or better, put another way: Ratherius's reforming zeal corresponds exactly with his problems and his aspirations to rule and to be powerful" (translation mine). Ratherius's obsession with controlling his clergy was "political": it was about governance and power. But such politics in the tenth century were grounded in a religious worldview, one that saw the emperor as the "Lord's annointed one" (*unctus domini*) and expected all good governance and just exercise of power to contribute to the salvation of mankind. Control of his clergy would have increased Ratherius's personal power, but it would also have facilitated reform and the proper administration of the sacraments upon which individual salvation depended. For the "pregregorian" reformer interpretation, see Fliche, *La réforme* 1: 74–92 and Cavallari, *Raterio*, pp. 18, 22–24. Giovanni Miccoli, "Raterio, un riformatore?" *Raterio da Verona* (Todi, 1973), pp. 97–136, quote above p. 123. On tenth-century politics and religion, see Karl J. Leyser on "Sacral Kingship," *Rule and Conflict in an Early Medieval Society* (London, 1979), pp. 75–107.

82. Fliche, *La réforme*, 1: 7–17, 129–30.

83. Fliche, *La réforme* 1: 82–88; Miccoli, "Raterio, un riformatore?" pp. 109–15.

which the Lord made His ascent, the pedestals upon which rest the whole structure of God's temple.[84]

Ratherius quotes numerous passages from scripture in support of this view, but the historian must ponder the circumstances that encouraged such Biblical interpretation. The most immediate are those we know Ratherius experienced: the patronage of the most powerful ruler in Europe; the company of an intellectual and social elite; control of an immense patrimony, a sizable army, and numerous regalian rights. He and his colleagues in imperial sees enjoyed the traditional right and responsibility of admonishing the emperor himself.[85] Little wonder he thought so highly of his calling. This expansive view of the episcopal office was certainly one of the *Reichskirchensystem*'s bequests to eleventh- and twelfth-century ecclesiology.[86] The fate of this ideal, once Verona's bishops were no longer imperial, now invites our attention.

The most immediate local effect of the resolution of the investiture conflict was a dramatic change in the character of Saint Zeno's successors. New kinds of men became bishops, local Veronese clerics from leading families in the city. They inherited the immense wealth, lordly dominion, and expectations of authority enjoyed by their predecessors. But the guarantor of that authority was gone. The city was no longer ruled by the emperor but by a communal government. In the early twelfth century, Verona's bishops had to redefine their position in the city. At the same time, the continuing work of reform and the results of more than a century of growth in the diocese demanded that the bishop clarify spiritual and proprietary jurisdictions within his diocese. This process of clarification brought the see into more frequent contact with the papacy.

Both the new political context of the see and the religious needs facing it

---

84. *Praeloquia* III.12 (p. 86).

85. This book of the *Praeloquia* is, in fact, addressed to kings and should be interpreted in this context. Leyser, *Rule and Conflict*, pp. 78–79.

86. It was also one of the roots of opposition to Gregory VII. The pontiff's disregard for traditional rights of the episcopate and his tendency to treat bishops as mere subordinates quickly alienated many. Those who renounced their obedience to Gregory at Worms in 1076 did so because of the pope's mistreatment of the episcopate, not because of any threats to royal authority. See I. S. Robinson, " 'Periculosus homo': Pope Gregory VII and Episcopal Authority," *Viator* 9 (1978): 103–31.

seem to have heightened the tensions inherent in the episcopal office. They erupt with particular force and clarity in the episcopate of Bishop Tebaldus (1135–1157). His career began in the cathedral chapter of Verona. In 1118 he was identified simply as a priest, but by 1120 he had assumed leadership of the canons as archpriest of the chapter. When Bishop Bernard died in November of 1135, Tebaldus was elected to the Veronese see.[87]

The numerous parchments of Verona's Capitular Archive reveal an active and contentious episcopate. From his elevation in 1135 until 1138 he was embroiled in a legal battle with the canons over jurisdiction (*districtus*) in Porcile. The case was settled in favor of the canons by the judgment of Pope Innocent II and the patriarch of Aquileia.[88] From 1139 to 1145 Tebaldus was involved in another, more successful, litigation with the abbot of Nonantola, a monastery just beyond the bounds of the Veronese diocese. In contention was the baptismal church of Nogara; again, the case was resolved only with papal intervention.[89]

During this same period, Bishop Tebaldus was still not on good terms with the canons. The canons accused the bishop of being behind a very obscure misdeed committed by two clerics from other urban churches— some sort of desecration of the altar in the canons' church of San Giorgio— and the chapter called in the patriarch of Aquileia to reconsecrate the chapel.[90] The canons then refused to participate in the annual rogation procession. Tebaldus put them under interdict.[91] By 1145, the bishop and the canons were involved in an even more bitter and protracted suit over a castle at Cerea.[92] Siding with the bishop in this quarrel was Verona's comital family, which had once controlled the castle and wanted it back. Bishop Tebaldus lost his bid for Cerea in 1145, but his allies, the counts of San Bonifacio, and their vassals continued to press the canons. Tebaldus ended up putting the counts under interdict for continued violence against the canons and Pope Eugene III chimed in, excommunicating them.[93] Open

87. ACV, III–7–5r (BC 33 m5 n2); (AC 53 m2 n6), transcription in Muselli, *Memorie*, volume DCCCXXXVI at 1120; MGH SS 19: 2; ACV, III–7–8r (BC 36 m4 n14).
88. ACV, II–7–1r (AC 53 m2 n1).
89. See above, Chapter 5, pp. 131–33.
90. IS 5: 778–81.
91. *VerST* 2: 252.
92. ACV, III–7–8r (BC 15 m2 n12); I–8–6v (AC 65 mp n12?); I–8–6v (AC 59 m2 n9); II–7–3 (BC 45 mp n13); II–7–3v (BC 45 mp n4); II–7–4r (AC 37 m2 n1); I–6–5v (BC 44 m4 n10).
93. Kehr, IP 7.1: 236–39.

factional conflict then erupted in the city. Verona's annals cryptically record the burning of the neighborhood around San Zeno and the destruction of the most fortified part of the city, Castel San Pietro. The arrival of Frederick Barbarossa in the 1150s coincided in the annals with more (seemingly) spontaneous combustion of castles and suburbs. Tebaldus died in the midst of all this turmoil in 1157.[94]

Veronese historians have regarded Tebaldus's career with puzzlement. This century's most esteemed historian of medieval Verona, Luigi Simeoni, saw him as a major contributor to the violent disorders that marked the commune's early years. Simeoni described as "rather strange" both Tebaldus's continuous involvement in litigations with other ecclesiastical institutions and his participation in factional infighting on the side of the city's comital family. This supposedly unbecoming behavior Simeoni contrasted sharply with Tebaldus's comportment as archpriest of the cathedral chapter before his elevation to the see. As archpriest, Tebaldus had vigorously defended the canons' rights and worked to recover lands usurped by lay lords—behavior Simeoni characterized as appropriate. It was "rather strange," marveled Simeoni, that upon his election as bishop Tebaldus began working strenuously to violate the privileges of the cathedral canons and that by the end of his pontificate he had alienated large amounts of episcopal property, mostly into the hands of his nephew.[95]

A particular sense of disappointment pervades Simeoni's assessment of Tebaldus because this bishop was the first Veronese cleric in centuries to be elected to the see. Finally, a Veronese bishop of Verona and, alas, he turned out to be a greedy nepotist! Tebaldus indeed was from a local knightly family that held lands in fief from the see.[96] This did make a difference, but not such a negative one as Simeoni implied. Although Tebaldus's predecessor was the first bishop elected by the cathedral chapter after the Concordat of Worms ended imperial control, Bishop Bernard (1122–1135) was from a Brescian noble family.[97] He figures somewhat differently from Tebaldus in the documents. Bishop Bernard usually appears alone or with clerics;[98] Tebaldus usually appears flanked not only by clerics, but by vassals, lay counsellors, leading men of the city, and consuls of the com-

94. MGH SS 19: 3.
95. VerST 2: 249–55.
96. IS 5: 797; Andrea Castagnetti, La società veronese nel medioevo II: Ceti e famiglie dominanti nella prima età comunale (Verona, 1987), p. 33.
97. Ederle, Dizionario, p. 39.
98. ASV, Fondo Veneto, no. 6886; ACV, II–6–7v (BC 17 m4 n7).

mune.[99] Tebaldus, the local Veronese cleric become bishop, appears in the office as a man much more embedded in local society than Bernard. That involvement—like imperial control—had advantages and disadvantages. Simeoni saw Tebaldus's local family connections as a motivating factor in his litigious assault on the canons' patrimony. A closer look at Tebaldus's litigations, however, reveals a far more complex picture.

Were greed and family ambition the driving forces behind the bishop's lawsuits, as Simeoni implied? I think not. The more complex demands of the episcopal office in the period of transition were at the root of Tebaldus's contentiousness. First, we have already seen how in the twelfth century the bishop struggled to assert his authority over the diocese. This involved litigation, and the close association of seigneurial and ecclesiastical authority meant that property and regalian rights were often sought. They brought ecclesiastical authority with them. Part of the bishop's litigiousness was rooted in the very Gregorian idea that the bishop should supervise the churches of his diocese.

Tebaldus's search for ecclesiastical control, however, went hand in hand with a broader effort to secure, protect, and extend the see's patrimony. In this effort, Tebaldus was not alone; bishops throughout northern Italy were expanding and consolidating their patrimonies.[100] If we look beyond Tebaldus's lawsuits, we see the bishop petitioning not only several popes but also the emperor for confirmation of the see's possessions. The imperial confirmation Tebaldus obtained from Frederick Barbarossa was clearly not about ecclesiastical control.

We also know that Tebaldus borrowed a significant sums of money.[101] He needed these resources for several purposes, most relating to the dignity of the see and the demands of the episcopal office. The first was a significant building campaign.[102] Much of Verona had been leveled by an

99. *ASVR*, S. Silvestro, no. 5 app.; Ospitale Civico, no. 73; SS. Nazaro e Celso, nos. 635.a, 1472; *ACV*, II-7-4r (AC 37 m2 n1) with consuls; II-7-1r (AC 53 m2 n1) with vassals; (AC 65 mp nr) transcription in Muselli, *Memorie*, at 1145 with "peers" (*paribus*); II-7-3v (BC 45 mp n4).

100. Dameron, *Episcopal Power*, pp. 77–85; Duane J. Osheim, *An Italian Lordship* (Berkeley and Los Angeles, 1977), pp. 24–26; G. A. Loud, *Church and Society in the Norman Principality of Capua*, 1058–1197 (Oxford, 1985), pp. 225–27. The expansionist claims of the bishops of Mantua, Ferrara, and Verona collided at Ostiglia in the mid-twelfth century: Adriano Franceschini, *Giurisdizione episcopale e comunità rurali altopolesane* (Bologna, 1986), pp. 77–96.

101. By the canons' reckoning, about 2000 Veronese pounds. *IS* 5: 797; BAV, Cod. Vat. Lat. no. 1322A, fols. 284r–285r.

102. On the "immobilization" of capital such building campaigns caused, see Robert Sabatino

earthquake in 1117 and, as the examples of Bishops Walther and Notker suggest, bishops were expected to do their utmost to alleviate its effects.[103] As archpriest of the cathedral chapter, Tebaldus had led the rebuilding of the canons' cloister. When he became bishop he immediately turned his efforts to the cathedral church, Santa Maria Matricolare.[104] Between 1139 and 1153, he rebuilt the entire cathedral on a larger scale. The beautiful carved portal of the church, the work of the master sculptor Nicolò, still stands today as a monument to the bishop's efforts.[105] Tebaldus also organized the construction of a new episcopal residence—many of the documents that illumine his later career were redacted in "palatio episcopi Tebaldi."[106]

The second financial need behind Tebaldus's maneuverings brings us to a consideration of the new political position of the bishop. While Professor Simeoni seemed dismayed at Tebaldus's "mixing himself up" in politics, it is clear from the foregoing discussion that Verona's bishops had for centuries been political as well as religious forces. From the eighth century through the eleventh, however, the bishops had been the emperor's men in the city. These bishops did, of course, wield power on a local level, but always as imperial representatives, with the emperor's financial and military resources behind them.

This changed in the early twelfth century, and the change in the bishop's political position is the root of both Simeoni's discomfiture and Tebaldus's efforts to expand his see's patrimony. Over the first half of the twelfth century, the emperor's control of the city slackened, a free commune emerged,[107] and after the Concordat of Worms in 1122, the cathedral chapter gained control of episcopal elections. As a result, the political

Lopez, "Économie et architecture médiévale. Cela aurait-il tué ceci?" *Annales: Économies, sociétés, civilisations* 7 (1952): 433–38.

103. Building and rebuilding churches are depicted in episcopal *gesta* as ways in which the bishop provides for his people: Ursus, the bishop of Ravenna, "began to build a temple of God here so that this most pious pastor might gather together the Christian people, who were wandering among several separate canopies, into one flock" ("hic initiavit templum construere Dei, ut plebs christianorum, quae in singuli teguriis vagabat, in unum ovile piisimus collegeret pastor"). Sot, "Historiographie épiscopale," p. 443 and note 46, p. 449.

104. *VerST* 2: 250.

105. Edoardo [Wart] Arslan, *L'architettura romanica veronese* (Verona, 1939), pp. 108–10.

106. ACV, (AC 65 mp nr), transcription in Muselli, *Memorie*, DCCCXXXVI at 1145.

107. Luigi Simeoni, "Le origini del comune di Verona," *Studi storici veronesi* 8–9 (1957–58): 87–151.

position of Verona's bishop changed dramatically. First, the bishop no longer exercised power as an imperial representative; the emperor no longer really controlled the city. In this period the emperor became a distant authority variously entreated or ignored by local factions. The only twelfth-century diploma to the see came late in Tebaldus's pontificate (1154), and secured only the temporary allegiance of the city.[108] During the first half of the century, Verona's bishops became free agents. It is not surprising, therefore, that they suddenly seem mired in local factional infighting. If the bishop was to remain a force in the city he had to ally himself with the most powerful elements forming the new communal government. This was exactly what Tebaldus did. His pursuit of litigation with the canons over Cerea was supported by Verona's comital family, the leaders of the dominant faction in the early commune. Tebaldus's chief counsellors and vassals were Alberto Tenca and Eliezar, tutors of the young count Boniface and consuls of the commune.[109] It is this local political arena that most concerned Tebaldus.

The bishop's involvement with the comital faction, in fact, coincides with the first real evidence of communal government. There is earlier evidence of independent diplomatic action on the part of citizens. In 1107 a group of forty Veronese had entered into a treaty with Venice pledging the city's military help against Padua and Treviso in return for reduced tolls for Veronese merchants in Venice.[110] But evidence of governmental institutions, of communal officials or consuls, does not appear until 1136.[111] It was probably no coincidence that the first evidence of communal government immediately followed Tebaldus's election to the see. Tebaldus threw in his support with his vassals, with the comital family, and with the leading knights and merchants of the city to assert the independence of the commune.[112]

---

108. *MGH DD* 10.1: 143–47 (no. 88); *VerST* 2: 255–66.

109. *ACV*, II–7–3v (BC 45 mp n4); *ASVR*, S. Silvestro, no. 5 app; Castagnetti, *La società* II, pp. 14, 52.

110. Andrea Castagnetti, *La società veronese nel medioevo I: La rappresentanza veronese nel trattato del 1107 con Venezia* (Verona, 1983), pp. 30–37.

111. Simeoni, "Le origini," p. 144.

112. Simeoni attributes the emergence of the commune to only the *negotiatores* and *milites*, even though he notes their relation to the bishop, the appearances of consuls meeting "in sala episcopi" before the commune had its own buildings, and even Tebaldus's representation of the city in 1156 in a meeting with Frederick Barbarossa. The list of Tebaldus's debts in *ASV*, Cod. Vat. Lat. 1322A, fols. 284r–285r, also includes 173 Veronese pounds "quas dedit consulibus" (285r). Since Simeoni's work, numerous studies of other cities have acknowledged the key role played by bishops in the emergence of free communes. Theseider, "Vescovi e città," pp. 80–81,

How did all this create new financial needs for Tebaldus? To build his faction, and therefore his leverage within the commune, Tebaldus needed vassals. Several pieces of evidence attest to this need. The bishop's struggle for Cerea is again significant: if Tebaldus had been able to wrest Cerea from the canons, he could have granted it to the counts of San Bonifacio as a fief, binding them and their vassals to the see.[113] This would have strengthened the see tremendously, ensuring it a dominant role in the city's government. Another piece of evidence: a document emanating from the cathedral chapter accused Tebaldus of alienating the lands of the see. The lands Tebaldus alienated were in fact fiefs—the document clearly identifies them as such. Now, all large ecclesiastical institutions during this period had vassals and invested them with fiefs; in fact, among the witnesses to this document were the vassals of the cathedral canons. What the canons objected to was Tebaldus's investitures of episcopal lands that had never before been used as fiefs. "The house at the head of the bridge," they protested, "which Bishop Bernard intended to grant to no one, he [Tebaldus] gave as a fief for money."[114] Tebaldus was using more of the see's property to create more vassals. Yet another kind of evidence reveals that the bishop was trying to bind allies to the see. He began using the formula of feudal investiture and its rituals in all kinds of transactions, most notably in exchanges of land.[115] All this evidence considered, it seems that Tebaldus was trying to build up his faction by securing more supporters. Obviously, this effort to assert a major role for the episcopate in the commune had a cost. Just as clearly, it was not accomplished with economic resources alone.

We return to Tebaldus's family background, to his place in Veronese

84–85; Reinhold Schumann, *Authority and the Commune, Parma 833–1133* (Parma, 1973); Giovanni Tabacco, "Vescovi e comuni in Italia," I *poteri temporali dei vescovi*, pp. 253–82; Lauro Martines, *Power and Imagination* (New York, 1979), pp. 19–21; Pierre Racine, "Évêque et cité dans le royaume d'Italie: Aux origines des communes italiennes," *Cahiers de civilisation médiévale* 27 (1984): 129–39.

113. The counts were clearly the ones who wanted the castle, as they continued to harry the canons after Tebaldus's suit was denied. Kehr, IP 7.1: 236–39.

114. "Domum quoque de capite pontis quam Episcopus Bernardus nulli concedere voluit, accepta pecunia pro feudo dedit." *BAV*, Cod. Vat. Lat. no. 1322A., fol. 284r.

115. *ACV*, III–7–8r (BC 36 m4 n14). During the same period, Padua's bishops tried to stem the decline of their power in the face of rising communal organization by creating lesser vassals and ceding them fiefs consisting of tithes. Gerard Rippe, "Commune urbaine et féodalité en Italie au nord: L'exemple de Padoue (Xe siècle—1237)," *Mélanges de L'École française de Rome: Moyen age—temps modernes* 91 (1979): 683.

society. Simeoni was correct in asserting that Tebaldus's family connections were a factor in his litigations and in his involvement in the politics of the early commune. But his lawsuits and political maneuvering cannot be attributed entirely to personal or familial greed and ambition. It is true that as Tebaldus propelled the see into the politics of the new government, he improved his family's position. His nephew Pecorarius, who received several episcopal fiefs, became a consul in 1150 and his descendants were very active in communal politics in the early thirteenth century.[116] But more than family ambition was behind Tebaldus's maneuvering. The bishop's attempts to enlarge the see's patrimony were rooted in the demands of the office. Most obvious were the financial demands of rebuilding the cathedral. The tradition of the office and the political changes of the early twelfth century created other demands. The early medieval heritage of the episcopal office had endowed it with some public authority. Tebaldus maintained that authority as political circumstances changed, but to do so required resources both economic and social. His familial ties certainly helped him assert a role for the see in the new communal government.

Tebaldus's difficulties in forging a new role for the bishop in local politics point out one of the paradoxes of the Gregorian Reform. The compromise won by the reformers in the Concordat of Worms was, in fact, a mixed blessing on the local level.[117] The reform threw the Veronese episcopate into an entirely new political arena, one created by the social, economic, and political changes of the eleventh and twelfth centuries. Verona's bishops were "freed" from imperial control, but were suddenly much more politically vulnerable. Although the reformers' aim in opposing lay investiture was to free the bishop from lay political control, the result in Verona was a much more intense and precarious involvement in local politics.

It would, however, be a mistake to view Tebaldus, as Simeoni did, chiefly

---

116. Castagnetti, *La società II*, p. 33. The importance of Veronese ecclesiastical institutions as centers of power and wealth for local elites markedly increased in the twelfth century as a result of the political changes under discussion. In regions where imperial authority waned earlier, the interests of local patrilineages were already inextricably intertwined with ecclesiastical institutions. Dameron, *Episcopal Power*, pp. 24–49.

117. Other scholars have noted this paradoxical result: Antonio Rigon, "I vescovi veneziani nella svolta pastorale dei secoli XII e XIII," *La Chiesa di Venezia nei secoli XI–XIII*, ed. Franco Tonon (Venice, 1988), pp. 33–34.

as a political figure.[118] Even considering his social connections and economic situation is not enough; Bishop Tebaldus was also a spiritual leader.
Amid the rolls of repetitious litigation proceedings, a religious figure
emerges. One of Tebaldus's chief interests in the litigation for Nogara was
control of its clergy, those who tended the souls commended to the
bishop's care. We know he held them accountable. In three parchments of
testimony in the mid-twelfth-century dispute over Ostiglia, witness after
witness spoke of the bishop's pastoral efforts. Episcopal synods come to
life in their words: "I know," said the priest Reginzo, that the church of
Ostiglia was part of the diocese, "because our Veronese Church is accustomed to celebrate synods every year for three days during the first full
week of Lent. Each *plebs* is called out and when each archpriest hears the
name of his *plebs* he rises with a loud voice."[119]

The other evidence these witnesses recalled also focused on the bishop's pastoral duties. "Two times," said the archpriest of Isola della Scala, "I
went to Rome with Bishop Tebaldus. I always saw him confirm the children of Saint Romanus and Ostiglia at Ostiglia."[120] Another witness,
Stefanus de Atalamasia, said of Tebaldus, "Twice he had been received in
Ostiglia with ringing bells, with holy water, and with incense. Once the
men of Ostiglia gave one pig and one tallage to him. When he was archpriest [of the cathedral chapter] and after, when he began to be bishop, the
monks came to Ostiglia to him for advice, since the men of Ostiglia had

118. Simeoni was not alone in this interpretive tendency. See Rigon, "I vescovi veneziani," p. 31
and literature discussed in note 5, pp. 45–46.

119. "Presbyter Reginzo da domo: Scio quia ecclesia nostra veronensis consuevit celebrare
sinodum singulis annis tribus diebus prime ebdomade maioris. xl. quadragesime. Singuli
plebes in ea nominantur et cum unusquisque archipresbyter audit nominem sue plebis, surgit
cum voce plene." Reginzo was not the only witness to recall episcopal synods. Stefanus de
Atalamasia recalled those of Tebaldus, as well as those of his predecessors Wolftrigel (1102) and
Bernard (1122–1135). Bishop Bernard, Stefanus tells us, held synods twice a year (during Lent
and after Pentecost). Zeno, the archpriest of Trevenzuolo, recalled the synod of Bishop
Ubertus (1111), who had made him an acolyte. ASVR, Ospitale Civico, no. 1 app.

120. Ibid. "Duabus vicibus ivi cum episcopo T[ebaldo] Romam. Semper vidi eum confermare
pueros sancti romani et ostilie in ostiglia." Another parchment of testimony in the same case—
ASVR, Ospitale Civico, no. 223—recorded the words of the *gastaldus* of Ostiglia, Gerard: "I saw
Bishop Tebaldus, who came to Ostiglia before, similarly received and lodged, and [I saw him]
confirm children. He came another time and similarly confirmed children and I myself held
the son of Hubert who lived at this place" ("Vidi episcopum Tebaldum quem prius venit
ostiliam similiter susceptum et ospitatum et pueros confirmare [sic]. Alia vice venit et similiter
pueros crismavit, et egomet tenui filium uberti qui adhuc vivit").

been manifestly falling into disrepute.[121] The bishop's advice was not recorded. But early records of episcopal visitations follow a similar pattern: the bishop arrived, he made inquiries, sometimes he was approached by those with grievances, more often he listened as the local clergy poured out complaints against the villagers in what must have been very tense sessions.[122]

The bishop's struggle for control over the churches in his diocese was slowly won through these minute accounts of where he confirmed, where the bells were rung, and where chrism was brought. Witness after witness tired notarial hands; for whom did these notaries write? Most of these rolls of testimony sooner or later must have been unfurled for papal legates and judges. It was under Bishop Tebaldus that the Veronese see increasingly resolved its problems in Rome. Papal letters and legates resolved the disputes over Porcile, Cerea, and Nogara. And two times, the archpriest of Isola della Scala reminds us, he went with Bishop Tebaldus to Rome. The closer ties with the papacy that bishops had to cultivate in the post-Gregorian era carried a cost. At least some of the debts for which the canons condemned Tebaldus were incurred to finance these expeditions to the Holy See.[123]

Even as the bishop was slowly bringing existing churches under his control, going back and forth to Rome and sending notaries here and there to record testimony about his pastoral activities, new and sometimes novel

121. "bis fuit susceptus in ostilia sonantibus campanis cum aqua benedicta et incenso et semel dedent ei porcum .1. et talliam .1. homines ostilie. et quando archipresbyter erat et postea cum episcopus esse cepit monachi qui ostiliam veniebant ad eum pro conscilium quoniam homines ostilie in criminibus manifeste cadebant." The final phrase could also mean "openly committing crimes," but in any case the important point here is that the bishop's counsel was sought about something the men of Ostiglia were doing. *ASVR*, Ospitale Civico, no. 1 app.

122. *Riforma pretridentina della diocesi di Verona* (Vicenza, 1989) 2: 450–53, 514–21, 537–38, 761 (just a few examples).

123. Ughelli published in *Italia Sacra* only half of the canons' lament against Bishop Tebaldus: the part concerning fiefs. The other half, a long list of debts incurred by the bishop, included some indications of why the bishop borrowed these sums. "Thirty-one pounds in Veronese coin which Hugo had given to the men who were staying with Bishop Tebaldus in Rome." "Eleven pounds in Veronese coin in exchange for three pounds in Luccan coin which Gerard, priest of San Tommaso, had when he wanted to go to Rome" ("XXX et I libre veronensis monete quas Ugo fecit dare hominibus qui staverant ipsos tebaldo episcopo rome." "XI. libra veronensis monete pro tribus libris lucensis monete quas habuit presbyter gerardus de sancto thome quando voluit ire romam"). *BAV*, Cod. Vat. Lat. no. 1322A, fol. 284v.

religious institutions were forming in his diocese. These new institutions, and the novel visions of the Christian life they elaborated, posed serious institutional and spiritual challenges. No document tells us of Tebaldus's initial reaction to the group of lepers settled outside the Porta San Fermo; we only know that in 1141 he consecrated Santa Croce for them. But Tebaldus did more than just consecrate the church. He also enjoined the entire community to support the lepers and called upon all Christian men and women of the city to come to Santa Croce every year on the anniversary of its consecration.[124]

This was a strong endorsement, one he did not back away from when scandal erupted in the house five years later over the lepers' right to Santa Croce's property. Confronted with conflicting claims in a developing institutional form, Bishop Tebaldus clarified the roles and rights of the various parties. He awarded the property and goods of the house to the institution and control of those goods to the rectors of the institution, not to its "guests," the lepers. In doing so he established a precedent that was invoked by his successors, as the number of hospitals for lepers and the poor multiplied in the city during the late twelfth century and throughout the thirteenth.[125] In both roles—exhorting his flock and correcting the lepers—the bishop was called upon to define the Christian life, to identify and advocate how to follow Christ.

These many changes in the episcopate were related to changes in the Church as well as changes in the world. Papal victory in the investiture struggle made it possible for a local Veronese cleric like Tebaldus to be elected bishop by the cathedral chapter. It made pope rather than emperor the outside power to whom the bishop and the institutions in his diocese appealed. The investiture victory and diminished imperial influence in Italy also led to his immersion in local political struggles as an independent force. The new local political landscape confronting the bishop, however, was the result of tremendous changes in Veronese society. Demographic growth and economic development had given rise to a thriving urban center. Its new urban professionals—merchants and craftsmen, notaries and judges—were a key faction in the formation of the new communal government. Its new urban poor prompted the rise of new religious institutions like Santa Croce. This growth and development also yielded

124. *ASVR*, S. Silvestro, no. 5 app.
125. *ASVR*, Istituto Esposti, no. 4.

many new churches, which the bishop struggled to place under his authority. The movement for reform created the demand that he undertake that struggle in order to supervise and correct his clergy.

All of these changes, from above and from below, contributed to tensions in the episcopacy. On the one hand, the reform movement and the more intense spirituality fueling it demanded that the bishop more than ever be a spiritual leader, sometimes even a spiritual arbiter. But, on the other hand, the demands of reform as well as the new political position of the bishop required that he be a shrewd administrator, deft politician, and very frequently a tireless litigator.[126] This tension is clear in the very different images of Bishop Tebaldus in the sources: consecrating the leper hospital at Santa Croce and litigating incessantly with the cathedral canons. It is also suggested by the varying final notices Veronese annals offered on the bishop's demise. When Tebaldus died on May 10, 1157, most local annals simply recorded that "Tebaldus, the bishop of Verona, died."[127] One chronicler, however, added an interesting phrase: "Bishop Tebaldus, who was a holy man (*qui fuit homo sanctus*), died."[128] Limited as they are, these varying contemporary assessments of the bishop point to this tension. The new demands of the episcopal office after the Gregorian Reform, and the enormous changes remaking the world in which the Church struggled, made it increasingly difficult for a bishop to defend his see and still be called at his death "homo sanctus," a holy man.

126. Constance Brittain Bouchard finds overwhelming evidence of this tension in a series of twelfth-century episcopal biographies from Auxerre, *Spirituality and Administration, The Role of the Bishop in Twelfth-Century Auxerre* (Cambridge, Mass., 1979). See especially pp. 51–67, the biography of Bishop Hugh of Macon, an exact contemporary of Tebaldus with a similarly contentious pontificate. By the mid-twelfth century this tension also came to influence the canonists' definition of the office, some emphasizing its administrative functions over its sacramental character. On these developments and their long-term significance, see John Gilchrist, "The Office of the Bishop in the Middle Ages," *Tijdschrift voor Rechtsgeschiedenis* 39 (1971): 88, 91–99. For other examples of this tension, see Rigon, "I vescovi veneziani," pp. 33–34; Rossetti, "Origine sociale," p. 83.

127. The *Annales Sanctae Trinitatis* recorded "Tebaldus Veronensis episcopus obiit," *MGH SS* 19: 3; two others entered similarly terse statements, Carlo Cipolla, "Annales veronenses antiqui," *Bullettino dell'Istituto storico italiano* 29 (1908): 36.

128. Cipolla, "Annales veronenses antiqui" p. 36 (Chron. Campagnola).

# CONCLUSION

**C**ONTEMPORARY chroniclers expended very few words on the end of Bishop Tebaldus's episcopate. I, however, will not be quite so reticent. The historian's perspective allows certain moments to be invested with special significance, and I would identify Tebaldus's demise as a turning point in the history of the Veronese Church. However one judges Tebaldus's character, his death marks the end of a period of remarkable change in every aspect of Veronese ecclesiastical life.

From the mid-tenth to the mid-twelfth century, new ideals had emerged for both clergy and laity. The great challenge posed by the expansion of pastoral care invested the priesthood with new importance; it provoked higher standards for the personal deportment of the clergy and more urgent insistence that pastoral duties be fulfilled. The organizational structure of the Church was modified to enforce these higher expectations. In Verona, the cathedral chapter's dominance of the clergy was broken; new institutions (*scole*, clerical Congregations) emerged for the education, representation, and supervision of the secular clergy; and the bishop gained control of nearly all the churches responsible for pastoral care in the diocese. Religious values and institutions became more inclusive. The new spirituality of the twelfth century embraced the most vulnerable and reviled members of the community, focusing new attention on the relief of suffering in this world. New institutions made religious life accessible to a broader social spectrum, so that the pursuit of holiness was no longer a prerogative of the nobility. Lay persons also became more involved in their local churches through the formation of confraternities. Both clergy and laity contributed to the development of these new ideals and the many new institutions that embodied and propagated them.

How should we characterize these manifold changes and their effects? Elisabeth Magnou-Nortier, in her study of the ecclesiastical province of Narbonne in the tenth and eleventh centuries, prefers the term "Gregorian Crisis" to Fliche's "Gregorian Reform." The development of the Narbonnaise Church, she argues, was "brutally" disrupted by the activities of papal legates and local advocates of the Roman reform circle. Much of what was vital and distinctive about this local Church was damaged or lost as a result of Roman intrusions into ecclesiastical life in the name of "reform."[1] Verona's experience was different, however, and neither "Gregorian Reform" nor "Gregorian Crisis" satisfactorily describes it. Reform did occur, but other, equally important kinds of changes took place as well. Nor were the changes that transformed the Veronese Church the result of a "crisis" provoked by outsiders. Most of the forces propelling change came from within the diocese. Some ideas and practices advocated by outsiders were adopted, but there is no evidence that they were brutally forced upon an unwilling local Church. Rapid change was accompanied by tensions and conflicts, but this ecclesiastical community seems to have retained strong local traditions even as it interacted with both papacy and empire.

The character of ecclesiastical change in Verona might best be described as urgently innovative. The most striking quality informing all the changes of this period is a strong sense of possibility; a sense that the Church could effectively minister to all souls and that all individuals could live a Christian life. These beliefs may appear remarkably naive, but it was in the two centuries considered here that the resources, both human and material, were first available even to attempt the realization of such goals. Resources were key. Wealth and power in these centuries could still be regarded as liberating and salvific, as sources of opportunity and instruments of divine dispensation. The sense of possibility pervading this period had its roots in economic growth and innovation.

Its sense of urgency springs from a different kind of growth. The formation of new communities, a new abundance of humanity, posed a real challenge to the rather loosely organized group of institutions that comprised the Veronese Church in the early Middle Ages. It was the very lack of rigid structures, in fact, which allowed an enormously creative response to this challenge. Creativity is evident in new institutions. Churches were built in new communities, monasteries in even the most desolate reaches of the diocese. Creativity is even more clearly demonstrated in novel institutional forms. Twelfth-century documents bristle with a whole new vocabulary to describe the ways men and women expressed and practiced their faith: *scola, congregatio, hospitalis, canonica, convivium.*

---

1. Elisabeth Magnou-Nortier, *La société laïque et l'Église dans la province ecclésiastique de Narbonne (zone cispyrénéene) de la fin du VIIIe à la fin du XIe siècle* (Toulouse, 1974), pp. 445–47, 458–518, 550–64.

All these new institutions were bound firmly one to another to form a cohesive and distinctive whole. A kind of quickening had occurred, provoked in large part by the multiplication of souls in the diocese. A weighty sense of responsibility for these souls slowly ordered the pastoral system; it defined and apportioned both duty and authority within the diocese. Law was increasingly invoked to define and solidify the ties between ecclesiastical institutions, to order them under the bishop's authority. More clearly and more self-consciously, by the mid-twelfth century these institutions formed a Church. This Church—in its organization, its institutional forms, and its spirituality—is much more familiar than that of the early Middle Ages. Its emergence was relatively rapid. Although it responded to demographic, social, and economic forces, the transformation of the Veronese Church was not a glacial, Braudelian evolution. The quickening was more swift, beginning in the late tenth century and becoming most intense from the mid-eleventh century to the mid-twelfth. This, not the thirteenth century, was the critical period of creative ferment in the formation of the medieval Church.

Historians underestimate the importance of this ferment when they characterize it as reform. This is, indeed, a limited description of what the men and women of this period achieved. For this reason, both "Gregorian Reform" and "Gregorian Crisis" fail to capture what is most significant about these two centuries. When one considers what was accomplished, this period has more in common with Charles Homer Haskins's "age of new creation."[2] Haskins did not include the Church in his *Renaissance of the Twelfth Century*, but it is not surprising that scholars since have tried to expand his original framework to include religion.[3] Haskins's rich language of new abundance and variety, of old forms taking on "greater breadth and fulness," of the development of new forms, and of "a general quickening of the spirit"[4] captures the character of ecclesiastical change in this period with greater accuracy and more descriptive force than traditional designations. His vision of change is both broad and positive. The formation of this one local Church suggests the need to reconsider the evolution of western Christianity in the same light.

2. Charles Homer Haskins, *The Renaissance of the Twelfth Century* (Cambridge, Mass., 1927), p. 190.
3. They also see the early twelfth century as its "center of gravity" and the mid-twelfth as its conclusion. *Renaissance and Renewal in the Twelfth Century*, ed. Robert L. Benson and Giles Constable with Carol D. Lanham (Cambridge, Mass., 1982), pp. xxiii, xxvii.
4. Haskins, *Renaissance*, pp. 13, 224.

# APPENDIX A. SOURCES

## Charters

To 961: These materials are published in the two-volume *Codice diplomatico veronese*, edited by Vittorio Fainelli. Fainelli's compilation of 562 documents includes private notarial charters, plus imperial diplomata, papal letters and bulls, and notices of Veronese bishops in conciliar sources.

962–1158: Three major collections of Veronese charters exist for this period.

1. Archivio di Stato, Verona (ASVR). When most ecclesiastical and pious institutions were suppressed in the Napoleonic era, their records came into the possession of the city government. These records came to form the "Antichi Archivi Veronesi," originally housed in the Biblioteca Civica (now in the Archive on Via Franceschine).[1] The various *fondi* are still arranged by ecclesiastical institution, although the bulk of the materials concerning the monastery of San Zeno is in the collections Ospedale Civico and Orfanotrofio Femminile under the series Opere Pie.[2] Only one collection, Clero Intrinseco, consists of late register copies and summaries[3]; the rest are original or medieval exemplar parchments (totaling more than 500 for the period). The following *fondi* contain charters from 962 to 1158: Bevilacqua, Compagna-Vari, Clero Intrinseco, Istituto Esposti, Maggio, Malaspina, Mensa Vescovile, Orfanotrofio Femminile, Ospedale

---

1. On the history of these collections, see Mario Carrara, "La biblioteca del Monastero di S. Zeno Maggiore di Verona," *Rivista di storia della Chiesa in Italia* 6 (1952): 411–26; Vittorio Fainelli, "Gli «Antichi archivi veronesi» annessi alla Biblioteca Comunale dalle origini dell'istituzione al 1943," *AMAV* 135 (1958–59): 96–151; Giulio Sancassani, "Il centenario degli antichi archivi veronesi (1869–1969)," *Vita veronese* 22 (1969): 339–43. Systematic descriptions of these holdings may be found in Carlo Cipolla, [Statistica degli archivi della città e provincia di Verona], in R. Sovrintendenza agli archivi veneti, *Gli archivi della regione veneta*, 3 vols. (Venice, 1881) 2: 197–371 and more recently, *Archivio di Stato di Verona* (Verona, 1960).

2. A more detailed survey of materials concerning the monastery of San Zeno may be found in Giulio Sancassani, "Le fonti archivistiche relative al Monastero e all'Abbazia di S. Zeno di Verona," in *Studi Zenoniani in occasione del XVI centenario della morte di S. Zeno* (Verona, 1974), pp. 49–63.

3. No original parchments survive in this collection. The Clero Intrinseco *fondo* is entirely registers, the earliest from the fourteenth century, containing copies and summaries of charters.

Civico, VIII Vari, Portalupi, Sandrà, Scalzi, Sant'Anastasia, San Domenico, Sant'Eufemia, San Fermo, San Giovanni in Valle, Santi Giuseppe e Fidenzio, San Lorenzo, Santa Maria della Ghiara, Santa Maria in Organo, San Martino d'Avesa, San Michele in Campagna, Santi Nazaro e Celso, San Nicolò, San Pietro in Monastero, San Salvar Corte Regia, San Silvestro, Santo Spirito, Santo Stefano, Santi Apostoli, San Tomaso Apostolo, San Zeno. In addition, one uncataloged collection, Dionisi Piomarta, yielded several charters for this period. I have also searched the late twelfth-century materials in several collections (Clero Intrinseco, Istituto Esposti, San Silvestro).

2. Archivio Capitolare, Verona (ACV). In existence from the eighth century, Verona's capitular library has the distinction of being the oldest still-functioning library in Europe. Its medieval charters (all originals or medieval exemplars) are essentially those of the cathedral chapter, but some episcopal documentation also survives here.[4] The collection suffered considerable damage in a flood of the Adige in 1882. Luckily, eighteenth-century copies of many of the documents rendered illegible by water damage may be found in Giuseppe Muselli, *Memorie istoriche, cronologiche, diplomatiche, canoniche, e critiche del Capitolo e Canonici della Cattedrale di Verona* (cartaceo, 17 buste: DCCCXXXII–DCCCXLVIII). Monsignor Turrini, who became librarian of the Capitolare in 1922, oversaw a tremendous effort to restore and reorganize this precious collection. Under his supervision all of the parchments were flattened and organized by size into three series (*formati*). Special cardboard portfolios (*cartelle*) were constructed for each series, each portfolio containing eight to ten pages. Protective envelopes were made for each parchment and then these were affixed to the pages of the *cartelle*.[5] The citations to these parchments begin with a roman numeral indicating one of the three series of *cartelle* (I = large, II = medium, III = small). This roman numeral is followed by an arabic numeral indicating the number of the portfolio in the series, and a second arabic numeral indicating the page in the portfolio ("r" and "v" indicating "recto" or "verso" of the page). Since several parchments may be found on any one page, I have also included the old enumeration (AC or BC + *calto* + *mazzo* + parchment numbers) from the back of the parchment in parentheses after the Turrini designation.

In addition to the chapter's documents, the archive holds several smaller collections of parchments.[6] Only one, Santo Stefano, contains twelfth-century materials.

---

4. The episcopal documents found in the Archivio Capitolare are mainly decrees. Since the episcopal patrimony was separate from that of the canons from the ninth century, a separate collection of materials should exist. The Archivio Storico della Curia Vescovile di Verona, however, holds no parchments earlier than the thirteenth century—despite what the guide says: Franco Segala, *L'Archivio storico della curia vescovile di Verona* (Verona, 1986), p. 19—and the fondo "Mensa vescovile" in the Archivio di Stato contains only six pre-thirteenth-century parchments. The earliest is the original of the 1145 bull of Eugene III to Bishop Tebaldus.

5. Giuseppe Turrini, "Communicazione [letter addressed to Prof. L. Schiaparelli, 12 November 1926]," *Archivio storico italiano*, ser. 7, 7 (1927): 110–14; Vittorio Cavallari, "Profilo di Mons. Giuseppe Turrini," *AMAV* 154 (1977–78): 17–44. The most lucid guide to the archive's holdings has been written by the present librarian, Don Giuseppe Zivelonghi, "Strumenti e spunti di ricerca nei documenti dell'Archivio Capitolare di Verona," pp. 117–76 in *Verona dalla caduta dei Carolingi al libero comune* (Verona, 1987).

6. Zivelonghi, "Strumenti," pp. 122–23.

There are approximately 350 parchments in the Archivio Capitolare for the period 962–1158. In addition to these materials, I have also consulted the charters for the period 1158–1185 (the pontificate of Bishop Omnebonus).

3. Archivio Segreto Vaticano, L'Archivio della Cancelleria della Nunziatura Veneta (ASV, Fondo Veneto). This immense collection of 16,511 medieval parchments contains the documentation of several Veronese religious houses that became affiliated with Venetian ecclesiastical institutions. When religious houses were suppressed in the Napoleonic era, the records of these Veronese houses devolved to their Venetian affiliates and ultimately to the Apostolic Nuncio in Venice. They remained in the palazzo of the Nunziatura until 1835, when they were transported to Rome and ultimately joined to the Vatican Archive.[7] Two collections, San Pietro in Castello and San Giorgio in Braida, contain Veronese materials for the period 962–1185, a total of 787 parchments.[8]

4. Other minor charter collections for the period 962–1158. Two very important documents concerning Bishop Tebaldus of Verona (1135–1157) survive in the Biblioteca Apostolica Vaticana, Cod. Vat. Lat. 1322A. The Veronese materials in the Venetian State Archive were trans-

---

7. For the history of this collection and a guide to it, see Pio Cenci, "L'Archivio della Cancelleria della Nunziatura veneta," in *Miscellanea Francesco Ehrle*, 5 vols. (Rome, 1924) 5 : 273–330. Monsignor Cenci compiled the card file index of the collection.

8. Only a tiny fraction of these materials has been published. Monsignor Cenci published thirty-four relating to Cadalus and the foundation of San Giorgio in Braida in *Archivio storico per le province parmensi* n.s. 23 (1923): 183–223 and 24 (1924): 309–44. These were republished with another eight documents by Vittorio Cavallari in "Cadalo e gli Erzoni," *Studi storici veronesi* 15 (1965): 59–170. Egidio Rossini has published several early medieval parchments from the collection in "Documenti per un nuovo codice diplomatico veronese (dai fondi di San Giorgio in Braida e di San Pietro in Castello (803 c.–994)," *AMAV* 143 (1966–67): 137–208. The following publications contain transcriptions of a few documents: Gerolamo Biscaro, "Attraverso le carte di S. Giorgio in Braida di Verona esistenti nel Archivio Vaticano," *Atti del Reale istituto veneto di scienze, lettere, ed arti* 92 (1932–33): 982–1051 published parchment numbers 6742, 6758, 6759, 6763, 6782, 8117; Andrea Castagnetti, *La società veronese nel medioevo II: Ceti e famiglie dominanti nella prima età comunale* (Verona, 1987) published 7238; Andrea Castagnetti, *«Ut nullus incipiat hedificare forticiam»: Comune veronese e signorie rurali nell'età di Federico I* (Verona, 1984) published 7010; Andrea Castagnetti, *La Valpolicella dall'alto medioevo all'età comunale* (Verona, 1984) published 6843, 6882, 6968, 6971, 7022, 7557, 7187, 7299, 7499; Carlo Cipolla, "I primi accenni alla organizzazione comunale in un piccolo villaggio presso Cologna Veneta; dalla pace di Venezia a quella di Costanza," pp. 203–40 in *Miscellanea di studi storici in onore di Giovanni Sforza* (Lucca, 1915) published four documents from 1177 and 1184; Carlo Cipolla, ["Verona e la guerra contra Federico Barbarossa,"] *Nuovo archivio veneto* 10 (1895): 405–504 published one document dated 13 June 1158; Walter Hotzmann, "Anecdota Veronensia," pp. 369–75 published five documents from the 1180s and 1190s, and Fedor Schneider, "Aus San Giorgio in Braida zu Verona," pp. 185–206 published eight (most also published in Cenci and Biscaro) in *Papsttum und Kaisertum: Forschungen zur politischen Geschichte und Geisteskultur des Mittelalters Paul Kehr zum 65. Geburtstag dargebracht,* ed. Albert Brackmann (Munich, 1926); Luigi Simeoni, "Documenti e note sull'eta precomunale e comunale a Verona," *Studi storici veronesi* 8–9 (1957–58): 41–73 published numbers 6876, 6896, 7005, and 7081.

ferred to Verona in 1964, and those from other local archives are largely published. I have found and included Veronese materials from the *Codice diplomatico padovano*; *Regesto mantovano*; Federico Odorici's *Storie bresciani* (volumes 3–5); G. Tiraboschi's *Storia dell'augusta badia di S. Silvestro di Nonantola*; Johanne-Benedicto Mittarelli and Anselmo Costadoni's *Annales Camaldulenses Ordinis Sancti Benedicti*; *I placiti del «regnum italiae»*; J. D. Mansi's *Sacrorum conciliorum nova et amplissima collectio*; and imperial diplomata through the reign of Frederick Barbarossa, *Monumenta Germaniae historica, Diplomata*, volumes 1–10.

In addition, eighteenth-century copies of several documents now lost survive in the manuscripts of Lodovico Perini.[9] These are today found in the manuscripts division of the Biblioteca Civica di Verona.[10]

## Narrative Sources

Verona's narrative sources are better for the early medieval period than for the eleventh and twelfth centuries. The earliest extant sources are probably the sermons attributed to Saint Zeno.[11] Another important early source is the *Versus de Verona*, a metrical poem celebrating the eighth-century return of the relics of Saints Firmus and Rusticus to Verona, which provides a valuable description of the city's ecclesiastical topography.[12] The most informative early narrative source, however, is the collected works of the tenth-century bishop Ratherius of Verona. His letters, sermons, decrees, and literary works are of inestimable value not only for the light they shed on the Veronese Church but also for what they reveal about Veronese society. Fritz Weigle has published critical editions of Ratherius's letters and decrees.[13] New editions of the *Praeloquia* and *Phrenesis*, as well as some minor literary works, have been edited by Peter L. D. Reid in the Corpus Christianorum series.[14] Reid's translation of Ratherius's works[15] appeared too late to be used in this book; the translations here are my own.

For the eleventh and twelfth centuries several annals are extant. The *Annales Breves* cover the

---

9. Perini is chiefly famed as an architect. He designed the Teatro Filarmonico and the Seminario Vescovile in Verona, but late in his life turned to historical pursuits. He published only one complete work, *Istoria delle monache di S. Silvestro* (Padua, 1720), but his manuscripts were used by G. B. Biancolini in compiling his *Notizie storiche delle chiese di Verona*. See G. Sancassani, "L'opera di archivista di Lodovico Perini, architetto veronese dei primi decenni del '700," *Vita veronese* 9 (1957): 356–57 and Luigi Simeoni, "Rapporti tra le opere dei due eruditi veronesi L. Perini e G. B. Biancolini," *Atti del Reale istituto veneto di scienze, lettere, ed arti* 88/2 (1928–29): 1033–48.

10. A brief description of the collection may be found in Giuseppe Biadego, *Catalogo descrittivo dei manoscritti della Biblioteca Comunale di Verona* (Verona, 1892).

11. S. Zeno, *Tractatus*, ed. B. Löfstedt, Corpus Christianorum, Series Latina 22 (Turnhout, 1971).

12. *Versus de Verona. Versum de Mediolano civitate*, ed. G. B. Pighi (Bologna, 1960).

13. *Die Briefe des Bishofs Rather von Verona* (Weimar, 1949); rpt. MGH, *Die Deutschen Geschichtsquellen des Mittelalters 500–1500*, volume 1 (Munich, 1977); "Urkunden und Akten zur Geschichte Rathers in Verona," *Quellen und Forschungen aus italienischen Archiven und Bibliotheken* 29 (1938–39): 9–40.

14. The *Praeloquia* and the *Phrenesis* are in Corpus Christianorum, continuatio mediaevalis volume 46A (Turnhout, 1984) and the sermons and minor works are in volume 46 (Turnhout, 1976).

15. *The Complete Works of Rather of Verona*, trans. Peter L. D. Reid (Binghamton, N.Y., 1991).

period 1095–1178 and the *Annales Sanctae Trinitatis* from 1117 to 1206, with a continuation to 1223. There are some scant eleventh- and twelfth-century notices included in the thirteenth-century chronicle of the Veronese notary Paride da Cerea as well. These three annals are edited by G. H. Pertz in the *Monumenta Germaniae historica, Scriptores*, volume 29. Carlo Cipolla, certainly the expert on Veronese annals and chronicles, has also edited an early series of annals from a Sarzan manuscript; his notes comparing its entries to other annals are particularly helpful.[16] Generally, these annals do not offer more than sparse laconic remarks until the very end of the twelfth century.

Also not very discursive, but still useful, are several liturgical sources. The *Carpsum*, an eleventh-century manual of the chapter's liturgies, mentions several new eleventh-century churches and describes the celebration of the great feasts of the Christian year.[17] Several liturgical calendars also offer evidence of changing hagiographical preferences in the celebration of feast days.[18]

---

16. "Annales veronenses antiqui," ed. Carlo Cipolla, *Bollettino dell'Istituto storico italiano* 29 (1908): 7–81.

17. *L'orazionale dell'arcidiacono Pacifico e il Carpsum del cantore Stefano*, ed. G. G. Meersseman et al. (Fribourg, 1975).

18. Antonio Spagnolo, "Tre calendarii medioevali veronesi" *AMAV* 90 (1913–14): 161–239.

# APPENDIX B. DATABASES

## Computer Analysis of Charters

All the charters used in this study were collected on a very simple database program called "Nutshell." My aim in doing this was both to keep track of documents (since several copies sometimes exist) and to allow systematic searches for names, dates, objects, places, and special terms.

Each document was entered as a record and each record contained the following fields: archive, collection, document number, printed edition (if any), location, date, Latin date, notary, witnesses, type of document (sale, donation, rental, etc.), executor, recipient, "pro" (for donation documents: whose souls, if any, were to receive prayers), object-what (what was being given, sold, rented), object-location, boundaries,[1] "estimatori" (names of those who estimated the value of the property in exchanges), price-rent. A miscellaneous field was also defined so that interesting pieces of formulary or other observations could be recorded.[2]

Standard abbreviations for common terms were used to facilitate searches. Otherwise, the original Latin text of the document was retained.

## Database of Veronese Ecclesiastical Institutions

The original source for the compilation of this database was G. B. Biancolini's *Notizie storiche delle chiese di Verona*. All the churches listed and discussed by Biancolini were entered as records, each record containing the following information:

—Name of the institution
—Type (chapel, church, monastery etc.; if secular, whether it was a parish; if religious, what order held it, what rule was followed, whether a male or female house)
—Location (whether urban, suburban, or rural; plus specific place name)
—Foundation date (or earliest evidence of its existence)
—Changes in the institution (refoundation, merged with another, destroyed, etc.)

---

1. Fields were also defined so that multiple objects in a single donation, sale, or rental could be recorded.

2. Some documents that were too complicated to be entered into these fields were completely transcribed in a word-processing file. A record, however, was entered in the database with its identifying information and location.

—Institution to which it was subjected, if any

—Founders, if known.

This original base was then systematically corrected against both primary sources and more recent secondary sources. The group of primary sources included all Veronese charters before 1158, imperial diplomata and placita, the works of Bishop Ratherius (932–968), annals, communal statutes, canons of church councils and episcopal synods. In the search of secondary literature I concentrated on two areas. First, I surveyed works on the later period (thirteenth–fifteenth centuries), generally more thoroughly studied than the eleventh and twelfth centuries. Second, I sought nondocumentary sources of information on churches: inscriptions, archeological reports, and studies of art and architecture.

Several definitions used in the compilation of this database should be noted. First, the geographical extent of Verona and its diocese has been defined as the extent of the diocese in the mid-twelfth century. In several areas, the twelfth-century diocese differs from the comitatus or districtus. The diocese did not include the stronghold of the Veronese comital family, San Bonifacio, and the zone immediately to the east of it (as far as Lonigo, extending from Montecchia di Crosara in the north to Roveredo di Guà in the south). It did include two areas not part of the comitatus: to the north, the diocese extended beyond Malcesine to include Brentonico; to the west, it included the west shore of Garda as far north as Manerba. One area, that of Gusnago (west of the river Mincio, south of Garda), was originally part of Veronese territory and the Veronese diocese, but was ceded in 1037 to Mantua and therefore has not been included in the diocese on the database.

Second, since Verona's second (communal) set of walls was just being completed in the mid-twelfth century, all institutions outside the original Roman walls of the city but within the present city have been coded on the database as "suburban." Included in this suburban area are, to the west, the land in the crook of the Adige known in the Middle Ages as Sacco (today, Borgo Trento); to the south and southeast, the entire area enclosed by the city's fifteenth-century walls; to the east of the Adige, the area in the Middle Ages called Campomarzo as far as the present day Porto Vescovo; to the north, the hill of San Pietro, as far as, but not including, Quinzano.

Third, when a span of dates was given for the foundation of an institution, the median date was entered. When only an estimate by century was available, the middle of that century was entered as the foundation date (1050, for example, for an institution datable only as eleventh century).

The patterns indicated by this database are, of course, blunt rather than precise measures of change. Several factors, however, give me confidence in the broad patterns of change the database yields. First, there is a large amount of evidence (both documentary and physical) available concerning early medieval churches. Unlike Tuscany, where early medieval rural plebes were built of wood and vanished without a trace,[3] Verona's early medieval churches—urban and rural—were built of tufa (a soft red sandstone), limestone, or brick. Although most of these churches were rebuilt in the twelfth century (after the earthquake of 1117), parts of the older buildings were incorporated into the new structures.[4] Given the surviving evidence of

---

3. Duane J. Osheim, *An Italian Lordship* (Berkeley and Los Angeles, 1977), p. 21.

4. A few examples from different parts of the diocese: San Giorgio in Valpolicella contains columns, paving stones, and a ciborium from the original eighth-century Lombard church—

early churches, I am confident that the increase after the year 1000 shown by the database is real and not produced by a lack of early medieval evidence. Second, this increase is not a reflection of increased documentation either. A comparison of the number of new institutions per half century to the number of documents yields a correlation coefficient of $R = .487$, $R = .237$ (a statistically insignificant correlation given the small number of cases in the sample: $p = .22$).[5]

## Database of Place Names

Another database of all rural place names that occur in Veronese documents to 1150 provides information on settlement patterns. The definition of the extent of the diocese used in the database of ecclesiastical institutions was also used in the construction of this database of place names. In order to discern variations in settlement, I divided the diocese into zones (following the designations the notaries themselves used):

—Fines Gardenses or Iudicaria Gardensis and Vallis Caprinasca
—Vallis Provinianensis
—Vallis Veriacus
—Vallis Paltenate
—Vallis Pretoriensis and Vallis Fontensis
—Vallis Longazeria
—the plain
—the Lessinia

In addition to recording the place name and its location by zone, each record also contains the year of the document in which the place first appeared, how the place was described ("locus," "villa," "locus et fundus," "curtis") and any changes in description, later citations to the place, and whether a church or castle ever appear at the site (if so, the date was recorded).

Changes in the overall number of new placenames correlate with the number of documents ($R = .97$). This is not surprising since our documents, nearly all charters, were produced to record property transactions (and these transactions were rarely concerned with unsettled lands). I have used this database only to look at the geographical distribution of communities and types of lands.

---

Andrea Castagnetti, *La Valpolicella dall'alto medioevo all'età comunale* (Verona, 1984), p. 141; San Zeno in Bardolino also contains fragments of the earlier church—Luigi Simeoni, *Verona: Guida storico-artistica della città e provincia* (Verona, 1953), p. 248; S. Michele in Porcile, rebuilt in 1143, retains sections of wall and many column capitals from the eighth century—Simeoni, *Guida*, p. 276; Santa Maria Maggiore in Gazzo has several inscriptions from the eighth century in addition to ninth-century mosaics—Alessandro Da Lisca, "La chiesa di S. Maria Maggiore al Gazzo Veronese," *AMAV* 119 (1940–41): 135–37, 142–48; San Pietro in Valle, also in the *basse*, still contains some of the original ninth-century walls—*VerST* 2: 499.

5. These figures exclude one case having undue influence on the regression line. That case, the number of documents compared to the number of churches 1101–1150, is different from the others in a significant way: one document, a papal bull listing all of the churches subject to Verona's bishop, accounts for most of the churches in this case.

# SELECT BIBLIOGRAPHY

## Primary Sources (Published)

*Acta sanctorum quotquot toto orbe coluntur.* Edited by Jean Bolland et al. New edition. Paris and Rome: Victor Palmé, 1863–.

Adelard of Verona. *Carmen de Adalhardo episcopo Veronensi. Monumenta Germaniae historica, Poetae Latini aevi Carolini* 3: 693–95. Edited by L. Traube. Berlin: Weidmannos, 1896; reprinted, 1964.

"Alcuni documenti inediti fino all'anno mille." Edited by Egidio Rossini. In *Studi storici Luigi Simeoni,* 39 (1989): 49–73.

*Annales veronenses.* In *Monumenta Germaniae historica, Scriptores,* 19: 1–18. Edited by G. H. Pertz. Hannover, 1866. Reprinted, Stuttgart: Anton Hiersemann; New York: Kraus, 1963.

"Annales veronenses antiqui." Edited by Carlo Cipolla. *Bollettino dell'Istituto storico italiano* 29 (1908): 7–81.

Anselm of Lucca. *Collectio canonum una cum collectione minore.* Edited by Fridericus Thaner. 2 volumes. Innsbruck: Librariae Academicae Wagnerianae, 1906–15.

Benedict of Nursia. *Sancti Benedicti Regula monachorum.* Edited by Cuthbert Butler. Fribourg: Herder, 1927.

*Le carte dei lebbrosi di Verona fra XII e XIII secolo.* Edited by A. Rossi Saccomani. Fonti per la storia della terraferma veneta 4. Padua: Antenore, 1989.

"Cenni storici." [1145 bull of Eugene III.] Edited by G. B. Pighi. *Bollettino ecclesiastico veronese* 6 (1919): 150–57.

Chrodegang of Metz. *Regula canonicorum.* Edited by Wilhelm Schmitz. Hannover: Hahn'sche Buchhandlung, 1889.

*Codex regularum monasticarum et canonicarum.* Edited by Lucas Holstenius. 6 volumes. Augsburg: I. A. & F. A. Veith, 1759.

*Codice diplomatico longobardo.* Edited by Luigi Schiaparelli. 3 volumes. Fonti per la storia d'Italia 62, 63, 64. Rome: Istituto storico italiano/Tipografia del Senato, 1929–.

*Codice diplomatico padovano.* Edited by Andrea Gloria. 3 volumes. Venice: Deputazione di storia patria per le Venezie, 1877–81.

*Codice diplomatico veronese.* Edited by Vittorio Fainelli. 2 volumes. Venice: Deputazione di storia patria per le Venezie, 1940–63.

*The Collection in Seventy-four Titles: A Canon Law Manual of the Gregorian Reform.* Translated and annotated by John Gilchrist. Toronto: Pontifical Institute of Medieval Studies, 1980.

Damian, Peter. *Die Briefe des Petrus Damiani.* Edited by Kurt Reindel. 3 volumes. Munich: Monumenta Germaniae historica, 1983–89.

"Documenti per la storia del priorato di S. Columbano in Bardolino prima della sua trasformazione in commenda (secolo IX–XV)." Edited by Carlo Cipolla. *AMAV* 80 (1903–4): 89–227.

"Documenti per un nuovo Codice diplomatico veronese (dai fondi di San Giorgio in Braida e di San Pietro in Castello) (803 c.–994)." Edited by Egidio Rossini *AMAV* 143 (1966–67): 137–208.

*I diplomi di Berengario I.* Edited by Luigi Schiaparelli. Fonti per la storia d'Italia 35. Rome: Forzani, Tipografia del Senato, 1903.

*I diplomi di Guido e di Lamberto.* Edited by Luigi Schiaparelli. Fonti per la storia d'Italia 36. Rome: Forzani, Tipografia del Senato, 1906.

*I diplomi di Ugo e di Lotario, di Berengario II e di Adalberto.* Edited by Luigi Schiaparelli. Fonti per la storia d'Italia 38. Rome: Tipografia del Senato, 1924.

*I diplomi italiani di Lodovico III e di Rodolfo II.* Edited by Luigi Schiaparelli. Fonti per la storia d'Italia 37. Rome: Forzani e c., Tipografia del Senato, 1910.

*Inventari altomedievali di terre, coloni, e redditi.* Edited by Andrea Castagnetti, Michele Luzzati, Gianfranco Pasquali, and Augusto Vasina. Fonti per la storia d'Italia 104. Rome: Istituto storico italiano, 1979.

*I placiti del «regnum italiae».* Edited by Cesare Manaresi. 3 volumes. Fonti per la storia d'Italia 92, 96, 97. Rome: Tipografia del Senato, 1955–60.

*Italia sacra.* Edited by Ferdinando Ughelli. 9 volumes. Venice: Sebastianus Coleti, 1717–22.

*Libellus de diversis ordinibus et professionibus qui sunt in aecclesia.* Edited and translated by G. Constable and B. Smith. Oxford: Clarendon Press, 1972.

*L'orazionale dell'arcidiacono Pacifico e il Carpsum del cantore Stefano. Studi e testi sulla liturgia del duomo di Verona dal IX all'XI secolo.* Edited by G. G. Meersseman, E. Adda, and J. Deshusses. Spicilegium Friburgense 21. Fribourg: Editions universitaires, 1974.

*Monumenta Germaniae historica, Diplomatum regum et imperatorum Germaniae.* Berlin: Weidmannsche Verlagsbuchhandlung, 1879–.

*Monumenta Germaniae historica, Legum sectio III: Concilia.* 3 volumes. Hannover and Leipzig: Bibliopolius Hahnianus, 1906–24.

*Monumenta Germaniae historica, Legum sectio IV: Constitutiones et acta publica imperatorum et regum.* 5 volumes. Hannover: Bibliopolius Hahnianus, 1893–.

*Monumenta Germaniae historica, Libelli de lite imperatorum et pontificum saeculis XI et XII conscripti.* 3 volumes. Hannover: Bibliopolius Hahnianus, 1891–97.

*Monumenta Germaniae historica, Scriptores rerum Germanicarum.* Hannover: Bibliopolius Hahnianius, 1826–. Reprinted, Stuttgart: Anton Hiersemann, New York: Kraus, 1903–.

Otto of Freising. *Gesta Frederici I Imperatoris. Monumenta Germaniae historica, Scriptores rerum Germanicarum,* vol. 7. Berlin: Weidmannsche Buchhandlung, 1930.

*Papsturkunden in Italien: Reiseberichte zur Italia Pontificia.* Edited by Paul F. Kehr. 6 volumes. Acta Romanorum Pontificum 1–6. Città del Vaticano: Biblioteca apostolica Vaticana, 1977.

*Patrologiae cursus completus. Series Latina.* Edited by J. P. Migne. 221 volumes. Paris: Garnier, 1844–64.

Peter the Venerable. *The Letters of Peter the Venerable.* Edited by Giles Constable. 2 volumes. Harvard Historical Studies 78. Cambridge, Mass.: Harvard University Press, 1967.

Ratherius of Verona. *Die Briefe des Bishofs Rather von Verona.* Edited by Fritz Weigle. Weimar, 1949. Reprinted as Volume 1 of the series *Monumenta Germaniae historica, Die Deutschen Geschichtsquellen des Mittelalters 500–1500.* Munich: Monumenta Germaniae historica, 1977.

———. *The Complete Works of Rather of Verona*. Translated by Peter L. D. Reid. Medieval and Renaissance Texts and Studies 76. Binghamton, N.Y.: Medieval and Renaissance Texts and Studies, 1991.

———. *Opera minora*. Edited by Peter L. D. Reid. Corpus Christianorum, continuatio mediaeualis 46. Turnhout: Brepols, 1976.

———. *Praeloqviorvm libri VI—Phrenesis*. Edited by Peter L. D. Reid. Corpus Christianorum, continuatio mediaeualis 46A. Turnhout: Brepols, 1984.

———. "Urkunden und Akten zur Geschichte Rathers in Verona." Edited by Fritz Weigle. *Quellen und Forschungen aus italienischen Archiven und Bibliotheken* 29 (1938–39): 1–40.

*Regesta pontificum romanorum. Italia pontificia*. Edited by Paul F. Kehr. 10 volumes. Berlin: Weidmannos, 1906–.

*Regesto mantovano*. Edited by Pietro Torelli. Regesta chartarum Italiae 12. Rome: E. Loescher, 1914.

*Rerum italicarum scriptores*. Edited by Lodovico Antonio Muratori. 25 volumes. Milan: Typographia Societatis palatinae, 1723–51.

*Riforma pretridentina della diocesi di Verona: Visite pastorali del vescovo G. M. Giberti 1525–1542*. Edited by Antonio Fasani. 3 volumes. Fonti e studi di storia veneta 13. Vicenza: Istituto per le ricerche di storia sociale e di storia religiosa, 1989.

*Sacrorum conciliorum nova et amplissima collectio*. Edited by J. D. Mansi. 53 volumes. Florence and Venice: Antonius Zata, 1759–98.

*Versus de Verona. Versum de Mediolano civitate*. Edited by G. B. Pighi. Studi pubblicati dall'Istituto di filologia classica 7. Bologna: Zanichelli, 1960.

Zeno, Saint. *Tractatus*. Edited by B. Löfstedt. Corpus Christianorum, Series Latina 22. Turnhout: Brepols, 1971.

## Secondary Sources

*Archivio di Stato di Verona*. Verona: Amministrazione della Provincia, 1961.

Arslan, Edoardo. *La pittura e la scultura veronese dal secolo VIII al secolo XIII*. Milan: Fratelli Bocca, 1943.

——— [Wart]. *L'architettura romanica veronese*. Verona: Tipografia Veronese, 1939.

Avril, Joseph. "Le IIIe concile du Latran et les communautés de lépreux." *Revue Mabillon* 60 (1981): 21–76.

Baker, Derek. "Crossroads and Crises in the Religious Life of the Later Eleventh Century." *Studies in Church History* 16 (1979): 137–48.

Bardy, Gustave. "Saint Grégoire VII et la reforme canoniale au XIe siécle." *Studi gregoriani* 1 (1947): 47–64.

Barraclough, Geoffrey. *The Medieval Papacy*. London: Thames and Hudson, 1968.

Bellotti, Luigi. "Gli statuti sinodali dei vescovi Adelardo II (1188–1214) e Norandino (1214–1224). In Luigi Bellotti, *Ricerche intorno alle costituzioni del capitolo della cattedrale di Verona nei secoli XIII–XV*, pp. 39–64. Venice: Deputazione di storia patria per le Venezie, 1943.

Beloch, Karl Julius. *Bevolkerungsgeschichte Italiens*. 3 volumes. Berlin, 1937–39. Reprinted, Berlin: W.de Gruyter, 1961.

Bennett, Ralph Francis. *The Early Dominicans; Studies in Thirteenth-Century Dominican History*. Cambridge: Cambridge University Press, 1937.

Berlière, U. "Le nombre des moines dans les anciens monastères." *Revue Bénédictine* 41 (1929): 231–61; 42 (1930): 19–42

Betto, Bianca. *Le nove congregazioni del clero di Venezia (sec. XI–XV): Ricerche storiche, matricole, e documenti vari.* Miscellanea erudita 41. Padua: Antenore, 1984.

Biadego, Giuseppe. *Catalogo descrittivo dei manoscritti della Biblioteca comunale di Verona.* Verona: G. Civelli, 1892.

Biancolini, G. B. *Dei vescovi e governatori di Verona.* Verona: Dionigi Ramanzini, S. Tomio, 1757.

——. *Notizie storiche delle chiese di Verona.* 8 volumes. Verona: A. Scolari, 1749–71.

Bienvenu, J.-M. "Les caractères originaux de la réforme grégorienne dans le diocèse d'Angers." *Bulletin philologique et historique (jusqu'à 1610) du Comité des travaux historiques et scientifiques* 2 (1968): 545–60.

Billo, Luisa. "Le iscrizioni veronesi dell'alto medioevo." *Archivio veneto* 16 (1934): 1–122.

Billo, Maria. "Origine e sviluppo delle parrocchie di Verona e variazioni nelle relative circoscrizioni territoriali." *Archivio veneto*, ser. 5, 29 (1941): 1–61.

Biscaro, Gerolamo. "Attraverso le carte di S. Giorgio in Braida di Verona esistenti nell'Archivio Vaticano." *Atti del Reale istituto veneto di scienze, lettere, e arti* 92 (1932–33): 983–1051.

——. "Le temporalità del vescovo di Treviso dal sec. IX al XIII." *Archivio veneto*, ser. 5, 18 (1936): 1–72.

Bizzocchi, Roberto. *Chiesa e potere nella Toscana del Quattrocento.* Annali dell'Istituto storico italo-germanico, Monografia 6. Bologna: Mulino, 1987.

Blumenthal, Uta-Renate. *The Investiture Controversy: Church and Monarchy from the Ninth to the Twelfth Century.* Philadelphia: University of Pennsylvania Press, 1988.

Bocchi, Francesca. "Monasteri, canoniche, e strutture urbane in Italia." In *Istituzioni monastiche e istituzioni canonicali in occidente (1123–1215)*, pp. 265–316. Atti della settima Settimana internazionale di studio, Mendola, 13 agosto–3 settembre 1977. Miscellanea del Centro di studi medioevali 9. Milan: Vita e Pensiero, 1980.

Bognetti, G. P. "I «loca sanctorum» e la storia della Chiesa nel regno dei Longobardi," *Rivista di storia della Chiesa in Italia* 6 (1952): 165–204.

Bogumil, Karlotto. *Das Bistum Halberstadt im 12. Jahrhundert.* Mitteldeutsche Forschungen 69. Cologne: Böhlau, 1972.

Bolton, Brenda. "Innocent III's Treatment of the Humiliati." *Studies in Church History* 8 (1972): 73–82.

Borders, James Matthew. "The Cathedral Chapter of Verona as a Musical Center in the Middle Ages: Its History, Manuscripts, and Liturgical Practice." 2 volumes. Ph.D. diss., University of Chicago, 1984.

Bouchard, Constance Brittain. "Merovingian, Carolingian, and Cluniac Monasticism: Reform and Renewal in Burgundy." *Journal of Ecclesiastical History* 41 (1990): 365–88.

——. *Spirituality and Administration: The Role of the Bishop in Twelfth-Century Auxerre.* Speculum Anniversary Monographs 5. Cambridge, Mass.: Medieval Academy of America, 1979.

——. *Sword, Mitre, and Cloister: Nobility and the Church in Burgundy, 980–1198.* Ithaca, N.Y.: Cornell University Press, 1987.

Boyd, Catherine E. *Tithes and Parishes in Medieval Italy: The Historical Roots of a Modern Problem.* Ithaca, N.Y.: Cornell University Press, 1952.

Brentano, Robert. "Italian Ecclesiastical History: The Sambin Revolution." *Medievalia et Humanistica* n.s. 14 (1986): 189–97.

——. *Two Churches: England and Italy in the Thirteenth Century.* Revised edition. Berkeley and Los Angeles: University of California Press, 1988.

Bresciani, Bruno. *Castelli veronesi.* Verona: Vita veronese, 1962.

Brooke, Christopher. "Monk and Canon: Some Patterns in the Religious Life of the Twelfth Century." *Studies in Church History* 22 (1985): 109–29

Brown, Peter. *The Cult of the Saints: Its Rise and Function in Latin Christianity.* Chicago: University of Chicago Press, 1981.

Brugnoli, Pier Paolo. *La cattedrale.* Verona: Vita veronese, 1955.

Bynum, Caroline Walker. "The Spirituality of the Regular Canons in the Twelfth Century: A New Approach." *Medievalia et Humanistica* n.s. 4 (1973): 3–24.

Cantor, Norman F. *Church, Kingship, and Lay Investiture in England, 1089–1135.* Princeton Studies in History 10. New York: Octagon Books, 1969.

——. "The Crisis of Western Monasticism, 1050–1130." *American Historical Review* 66 (1960): 47–67.

Capitani, Ovidio. "Episcopato ed ecclesiologia nell'età gregoriana." In *Le istituzioni ecclesiastiche della «societas christiana» dei secoli XI–XII: Papato, cardinalato, ed episcopato,* pp. 316–73. Atti della quinta Settimana internazionale di studio, Mendola, 26–31 agosto 1971. Miscellanea del Centro di studi medioevali 7. Milan: Vita e Pensiero, 1974.

——. "Esiste un' «età gregoriana»?" *Rivista di storia e letteratura religiosa* 1 (1965): 454–81.

——. "Storiografia e riforma della Chiesa in Italia (Arnolfo e Landolfo Seniore di Milano)." In *La storiografia altomedievale* 2: 557–629. Atti delle Settimane di studio del Centro italiano di studi sull'alto medioevo 17 (10–16 aprile 1969). Spoleto: Centro italiano di studi sull'alto medioevo, 1970.

Carrara, Mario. "La biblioteca del Monastero di S. Zeno Maggiore di Verona." *Rivista di storia della Chiesa in Italia* 6 (1952): 411–26.

——. "Novecento anni di vita sul Monte Oliveto. In *SS. Trinità in «monte oliveto» di Verona,* pp. 43–76. Verona: Stimmatini, 1974.

Carraro, Giannino. "I monasteri benedettini della diocesi di Padova." *Benedictina* 35 (1988): 87–152.

Castagnetti, Andrea. *I conti di Vicenza e di Padova dall'età ottoniana al comune.* Verona: Libreria Universitaria Editrice, 1981.

——. "Contributo allo studio dei rapporti fra città e contado. Le vicende del castello di Villimpenta dal X al XIII secolo." *Atti dell'Istituto veneto di scienze, lettere, ed arti,* Classe di scienze morali, lettere, ed arti 133 (anno accademico 1974–75): 81–137.

——. "Le dipendenze polironiane nella Marca Veronese fra XI e XII secolo." In *L'Italia nel quadro dell'espansione europea del monachesimo cluniacense,* edited by Cinzio Violante, Amleto Spicciani, and Giovanni Spinelli, pp. 105–15. Atti del convegno internazionale di storia medioevale, Pescia, 26–28 novembre 1981. Cesena: Badia di Santa Maria del Monte, 1985.

——. "La distribuzione geografica dei possessi di un grande proprietario veronese del secolo IX: Engelberto del fu Grimoaldo di Erbe." *Rivista di storia dell'agricoltura* 9 (1969): 15–26.

——. "Dominico e massaricio a Limonta nei secoli IX e X." *Rivista di storia dell'agricoltura* 8 (1968): 3–20.

——. "Le due famiglie comitali veronesi: I San Bonifacio e i Gandolfingi-di Palazzo." In *Studi sul medioevo veneto,* edited by Giorgio Cracco, pp. 49–93. Turin: Giappichelli, 1981.

——. "Enti ecclesiastici, canossa, estensi, famiglie signorili, e vassalatiche a Verona e Ferrara." In *Structures féodales et féodalisme dans l'occident méditerranéen (Xe–XIIIe siècles): Bilan et perspectives de recherches,* pp. 387–412. Section de L'École française de Rome 44. Rome: École française de Rome, 1980.

——. "La famiglia veronese degli Avvocati (secoli XI–XIII)." In *Studi sul medioevo cristiano offerti a*

*Raffaello Morghen per il 900 anniversario dell'Istituto storico italiano* (1883–1973) 1: 251–92. Istituto storico italiano per il medio evo, Studi storici 83–87. Rome: Istituto storico italiano per il medio evo, 1974.

——. *La Marca Veronese-Trevigiana.* Turin: UTET, 1986.

——. "Mercanti, società, e politica nella Marca Veronese-Trevigiana (secoli XI–XIV)." In *Mercanti e vita economica nella Repubblica Veneta (secoli XIII–XVIII)* 1: 107–93. Edited by Giorgio Borelli. Verona: Banca Popolare di Verona, 1985.

——. *L'organizzazione del territorio rurale nel medioevo: Circoscrizioni ecclesiastiche e civili nella «langobardia» e nella «romania».* Turin: G. Giappichelli Editore, 1979. Second edition, Bologna: Pàtron, 1982.

——. *La pieve rurale nell'Italia padana: Territorio, organizzazione patrimoniale, e vicende della pieve veronese di San Pietro di Tillida dall'alto medioevo al secolo XIII.* Italia Sacra 23. Rome: Herder, 1976.

——. "I possessi del monastero di S. Zeno di Verona a Bardolino." *Studi medioevali,* ser. 3, 13/1 (1972): 95–159.

——. "Primi aspetti di politica annonaria nell'Italia comunale: La bonafica della «palus comunis Verone» (1194–1199)." *Studi Medioevali,* ser. 3, 15/1 (1974): 363–481.

——. *La società veronese nel medioevo, I: La rappresentanza veronese nel trattato del 1107 con Venezia.* Verona: Libreria Universitaria, 1983.

——. *La società veronese nel medioevo, II: Ceti e famiglie dominanti nella prima età comunale.* Verona: Libreria Universitaria, 1987.

——. *«Ut nullus incipiat hedificare forticiam»: Comune veronese e signorie rurali nell'età di Federico I.* Verona: Libreria Universitaria, 1984.

——. *La Valpolicella dall'alto medioevo all'età comunale.* Verona: Centro di documentazione per la storia della Valpolicella, 1984.

——. *Il Veneto nell'alto medioevo.* Verona: Libreria Universitaria, 1990.

——. "I Veronesi da Moratica: Prestatori di danaro, signori rurali, esponenti della *pars comitum* (1136–1267)." In *Studi in onore di Gino Barbieri: Problemi e metodi di storia ed economica,* pp. 409–47. Pisa: IPEM, 1983.

Casto, Lucio. "Il fondamento patrimoniale della potenza vescovile di Asti." *Bollettino storico-bibliografico subalpino* 73 (1975): 5–58 and 74 (1976): 27–66.

Cavallari, Vittorio. "Cadalo e gli Erzoni." *Studi storici veronesi* 15 (1965): 59–170.

——. "Il Conte di Verona. Cronologia del comitato (fino all'inserimento dei Sambonifacio)." *AMAV* 139 (1962–63): 103–41.

——. "Il Conte di Verona. I Sambonifacio e i conti di Verona nel X secolo: Milone." *AMAV* 140 (1963–64): 207–46.

——. "Il Conte di Verona fra il X e l'XI secolo." *AMAV* 142 (1965–66): 61–105.

——. "Il Conte di Verona fra l'XI ed il XII secolo." *AMAV* 145 (1968–69): 203–74.

——. "Profilo di Monsignore Giuseppe Turrini." *AMAV* 154 (1977–78): 17–44.

——. *Raterio e Verona.* Verona: Istituto per gli studi storici veronese, 1967.

——. "Verona e San Zeno." *AMAV* 128 (1951–52): 185–262.

Cavazzocca Mazzanti, Vittorio. "La pieve di Cisano di Gardesana." *AMAV* 87 (1910–11): 263–80.

Cenci, Pio. "L'Archivio della Cancelleria della Nunziatura veneta." In *Miscellanea Francesco Ehrle* 5: 273–330. Rome: Biblioteca apostolica Vaticana, 1924.

——. "Documenti inediti su la famiglia e la giovinezza dell'Antipapa Cadalo." *Archivio storico per le province parmensi* n.s. 23 (1923): 185–223 and 24 (1924): 309–44.

Chapman, John. "The Origin of the Rules of St. Augustine." *The Downside Review* 49 (1931): 395–407.

Chenu, Marie Dominique. *Nature, Man, and Society in the Twelfth Century.* Edited and translated by Jerome Taylor and Lester K. Little. Chicago: University of Chicago Press, 1968; reprinted 1983.

Cherubini, Giovanni. "Qualche considerazione sulle campagne dell'Italia centro-settentrionale tra l'XI e il XV secolo." *Rivista storica italiana* 79 (1967): 111–57.

*La Chiesa di Venezia nei secoli XI–XIII.* Edited by Franco Tonon. Venice: Studium Cattolico Veneziano, 1988.

*Chiesa e riforma nella spiritualità del secolo XI.* Convegni del Centro di studi sulla spiritualità medievale 6 (13–16 ottobre 1963). Todi: Accademia Tudertina, 1968.

*Chiese e monasteri di Verona.* Edited by Giorgio Borelli. Verona: Banca Popolare di Verona, 1980.

*Chiese e monasteri nel territorio veronese.* Edited by Giorgio Borelli. Verona: Banca Popolare di Verona, 1981.

Cipolla, Carlo. "L'antichissima iconografia di Verona secondo una copia inedita." *Memorie della R. accademia dei Lincei, Classe di scienze morali, storiche, e filologiche* 8 (1909): 49–60.

——. "Di una iscrizione metrica riguardante Uberto vescovo di Verona." *Rendiconti della R. accademia dei Lincei, Classe di scienze morali, storiche, e filologiche* 5 (1896): 387–99.

——. "Una iscrizione medioevale a Cisano sul lago di Garda." *Atti della R. Accademia delle scienze di Torino* 29 (1894): 3–12.

——. *Le popolazioni dei XIII comuni veronesi: Ricerche storiche sull'appoggio di nuovi documenti.* Venice: Deputazione veneta sopra gli studi di storia patria, 1882.

——. "I primi accenni alla organizzazione comunale in un piccolo villaggio presso Cologna Veneta; dalla pace di Venezia a quella di Costanza." In *Miscellanea di studi storici in onore di Giovanni Sforza,* pp. 203–40. Lucca: Baroni, 1915.

——. "[Statistica degli archivi della città e provincia di Verona]." In *Gli archivi della regione veneta,* edited by R. Sovrintendenza agli archivi veneti, 2: 197–371. Venice: P. Naratovich, 1880–81.

——. *La storia politica di Verona.* Verona, 1899. Reprinted, Verona: Edizioni Valdonega, 1954.

——. "Il Velo di Classe." *Le gallerie nazionali italiane* 3 (1897): 194–249.

——. ["Verona e la guerra contro Federico Barbarossa."] *Nuovo archivio veneto* 10 (1895): 405–504.

Cohn, Samuel K., Jr. *Death and Property in Siena, 1205–1800: Strategies for the Afterlife.* Johns Hopkins University Studies in Historical and Political Science, 106th ser., vol. 2. Baltimore: Johns Hopkins University Press, 1988.

Constable, Giles. "The Study of Monastic History Today." In *Essays on the Reconstruction of Medieval History,* edited by Vaclav Mudroch and G. S. Couse. Montreal: McGill-Queen's University Press, 1974. Reprinted in *Religious Life and Thought* (11th–12th centuries). London: Variorum Reprints, 1979.

Cowdrey, H. E. J. "The Gregorian Reform in the Anglo-Norman Lands and in Scandinavia." *Studi gregoriani* 13 (1989): 321–52.

Cracco, Giorgio. "Dinamismo religioso e contesto politico nel medioevo Vicentino." *Ricerche di storia sociale e religiosa* 13 (1978): 121–37.

——. "La fondazione dei canonici secolari di S. Giorgio in Alga." *Rivista di storia della Chiesa in Italia* 13 (1959): 70–81.

——. "Movimenti popolari, movimenti religiosi del medioevo." *Rivista di storia e letteratura religiosa* 23 (1987): 133–41.

——. "Religione, Chiesa, pietà." In *Storia di Vicenza II: L'età medievale,* pp. 359–425. Vicenza: Accademia Olimpica, Neri Pozza, 1988.

———. "Riforma e decadenza nel monastero di S. Agostino di Vicenza." *Rivista di storia della Chiesa in Italia* 14 (1960): 203–34.

Cremonesi, Arduino. *L'eredità europea del patriarcato di Aquileia.* Second edition. Udine: Arti grafiche friulane, 1974.

*Cristianizzazione ed organizzazione ecclesiastica delle campagne nell'alto medioevo: Espansione e resistenze.* 2 volumes. Atti delle Settimane di studio del Centro italiano di studi sull'alto medioevo 28 (10–16 aprile 1980). Spoleto: Centro italiano di studi sull'alto medioevo, 1982.

Dal Forno, Federico. *La chiesa dei Santi Nazaro e Celso a Verona.* Verona: Fiorini, 1982.

Da Lisca, Alessandro. "La basilica di S. Stefano in Verona." *AMAV* 114 (1935–36): 45–119.

———. "La chiesa di S. Maria Maggiore al Gazzo Veronese." *AMAV* 119 (1940–41): 131–76.

———. "La chiesa di S. Teuteria e Tosca in Verona." *Madonna Verona* 7 (1913): 161–76; 8 (1914): 1–25.

———. "Le varie cinte murate di Verona." *Madonna Verona* 9 (1915): 11–72.

———. "Verona—S. Anastasia." *AMAV* 121 (1942–43): 33–65.

Dameron, George W. *Episcopal Power and Florentine Society, 1000–1320.* Cambridge, Mass.: Harvard University Press, 1991.

David, Tilla. "Una strana comunità benedettina-cistercense in Padova nel sec. XIII: Gli albi." In *Mélanges offerts à René Crozet à l'occasion de son soixante-dixième anniversaire,* edited by Pierre Gallais et Yves-Jean Riou, 2: 1079–84. Poitiers: Société d'Études Médiévales, 1966.

de Angelis D'Ossat, Guglielmo. "L'architettura del S. Giorgio di Valpolicella: Una chiesa castrense." In *Verona in età gotica e longobarda,* pp. 149–171. Atti del convegno 6–7 dicembre 1980. Verona: Accademia di agricoltura, scienze e lettere di Verona, 1982.

Delaruelle, Étienne. *La piété populaire au moyen âge.* Edited by Raoul Manselli and André Vauchez. Turin: Bottega d'Erasmo, 1975.

Dereine, Charles. "Chanoines." *Dictionnaire d'histoire et de géographie ecclésiastiques* 12: 353–405. Paris: Letouzey et Ané, 1912–.

———. "Odon de Tournai et la crise du cénobitism au XIe siècle." *Revue de moyen age latin* 4 (1948): 137–54.

de Sandre Gasparini, Giuseppina. "L'assistenza ai lebbrosi nel movimento religioso dei primi decenni del duocento veronese: Uomini e fatti." In *Viridarium floridum: Studi di storia veneta offerti dagli allievi a Paolo Sambin,* edited by Maria Chiara Billanovich, Giorgio Cracco, and Antonio Rigon, pp. 25–59. Medioevo e umanesimo 54. Padua: Antenore, 1984.

———. *Contadini, chiesa, confraternità in un paese veneto di bonifica: Villa del Bosco nel Quattrocento.* Padua: Antoniana, 1979.

———. "Per la storia dei penitenti a Verona nel secolo XIII. Primi contributi." In *Il movimento francescano della penitenza nella società medioevale,* edited by Mariano d'Alatri, pp. 257–283. Atti del 30 convegno di studi francescani, Padova, 25–26–27 settembre 1979. Rome: Istituto storico dei Cappuccini, 1980.

De Spiegeler, Pierre. *Les hôpitaux et l'assistance à Liège (Xe–XVe siècles): Aspects institutionnels et sociaux.* Bibliothèque de la Faculté de philosophie et lettres de l'Université de Liège 249. Paris: "Les Belles Lettres," 1987.

Devailly, G. "Une enquête en course: L'application de la réforme grégorienne en Bretagne." *Annales de Bretagne* 75 (1968): 293–316.

———. "Les restitutions de paroisses au temps de la réforme grégorienne. Bretagne et Berry: étude comparée," *Bulletin philologique et historique (jusqu'à 1610) du Comité des travaux historiques et scientifiques* 2 (1968): 583–98.

*Dictionnaire de droit canonique.* 7 volumes. Paris, Letouzey et Ané, 1935–65.

Dionisi, G. G. *De duobus episcopis Aldone et Notingo.* Verona: Antonius Andreoni, 1758.

——. *Dei Santi veronesi.* Verona: Per l'Erede Merlo alla Stella, 1786.

——. *Dell'origine e dei progressi della zecca di Verona.* Verona: Presso l'Erede di Agostino Carattoni, 1776.

Drew, Katherine Fischer. "The Italian Monasteries of Nonantola, S. Salvatore, and Santa Maria Teodota in the Eighth and Ninth Centuries." *Manuscripta* 9 (1965): 131–54.

Duby, Georges. *The Early Growth of the European Economy: Warriors and Peasants from the Seventh to the Twelfth Century.* Translated by Howard B. Clarke. London: Weidenfeld & Nicolson, 1974.

Duggan, Lawrence G. *Bishop and Chapter: The Governance of the Bishopric of Speyer to 1552.* New Brunswick, N.J.: Rutgers University Press, 1978.

Dunbabin, Jean. *France in the Making, 843–1180.* Oxford: Oxford University Press, 1985.

Ederle, G. *Dizionario cronologico bio-bibliografico dei vescovi di Verona.* Verona: Vita veronese, 1965.

Egger, Carlo. "Canonici regolari di Santa Maria in Porto." *Dizionario degli istituti de perfezione* 2: 147–8. Rome: Paoline, 1974–.

Faccioli, Vicenzo. *La chiesa di S. Michele Arcangelo in Angiari.* Verona: Tipografia Nigrizia, 1972.

Faè, Gianni. *Badia Calavena.* Collana "Le Guide" 69. Verona: Vita veronese, 1964.

Fainelli, Vittorio. "L'abbazia di San Zeno nell'alto medioevo." In *Miscellanea in onore di Roberto Cessi* 1: 51–62. Rome: Edizioni di Storia e letteratura, 1958.

——. "Gli «Antichi archivi veronesi» annessi alla Biblioteca Comunale dalle origini dell'istituzione al 1943." *AMAV* 135 (1958–59): 96–151.

——. "L'assistenza nell'alto medioevo: I xenodochi di origine romana." *Atti del Reale istituto veneto di scienze, lettere, ed arti* 92/2 (1932–33): 915–34.

——. "Chiese di Verona esistenti e distrutte. Contributo alla topografia storica veronese." *Madonna Verona* 13 (1910): 50–66.

——. "Consoli, podestà, e giudici di Verona fino alla Pace di Costanza." *Atti dell'Istituto veneto di scienze, lettere, et arti* 114 (1955–56): 217–53.

——. "La data nei documenti e nelle cronache di Verona." *Nuovo archvio veneto* n.s. 21 (1911): 128–77.

——. "Intorno alle origini dei comuni rurali veronesi." *Nuovo archivio veneto* n.s. 25 (1904): 381–444.

——. *Storia degli ospedali di Verona dai tempi di San Zeno ai giorni nostri.* Verona: Ghidini e Fiorini, 1962.

Fanning, Steven. *A Bishop and His World Before the Gregorian Reform: Hubert of Angers, 1006–1047.* Transactions of the American Philosophical Society 78, pt. 1. Philadelphia: American Philosophical Society, 1988.

Farmer, David Hugh. *The Oxford Dictionary of Saints.* Oxford: Oxford University Press, 1987.

Fasoli, Gina. "Per la storia di Vicenza dal IX al XIII secolo, Conti-Vescovi, Vescovi-Conti." *Archivio veneto,* ser. 5, 36–37 (1945): 208–41.

Ferrari, Gianino. "La campagna di Verona dal sec. XII alla venuta dei Veneziani (1405)." *Atti del Reale istituto veneto di scienze, lettere, ed arti* 74 (1914–15): 41–103.

Filippini, Vittorio. "Intorno alla chiesa di S. Elena." *Studi storici veronesi* 15 (1965): 5–57.

Fleckenstein, Josef. *Die Hofkapelle der deutschen Könige, I. Grundlegen: Die Karolingische Hofkapelle.* Schriften der Monumenta Germaniae historica 16/1. Stuttgart: Anton Hiersemann, 1959.

——. *Die Hofkapelle der deutschen Könige, II: Die Hofkapelle im Rahmen der Ottonisch-Salischen Reichskirche.* Schriften der Monumenta Germaniae historica 16/2. Stuttgart: Anton Hiersemann, 1966.

——. "Hofkapelle und Reichsepiskopat unter Heinrich IV." In *Investiturstreit und Reichsverfassung*, edited by Josef Fleckenstein. Munich: Jan Thorbecke, 1973.

——. "Zum Begriff der Ottonisch-Salischen Reichskirche." In *Geschichte, Wirtschaft, Gesellschaft: Festschrift für Clemens Bauer zum 75. Geburtstag*, edited by Erich Hassinger, J. Heinz Müller, and Hugo Ott. Berlin: Duncker & Humbolt, 1974.

Fliche, Augustin. *La réforme grégorienne*. 3 volumes. Spicilegium sacrum Lovaniense, Etudes et documents 6, 9, 16. Louvain: Spicilegium sacrum Lovananesis, and Paris: E. Champion, 1924–37.

Fonseca, Cosimo Damiano. "Gregorio VII e il movimento canonicale: Un caso di sensibilità gregoriana." *Benedictina* 33 (1986): 11–23.

Forchielli, Giuseppe. "Collegialità di chierici nel veronese dall'VIII secolo all'età comunale." *Archivio veneto*, ser. 5, 3 (1928): 1–117.

——. *La pieve rurale: Ricerche sulla storia della costruzione della chiesa in Italia e particolarmente nel Veronese*. Bologna: Nicola Zanichelli, 1938.

Forlati, Ferdinando. "La pieve di S. Andrea di Sommacampagna." *AMAV* 121 (1942–43): 163–76.

Fornasari, Giuseppe. "Coscienza ecclesiale e storia della spiritualità: Per una ridefinizione della riforma di Gregorio VII." *Benedictina* 33 (1986): 25–50.

——. "Fondazioni cluniacensi non dipendenti da S. Benedetto di Polirone nelle regioni venete: Un primo sondaggio." In *L'Italia nel quadro dell'espansione europea del monachesimo cluniacense*, edited by Cinzio Violante, Amleto Spicciani, and Giovanni Spinelli, pp. 105–15. Atti del convegno internazionale di storia medioevale, Pescia, 26–28 novembre 1981. Cesena: Badia di Santa Maria del Monte, 1985.

——. "La riforma gregoriana nel «Regnum Italiae»." *Studi gregoriani* 13 (1989): 281–320.

Fournier, Paul. "Les collections canoniques romaines de l'époque de Grégoire VII." *Mémoires de l'institut national de France—Académie des inscriptions et belles-lettres* 41 (1920): 271–395.

Franceschini, Adriano. *Giurisdizione episcopale e comunità rurali altopolesane: Bergantino, Melara, Bariano, Trecenta (Sec. X–XIV)*. Bologna: Pàtron, 1986.

Freed, John B. *The Friars and German Society in the Thirteenth Century*. Medieval Academy of America Publication 86. Cambridge, Mass.: Medieval Academy of America, 1977.

Fumagalli, Vito. "In margine alla storia delle prestazioni di opere sul dominico in territorio veronese durante il secolo IX." *Rivista di storia dell'agricoltura* 6 (1966): 115–27.

Gagliardo, Reno Scola. *La mensa vescovile di Verona*. Studi e documenti di storia e liturgia 5. Verona: Archivio Storico Curia Vescovile, 1987.

Garcìa y Garcìa, Antonio. "Reforma gregoriana e idea de la 'militia sancti Petri' en los reinos ibéricos." *Studi gregoriani* 13 (1989): 241–62.

Garzotti, Pietro. *Le pievi della città di Verona a la pieve d'Isola della Scala*. Verona: Tipografia A. Merlo, 1882.

Gaudemet, Jean. "La paroisse au moyen âge: État des questions," *Revue d'histoire de L'Église de France* 59 (1973): 5–21.

Giampaolini, Elisabetta Archetti. *Aristocrazia e chiese nella Marca del centro-nord tra IX e XI secolo*. Università di Macerata, Pubblicazioni della Facoltà di lettere e filosofia 38. Rome: Viella, 1987.

Gilchrist, John. "The Office of Bishop in the Middle Ages." *Tijdschrift voor Rechtsgeschiedenis* 39 (1971): 85–101.

——. "Was There a Gregorian Reform Movement in the Eleventh Century?" *The Canadian Catholic Historical Association, Study Sessions* 37 (1970): 1–10.

Giusti, Martino. "Le canoniche della città e diocesi di Lucca al tempo della riforma gregoriana." *Studi gregoriani* 3 (1948): 321–67.

Glaeske, Günter. *Die Erzbischöfe von Hamburg-Bremen als Reichsfürsten (937–1258)*. Quellen und Darstellungen zur Geschichte Niedersachsens 60. Hildesheim: August Lax, 1962.

Golinelli, Paolo. *Culto dei santi e vita cittadina a Reggio Emilia (secoli IX–XII)*. Modena: Aedes Muratoriana, 1980.

——. *«Indiscreta sanctitas.» Studi sui rapporti tra culti, poteri, e società nel pieno medioevo*. Studi storici 197–198. Rome: Istituto storico italiano per il medio evo, 1988.

Grégoire, Réginald. *La vocazione sacerdotale: I canonici regolari nel medioevo*. La spiritualità cristiana, storia e testi 7. Rome: Studium, 1982.

Groß, Thomas. *Lothar III. und die Mathildischen Güter*. Europäische Hochschulschriften ser. 3, 419. Frankfurt am Main: Peter Lang, 1990.

Grundmann, Herbert. *Religiöse Bewegungen im Mittelalter*. Berlin: Emil Ebering, 1935.

Guerrini, Paolo. "Un cardinale gregoriano a Brescia: Il vescovo Arimanno." *Studi gregoriani* 2 (1947): 361–85.

Guterman, Simeon L. "The Principle of the Personality of Law in the Early Middle Ages: A Chapter in the Evolution of Western Legal Institutions and Ideals." *University of Miami Law Review* 21 (1966): 259–348.

Hallinger, Kassius. *Gorze-Kluny: Studien zu den monastischen Lebensformen und Gegensätzen im Hochmittelalter*. 2 volumes. Studia Anselmiana 22–25. Rome: Herder, 1950.

——. "Progressi e problemi della ricerca sulla riforma pre-gregoriana." In *Il monachesimo nell'alto medioevo e la formazione della civiltà occidentale*, pp. 257–91. Settimane di studio del Centro italiano di studi sull'alto medioevo 4. Spoleto: Centro italiano di studi sull'alto medioevo, 1957.

Haverkamp, Alfred. *Medieval Germany 1056–1273*. Translated by Helga Braun and Richard Mortimer. Oxford: Oxford University Press, 1988.

Herlihy, David. "The Agrarian Revolution in Southern France and Italy, 801–1150." *Speculum* 33 (1958): 23–37.

——. "Demography." In *Dictionary of the Middle Ages* 4: 136–48. Edited by Joseph R. Strayer. New York: Charles Scribner's Sons, 1984.

——. *Medieval and Renaissance Pistoia: The Social History of an Italian Town, 1200–1430*. New Haven: Yale University Press, 1967.

——. "The Population of Verona in the First Century of Venetian Rule." In *Renaissance Venice*, edited by J. R. Hale, pp. 91–120. London: Faber & Faber, 1974.

Hill, Bennett D. *English Cistercian Monasteries and Their Patrons in the Twelfth Century*. Urbana: University of Illinois Press, 1968.

Hotzmann, Walther. "Anecdota Veronensia" In *Papsttum und Kaisertum; Forschungen zur politischen Geschichte und Geisteskultur des Mittelalters Paul Kehr zum 65. Geburtstag dargebracht*, edited by Albert Brackmann, pp. 369–75. Munich: Verlag Münchner Drucke, 1926.

Hove, Aloïs Van. *Prolegomena*. St. Mecheln and Rome: H. Dessain, 1945.

Howe, John. "The Nobility's Reform of the Medieval Church." *American Historical Review* 93 (1988): 317–39.

Hudson, Peter J. "La dinamica dell'insediamento urbano nell'area del cortile del Tribunale di Verona: L'età medioevale." *AMAV* 160 (1983–84): 383–414.

Imbart de la Tour, Pierre. *Les origines religieuses de la France: Les paroisses rurales du 4e au 11e siècle*. Paris, 1900. Reprinted, Paris: Picard, 1979.

Le istituzioni ecclesiastiche della «societas christiana» dei secoli XI–XII: Diocesi, pievi, e parrocchie. Atti della sesta Settimana internazionale di studio, Milano, 1–7 settembre 1974. Miscellanea del Centro di studi medioevali 8. Milan: Vita e Pensiero, 1977.

Jedin, Hubert and John Dolan, eds. Handbook of Church History. Translated by Anselm Biggs. 10 volumes. New York: Herder & Herder, 1965–70.

Johnson, Edgar N. "Bishop Benno II of Osnabrück." Speculum 16 (1941): 389–403.

Johnson, Penelope. Prayer, Patronage, and Power: The Abbey of la Trinité, Vendôme, 1032–1187. New York: New York University, 1981.

Lambert, Malcolm D. Franciscan Poverty; The Doctrine of the Absolute Poverty of Christ and the Apostles in the Franciscan Order, 1210–1323. London: SPCK, 1961.

Laudage, Johannes. Priesterbild und Reformpapsttum im 11. Jahrhundert. Beihefte zum Archiv für Kulturgeschichte 22. Cologne: Böhlau, 1984.

Lawrence, C. H. Medieval Monasticism. London: Longman, 1984.

Le Bras, G., Ch. Lefebvre, and J. Rambaud. Histoire du droit et des institutions de l'Eglise en occident, Volume VII: L'âge classique, 1140–1378: Sources et théorie du droit. Paris: Sirey, 1965.

Leclercq, Jean. "La crise du monachisme aux XIe et XIIe siècles." Bullettino dell'Istituto storico italiano per il medio evo e Archivio Muratoriano 70 (1958): 19–41. English translation: "The Monastic Crisis of the Eleventh and Twelfth Centuries." In Cluniac Monasticism in the Central Middle Ages, ed. Noreen Hunt (London: Macmillan, 1971), pp. 217–37.

——. "Gregorio VII nel nostro secolo." Benedictina 33 (1986): 117–23.

Leclercq, Jean, François Vandenbroucke, and Louis Bouyer. A History of Christian Spirituality. 3 volumes. New York: Seabury Press, 1963–69.

Lemarignier, J. F. "Hiérarchie monastique et hiérarchie féodale." Revue historique de droit française et étranger, ser. 4, 31 (1953): 171–74.

——. "Structures monastiques et structures politiques dans la France de la fin du X siècle et des débuts du XI siècle." In Il monachesimo nell'alto medioevo e la formazione della civiltà occidentale, pp. 357–400. Settimane di studio del Centro italiano di studi sull'alto medioevo 4. Spoleto: Centro italiano di studi sull'alto medioevo, 1957.

Lenotti, T. Chiese e conventi scomparsi. 2 volumes. Verona: Vita veronese, 1955.

Lesnick, Daniel R. Preaching in Medieval Florence: The Social World of Franciscan and Dominican Spirituality. Athens: University of Georgia Press, 1989.

Leyser, Henrietta. Hermits and the New Monasticism: A Study of Religious Communities in Western Europe 1000–1150. London: Macmillan, 1984.

Leyser, Karl J. Medieval Germany and its Neighbors, 900–1250. London: The Hambledon Press, 1982.

——. Rule and Conflict in an Early Medieval Society: Ottonian Saxony. London: Edward Arnold, 1979.

Little, Lester K. Liberty, Charity, Fraternity: Lay Religious Confraternities at Bergamo in the Age of the Commune. Smith College Studies in History 51. Northampton, Mass.: Smith College, and Bergamo: Pierluigi Lubrina, 1988.

——. Religious Poverty and the Profit Economy in Medieval Europe. Ithaca, N.Y.: Cornell University Press, 1978.

Lopez, Robert Sabatino. "Économie et architecture médiévale. Cela aurait-il tué ceci?" Annales: Économies, sociétés, civilisations 7 (1952): 433–38.

Loud, G. A. Church and Society in the Norman Principality of Capua, 1058–1197. Oxford: Clarendon Press, 1985.

Lynch, Joseph H. Simoniacal Entry into Religious Life from 1000 to 1260: A Social, Economic, and Legal Study. Columbus: Ohio State University Press, 1976.

Maccarrone, Michele. *Studi su Innocenzo III*. Italia Sacra 17. Padua: Antenore, 1972.

Maffei, Scipione. *Verona illustrata*. Verona: Vallarsi, 1731–32.

Magnou-Nortier, Elisabeth. *La société laïque et l'Église dans la province ecclésiastique de Narbonne (zone cispyrénéene) de la fin du VIIIe à la fin du XIe siècle*. Publications de l'Université de Toulouse-Le Mirail, ser. A, 20. Toulouse: Association des publications de l'Université de Toulouse-Le Mirail, 1974.

Manselli, Raoul. "La religione popolare nei secoli XII–XIII." In *Problemi di storia della Chiesa: Il medioevo dei secoli XII–XV*, pp. 73–89. Milan: Vita e Pensiero, 1976.

Mantese, G. *Memorie storiche della chiesa vicentina*. 2 volumes. Vicenza: Scuola Tipografia Istituto S. Gaetano, 1952–59.

Martines, Lauro. *Power and Imagination: City-States in Renaissance Italy*. New York: Knopf, 1979.

Mascanzoni, L. *Pievi e parrocchie in Italia: Saggio di bibliografia storica*. 2 volumes. Bologna: La Fotocromo Emiliana, 1988–89.

Mazzaoui, Maureen Fennell. "The Emigration of Veronese Textile Artisans to Bologna in the Thirteenth Century." *AMAV* 144 (1967–68): 275–321.

Meersseman, Giles Gerard. "Il codice XC della Capitolare di Verona." *Archivio Veneto*, ser. 5, 104 (1975): 11–44.

——. "Die Klerikervereine von Karl dem Großen bis Innocenz III." *Zeitschrift für Schweizerische Kirchengeschichte* 46 (1952): 1–42, 81–112.

——. *Ordo fraternitatis: Confraternite e pietà dei laici nel medioevo*. 3 volumes. Rome: Herder, 1977.

Meier, Gabriele. *Die Bischöfe von Paderborn und ihr Bistum im Hochmittelalter*. Paderborner Theologische Studien 17. Paderborn: Ferdinand Schöningh, 1987.

Miccoli, Giovanni. *Chiesa gregoriana: Ricerche sulla riforma del secolo XI*. Storici antichi e moderni n.s. 17. Florence: La nuova Italia, 1966.

Milo, Yoram. "From Imperial Hegemony to the Commune: Reform in Pistoia's Cathedral Chapter and its Political Impact." In *Istituzioni ecclesiastiche della Toscana medioevale*, pp. 87–107. Galatina: Congedo, 1980.

Mittarelli, Johanne-Benedicto and Anselmo Costadoni, eds. *Annales Camaldulenses Ordinis Sancti Benedicti*. 9 volumes. Venice: J. B. Pasquali, 1755–73.

Modena, L. "Vita difficile di un'antico pieve." *Vita veronese* 5–6 (1980): 106–8.

*Monasteri in alta Italia dopo le invasioni saracene e magiare (sec. X–XII)*. Relazioni e comunicazioni presentate al XXXII Congresso storico subalpino, III Convegno di storia della chiesa in Italia, Pinerolo, 6–9 settembre 1964. Turin: Deputazione subalpina di storia patria, 1966.

Monese Recchia, Valeria. "Aspetti sociali ed economici nella vita di un monastero benedettino femminile: S. Michele in Campagna di Verona dal secolo XI al periodo ezzeliniano." *Archivio veneto*, ser. 5, 98 (1973): 5–54.

——. "Il problema delle origini del monastero di S. Michele in Campagna di Verona." *Archivio Veneto*, ser. 5, 130 (1972): 15–24.

Moore, R. I. "Family, Community, and Cult on the Eve of the Gregorian Reform." *Transactions of the Royal Historical Society*, ser. 5, 30 (1980): 49–69.

——. *The Formation of a Persecuting Society: Power and Deviance in Western Europe, 950–1250*. Oxford: Basil Blackwell, 1987.

——. "New Sects and Secret Meetings: Association and Authority in the Eleventh and Twelfth Centuries." *Studies in Church History* 23 (1986): 47–68.

Moorman, John. *A History of the Franciscan Order from its Origins to the Year 1517*. Oxford: Clarendon Press, 1968.

Morghen, Raffaello. *Gregorio VII e la riforma della Chiesa nel secolo XI*. Palermo: Palumbo, 1974.

——. *Medioevo cristiano*. Rome, 1951. Reprinted Rome: Laterza, 1978.

——. *La riforma della Chiesa nel secolo XI*. Rome: Ateneo, 1952.

Morris, Colin. *The Papal Monarchy: The Western Church from 1050 to 1250*. Oxford: Clarendon, 1989.

Morrison, Karl. "Gregorian Reform." In *Christian Spirituality: Origins to the Twelfth Century*, edited by Bernard McGinn and John Meyerdorff, pp. 177–93. Volume 16 of *World Spirituality, An Encylopedic History of the Religious Quest*. London: Routledge & Kegan Paul, 1986.

Muncey, R. W. *A History of the Consecration of Churches and Churchyards*. Cambridge: W. Heffer & Sons, 1930.

Mundy, John Hine. "Charity and Social Work in Toulouse, 1100–1250." *Traditio* 22 (1966): 203–87.

Munerati, D. "Sulle origini dell'Antipapa Cadalo vescovo di Parma." *Rivista di scienze storiche* 3 (1906): 3–20.

Nagler, Georg Kaspar. *Neues allgemeines Künstlerlexicon*. 22 volumes. Munich: E. A. Fleischmann, 1835–52.

Nanni, Luigi. *La parrocchia studiata sui documenti lucchesi dei secoli VIII–XIII*. Analecta gregoriana 47. Rome: Gregorian University, 1948.

Odorici, Federico. *Storie bresciane*. 11 volumes. Brescia: Pietro di Lor. Gilberti, 1953–65.

Osheim, Duane J. *An Italian Lordship: The Bishopric of Lucca in the Late Middle Ages*. Berkeley and Los Angeles: University of California Press, 1977.

——. *A Tuscan Monastery and Its Social World: San Michele of Guamo (1156–1348)*. Italia Sacra 40. Rome: Herder, 1989.

Pahncke, Hans. *Geschichte der Bischöfe Italiens deutscher Nation von 951–1264, I: Teil, Einleitende Periode (951–1004)*. Berlin: Emil Ebering, 1913.

Paschini, Pio. *San Paolino patriarca e la chiesa aquileise alla fine del secolo VIII*. Udine, 1906. Reprinted, Udine: La Nuova Base, 1977.

——. "Le vicende politiche e religiose del Friuli nei secoli nono e decimo." *Nuovo archivio veneto* n.s. 21 (1911): 37–88, 399–435.

Penco, Gregorio. *Storia del monachesimo in Italia dalle origini alla fine del medio evo*. Rome: Pia Società San Paolo, 1961.

Pennington, Kenneth. *Pope and Bishops: The Papal Monarchy in the Twelfth and Thirteenth Centuries*. Philadelphia: University of Pennsylvania Press, 1984.

Perini, Lodovico. *Istoria delle monache di S. Silvestro*. Padua: Nella Stamperia del Seminario, 1720.

Perini, Quintilio. *Le monete di Verona*. Rovereto, 1902. Reprinted Bologna: Arnaldo Forni, 1981.

Peroni, G. and B. Polverigiani, eds. *Avesa: Studi, ricerche, cose varie*. Verona: La Consortia (Comunità) Stampe, 1978.

Picasso, Giorgio. "«Studi gregoriani» e storiografia gregoriana." *Benedictina* 33 (1986): 51–60.

*Pievi e parrocchie in Italia nel basso medioevo (secoli XIII–XV)*. Atti del VI Convegno di storia della Chiesa in Italia, Firenze, 21–25 settembre 1981. Italia Sacra 35–36. Rome: Herder, 1984.

*Pievi, parrocchie, e clero nel Veneto dal X al XV secolo*. Edited by Paolo Sambin. Miscellanea di studi e memorie della Deputazione di storia patria per le Venezie 24. Venice: Deputazione, 1987.

*I poteri temporali dei vescovi in Italia e Germania nel medioevo*. Edited by Carlo Guido Mor and Heinrich Schmidinger. Annali dell'Istituto storico italo-germanico, Quaderno 3. Atti della settimana di studio 13–18 settembre 1976. Bologna: Mulino, 1979.

*La povertà del secolo XII e Francesco d'Assisi*. Atti del II convegno internazionale, Assisi, 17–19 ottobre 1974. Assisi: Società internazionale di studi francescani, 1975.

Quilici, B. *Giovanni Gualberto e la sua riforma monastica*. Florence: Tipografia Salesiana, 1943.

Racine, Pierre. "Évêque et cité dans la royaume d'Italie: Aux origines des communes italiennes." *Cahiers de civilisation médiévale* 27 (1984): 129–39.

Ragnolini, Massimo. *Garda*. Collana "Le Guide" 91. Verona: Vita veronese, 1972.

*Raterio da Verona*. Convegni del Centro di studi sulla spiritualità medievale 10. Todi: L'Accademia Tudertina, 1973.

Rauty, Natale. *Storia di Pistoia I: Dall'alto medioevo all'età precomunale, 406–1105*. Florence: Felice Le Monier, 1988.

*Reich und Kirche vor dem Investiturstreit: Vorträge beim wissenschaftlichen Kolloquium aus Anlaß des achtzigsten Geburtstags von Gerd Tellenbach*. Edited by Karl Schmid. Munich: Jan Thorbecke, 1985.

Reid, Peter L. D. *Tenth-Century Latinity: Rather of Verona*. Humana Civilitas: Studies and Sources relating to the Middle Ages 6. Los Angeles: Center for Medieval and Renaissance Studies; Malibu: Undena publications, 1981.

*Renaissance and Renewal in the Twelfth Century*. Edited by Robert L. Benson and Giles Constable with Carol D. Lanham. Cambridge, Mass.: Harvard University Press, 1982.

Reuter, Timothy. "The 'Imperial Church System' of the Ottonian and Salian Rulers: a Reconsideration." *Journal of Ecclesiastical History* 33 (1982): 347–74.

——, ed. and trans. *The Medieval Nobility*. Amsterdam: North-Holland, 1978.

Richards, Peter. *The Medieval Leper and His Northern Heirs*. Cambridge: D. S. Brewer, 1977.

Riché, Pierre. *Education and Culture in the Barbarian West from the Sixth through the Eighth Century*. Translated by John J. Contreni. Paris: Editions du Seuil, 1962; Columbia: University of South Carolina Press, 1976.

Rigon, Antonio. *Clero e città: «fratalea cappellanorum», parroci, cura d'anime in Padova dal XII al XV secolo*. Fonti e ricerche di storia ecclesiastica padovana 22. Padua: Istituto per la storia ecclesiastica padovana, 1988.

——. "Le elezioni vescovili nel processo di sviluppo delle istituzioni ecclesiastiche a Padova fra XII e XIII secolo." *Mélanges de l'École française de Rome: Moyen âge—temps modernes* 89 (1977): 371–409.

——. "I laici nella chiesa padovana del duocento: Conversi, oblati, penitenti." *Contributi alla storia della chiesa padovana nell'età medioevale* 1 (1979): 11–81.

——. "Orientamenti religiosi e pratica testamentaria a Padova nei secoli XII–XIV (prime ricerche)." In *Nolens intestatus decedere: Il testamento come fonte della storia religiosa e sociale*, pp. 41–63. Atti del'incontro di studio, Perugia, 3 maggio 1983. Archivi dell'Umbria inventari e ricerche 7. [n.p.]: Regione dell'Umbria, 1985.

——. "Penitenti e laici devoti fra mondo monastico-canonicale e ordini mendicanti: Qualche esempio in area veneta e mantovana." *Ricerche di storia sociale e relgiosa* n.s. 17–18 (1980): 51–73.

——. *S. Giacomo di Monselice nel medio evo (sec. XII–XV): Ospedale, monastero, collegiata*. Fonti e ricerche di storia ecclesiastica padovana 4. Padua: Istituto per la storia ecclesiastica padovana, 1972.

Rippe, Gerard. "Commune urbaine et féodalité en Italie au nord: L'exemple de Padove (Xe siècle—1237)." *Mélanges de l'École française de Rome: Moyen âge—temps modernes* 91 (1979): 659–97.

Roberti, Mario Mirabella. "La basilica di San Salvatore a Sermione." In *Verona in età gotica e langobarda*, pp. 133–142. Atti del convegno 6–7 dicembre 1980. Verona: Accademia di agricoltura, scienze, e lettere di Verona, 1982.

Robinson, I. S. *Authority and Resistance in the Investiture Contest: The Polemical Literature of the Late Eleventh Century*. Manchester: Manchester University Press; New York: Holmes & Meier, 1978.

——. "Gregory VII and the Soldiers of Christ." *History* 58 (1973): 169–92.

——. "'Periculosus homo': Pope Gregory VII and Episcopal Authority." *Viator* 9 (1978): 103–31.

——. "Pope Gregory VII (1073–1085)." *Journal of Ecclesiastical History* 36 (1985): 439–83.

Ronzani, Mauro. "L'organizzazione della cura d'anime nella città di Pisa (secoli XII–XIII)." In *Istituzioni ecclesiastiche della Toscana medioevale*, pp. 35–85. Galatina: Congedo, 1980.

Rosenwein, Barbara. *Rhinoceros Bound: Cluny in the Tenth Century*. Philadelphia: University of Pennsylvania Press, 1982.

——. *To Be the Neighbor of Saint Peter: The Social Meaning of Cluny's Property, 909–1049*. Ithaca, N.Y.: Cornell University Press, 1989.

Rossetti, Gabriella. "Formazione e carattere delle signorie di castello e dei poteri territoriali dei vescovi sulle città nella langobardia del secolo X." *Aevum* 49 (1975): 241–309.

——. "Il matrimonio del clero nella società altomedievale." In *Il matrimonio nella società altomedievale* 1: 473–576. Settimane di studio del Centro italiano di studi sull'alto medioevo 24. Spoleto: Centro italiano di studi sull'alto medioevo, 1977.

Rossini, Egidio. "Il diploma di Lodovico II imperatore concesso nell'873 in favore della chiesa veronese (problemi e proposte)." *AMAV* 154 (1977–78): 137–55.

——. "I livelli di Ostiglia nel secolo IX." In *Contributi alla storia della agricoltura veronese*, pp. 11–136. Verona: Accademia di agricoltura, scienze, e lettere di Verona/Artegrafica, 1979.

——. "Società e burocrazia nel basso medioevo: Il collegio dei notai di Verona nei secoli XIII–XIV." *AMAV* 149 (1972–73): 211–59.

——. "Ugo 'gratia Dei gloriosissimus dux et marchio' e il monastero della Vangadizza." *Atti e memorie del Sodalizio vangadiciense* 2 (1982): 3–25.

——. "Uomini, terra e lavoro nel veronese del secolo XI." In *Verona dalla caduta dei Carolingi al libero comune*, pp. 273–335. Atti del convegno del 24–26 maggio 1985. Verona: Accademia di agricoltura, scienze, e lettere di Verona, 1987.

——. "Verona nelle carte cremonesi del medioevo (916–1329) (Appunti per un regesto)." *Studi storici veronesi* 19 (1968–69): 23–96.

Sala, Giuliano. *La chiesa di S. Severo a Bardolino nella storia e nell'arte*. Verona: Centro di studi per il territorio benacense, 1987.

Salvioli, Giuseppe. *Storia delle immunità delle signorie e giustizie delle chiese in Italia*. Le giurisdizioni speciali nella storia del diritto Italiano 2. Modena: G. T. Vincenzi e nipoti, 1889.

Sambin, Paolo. *Nuovi documenti padovani dei secoli XI–XII*. Monumenti storici n.s. 8. Venice: Deputazione di storia patria per le Venezie, 1955.

——. *L'ordinamento parrochiale di Padova nel medioevo*. Pubblicazioni della Facoltà di lettere e filosofia 20. Padua: CEDAM, 1941.

*San Proculo: Un recupero e un restauro*. Verona: Banca Popolare di Verona, 1988.

Sancassani, Giulio. "Abati del monastero e abbazia della SS. Trinità di Verona." In *SS. Trinità in «monte oliveto» di Verona*, pp. 79–125. Verona: Stimmatini, 1974.

——. "Il centenario degli antichi archivi veronesi (1869–1969)." *Vita veronese* 22 (1969): 339–43.

——. "I Da Palazzo nella bassa veronese nel medioevo." *AMAV* 157 (1980–81): 87–97.

——. "Documenti della Vangadizza nel fondo archivistico di S. Salvar Corte Regia di Verona." *Atti e memorie del Sodalizio vangadiciense* 1 (1975): 297–305.

——. "Documenti di Polverano abate della Badia della Vangadizza concernenti il monastero di S. Salvar Corte Regia di Verona." *Atti e memorie del Sodalizio vangadiciense* 2 (1982): 27–36.

——. "Le fonti archivistiche relative al Monastero e all'Abbazia di S. Zeno di Verona." In *Studi Zenoniani in occasione del XVI centenario della morte di S. Zeno*, pp. 49–63. Verona: Accademia di agricoltura, scienze e lettere di Verona, 1974.

——. "L'opera di archivista di Lodovico Perini, architetto veronese dei primi decenni del '700." *Vita veronese* 9 (1957): 356–57.

Sandri, Gino. "L'antica chiesa di S. Tommaso Cantuariense nell'isola di Verona." *AMAV* 123 (1944–47): 67–79.

*Santa Maria Novella, un convento nella città: Studie e fonti.* 2 volumes. Memorie Domenicane n.s. 11. Pistoia: Memorie Domenicane, 1980.

Sant'Ambrogio, Diego. "Donazione di San Stefano Veronese al monastero cluniacense ed a San Gabriele di Cremona." *Nuovo archivio veneto* n.s. 15/2 (1908): 377–89.

Sartori, Giuseppe. *Colognola ai Colli.* Collana "Le Guide" 58. Verona: Vita veronese, 1958.

Savio, Fedele. *Gli antichi vescovi d'Italia dalle origini al 1300 descritti per regioni, La Lombardia.* 2 volumes. Florence: Libreria Editrice Fiorentina, 1913; Bergamo: Tipografia Editrice S. Alessandro, 1932.

——. *Gli antichi vescovi d'Italia dalle origini al 1300 descritti per regione, Il Piemonte.* Turin: Fratelli Bocca, 1898.

Schneider, Fedor. "Aus San Giorgio in Braida zu Verona." In *Papsttum und Kaisertum: Forschungen zur politischen Geschichte und Geisteskultur des Mittelalters. Paul Kehr zum 65. Geburtstag dargebracht*, edited by Albert Brackmann, pp. 185–206. Munich: Münchner Drucke, 1926.

Schumann, Reinhold. *Authority and the Commune, Parma, 833–1133.* Parma: Deputazione di storia patria per le province parmensi, 1973.

Schwarzmaier, Hansmartin. "The Monastery of St. Benedict, Polirone, and Its Cluniac Associations." In *Cluniac Monasticism in the Central Middle Ages*, edited by Noreen Hunt, pp. 123–42. London: Macmillan, 1971.

*La scuola nell'occidente latino dell'alto medioevo.* Atti della XIX settimana di studio del Centro italiano di studi sull'alto medioevo, 15–21 aprile 1971. 2 volumes. Spoleto: Centro italiano di studi sull'alto medioevo, 1972.

Segala, Franco. *L'Archivio storico della curia vescovile di Verona.* Verona: Archivio storico curia vescovile, 1986.

——. *Il culto di San Zeno nella liturgia medioevale fino al secolo XII: Contributo allo studio e all'interpretazione delle messe in memoria del santo vescovo di Verona.* Studi e documenti di storia e liturgia 1. Verona: Archivio storico curia vescovile, 1982.

Settia, Aldo A. *Castelli e villaggi nell'Italia padana: Popolamento, potere, e sicurezza fra IX e XII secolo.* Naples: Liguori, 1984.

——. "Strade romane e antiche pievi fra Tanaro e Po," *Bollettino storico-bibliografico subalpino* 68 (1970): 5–108.

Simeoni, Luigi. "Antichi patti tra signori e comuni rurali nelle carte veronesi." *AMAV* 83 (1906–7): 51–67.

——. *La basilica di S. Zeno di Verona.* Verona: C. A. Baroni, 1909.

——. "Dazii e tolonei medievali di diritto privato a Verona." *Studi storici veronesi* 8–9 (1957–58): 191–248.

——. "Documenti e note sull'età precomunale e comunale a Verona." *Studi storici veronesi* 8–9 (1957–58): 41–85.

——. "Iscrizioni medievali di monumenti veronesi." *AMAV* 85 (1908–9): 69–89.

——. "Le origini del comune di Verona." *Studi storici veronesi* 8–9 (1957–58): 87–151.

——. "Rapporti tra le opere dei due eruditi veronesi: L. Perini e G. B. Biancolini." *Atti del Reale istituto veneto di scienze lettere ed arti* 88/2 (1928–29): 1033–48.

——. "Le sedi della cattedrale a Verona prima dell'attuale." *Studi storici veronesi* 4 (1953): 11–28.

——. *Verona; Guida storico-artistica della città e provincia.* Verona, 1909. Reprinted, Verona: Vita veronese, 1953.

——. "Verona nell'età precomunale." *Studi storici veronesi* 8–9 (1957–58): 7–39.

Simoni, Pino. "Un erudito del settecento: Giambattista Biancolini." *Studi storici veronesi* 33 (1983): 7–46.

Sot, Michel. "Historiographie épiscopale et modèle familial en occident au IXe siècle." *Annales: Économies, sociétés, civilisations* 33 (1978): 433–49.

Southern, R. W. *Western Society and the Church in the Middle Ages.* Harmondsworth, Penguin, 1970.

Spagnolo, Antonio. "L'avvento e le sue domeniche." *AMAV* 92 (1915–16): 185–90.

——. "Il clero veronese nella elezione del vescovo, 1080–1338." *AMAV* 84 (1907–8): 97–105.

——. "Le quattro tempora e un documento veronese." *AMAV* 92 (1915–16): 191–96.

——. *Le scuole accolitali in Verona.* Verona: G. Franchini, 1904.

——. "Tre calendarii medioevali veronesi." *AMAV* 90 (1913–14): 161–239.

Spufford, Peter. *Handbook of Medieval Exchange.* London: Offices of the Royal Historical Society, 1986.

——. *Money and Its Use in Medieval Europe.* Cambridge: Cambridge University Press, 1988.

Stoller, Michael. "Eight Anti-Gregorian Councils." *Annuarium historiae conciliorum* 17 (1985): 252–321.

*Storia di Brescia.* Edited by Giovanni Treccani degli Alfieri. 5 volumes. Brescia: Morcelliana, 1963–64.

*La storiografia italiana negli ultimi vent'anni,* edited by Luigi De Rosa. 2 volumes. Milan: Marzorati, 1971.

Tabacco, Giovanni. "Cristianità e impero fino al Concordato di Worms." In *La cristianità dei secoli XI e XII in occidente: Coscienza e strutture di una società,* pp. 3–25. Atti della ottava Settimana internazionale di studio, Mendola, 30 giugno–5 luglio 1980. Miscellanea del Centro di studi medioevali 10. Milan: Vita e Pensiero, 1983.

——. "Problemi di insediamento e di popolamento nell'alto medioevo." In *Rivista storica italiana* 79 (1967): 67–110.

——. "Vescovi e monasteri." In *Il monachesimo e la riforma ecclesiastica (1049–1122),* pp. 105–24. Atti della quarta Settimana internazionale di studio, Mendola, 23–29 agosto 1968. Miscellanea del Centro di studi medioevali 6. Milan: Vita e Pensiero, 1971.

Tachella, Lorenzo. "Le origini dell'abbazia dei SS. Nazaro e Celso di Verona." *Studi storici veronesi* 20–21 (1970–71): 5–105.

Tafi, Angelo. *La chiesa aretina dalle origine al 1032.* Arezzo: Tipografia Badiali di Arezzo, 1972.

Tedone, Cinzia Fiorio. "Tombe dipinte altomedievali rinvenute a Verona." *Archeologia veneta* 8 (1985): 251–88.

Tellenbach, Gerd. *Church, State, and Christian Society at the Time of the Investiture Conflict.* Translated by R. F. Bennett. Oxford, 1940. Reprinted, Atlantic Highlands, N.J.: Humanities Press, 1979.

——. "Il monachesimo riformato ed i laici nei secoli XI e XII." In *I laici nella «societas christiana» dei secoli XI e XII,* pp. 118–42. Atti della terza Settimana internazionale di studio, Mendola, 21–27 agosto 1965. Miscellanea del Centro di studi medioevali 5. Milan: Vita e Pensiero, 1968.

Terragnoli, P. "Appunti storici sulla pieve di Calavena." *Bollettino ecclesiastico veronese* 1 (1914): 119–20.

Tessari, Umberto Gaetano. *La chiesa di S. Nazaro*. Verona: Vita veronese, 1958.

Tillier, J.-C. "Les conciles provinciaux de la province ecclésiastique de Bordeaux au temps de la réforme grégorienne (1073–1100)." *Bulletin philologique et historique (jusqu'à 1610) du Comité des travaux historiques et scientifiques* 2 (1968): 561–82.

Tiraboschi, Girolamo. *Storia dell'augusta badia di S. Silvestro di Nonantola*. Modena: Società Tipografica, 1784–85.

Toubert, Pierre. *Les structures du Latium médiéval; Le Latium méridional et la Sabine du IXe siècle à la fin du XIIe siècle*. 2 volumes. Rome: École française de Rome, 1973.

Turrini, Giuseppe. "Communicazione [lettera indirizzata al Prof. L. Schiaparelli, 12 novembre 1926]." *Archivio storico italiano*, ser. 7, 7 (1927): 110–14.

Ullmann, Walter. *The Growth of Papal Government in the Middle Ages*. 2d edition. London: Methuen, 1962.

*Una città e il suo fiume: Verona e l'Adige*. Edited by Giorgio Borelli. 2 volumes. Verona: Banca Popolare di Verona, 1977.

*Un lago, una civiltà: Il Garda*. Edited by Giorgio Borelli. 2 volumes. Verona: Banca Popolare di Verona, 1983.

Van Engen, John. "The Christian Middle Ages as an Historiographical Problem." *American Historical Review* 91 (1986): 519–52.

——. "The 'Crisis of Cenobitism' Reconsidered: Benedictine Monasticism in the Years 1050–1150." *Speculum* 61 (1986): 269–304.

Varanini, Gian Maria. *Il distretto veronese nel quattrocento: Vicariati del comune di Verona e vicariati privati*. Verona: Fiorini, 1980.

——. "L'espansione urbana di Verona in età comunale: dati e problemi." In *Spazio, società, potere nell'Italia dei comuni*, edited by Gabriella Rossetti, pp. 1–25. Naples: Liguori, 1986.

——. "Per la storia dei Minori a Verona nel duecento." In *Minoritismo e centri veneti nel duecento, nell'ottavo centenario della nascita di Francesco d'Assisi (1182–1982)*, edited by Giorgio Cracco, pp. 92–125. Trent: Civis Studi e Testi, 1983.

Vasaturo, Nicola. "L'espansione della congregazione Vallombrosana fino alla metà del secolo XII." *Rivista di storia della Chiesa in Italia* 16 (1962): 456–85.

Vauchez, André. *Les laïcs au moyen âge: Pratiques et expériences religieuses*. Paris: Cerf, 1987.

Venarde, Bruce Lanier. "La réforme à Apt (Xe–XIIe siècles): Patrimoine, patronage, et famille," *Provence historique* 152 (1988): 131–47.

Venturini, Maria. *Vita ed attività dello «scriptorium» veronese nel secolo XI*. Verona: Tipografica Veronese, 1930.

*Verona e il suo territorio*. 7 volumes. Verona: Istituto per gli studi storici veronesi, 1960–69.

*Vescovi e diocesi in Italia nel medioevo (sec. IX–XIII)*. Atti del II convegno di storia della Chiesa in Italia (Roma, 5–9 sett. 1961). Italia Sacra 5. Padua: Antenore, 1964.

Violante, Cinzio. "La chiesa bresciana nel medioevo." In *Storia di Brescia*, edited by Giovanni Treccani degli Alfieri, 1: 1000–1124. Brescia: Morcelliana, 1963–64.

——. "I laici nel movimento patarino." In *I laici nella «societas christiana» dei secoli XI e XII*, pp. 597–687. Atti della terza Settimana internazionale di studio, Mendola, 21–27 agosto 1965. Miscellanea del Centro di studi medioevali 5. Milan: Vita e Pensiero, 1968.

——. "I movimenti patarini e la riforma ecclesiastica." *Annuario dell'Università Cattolica del Sacro Cuore*, 1955–56 and 1956–57, pp. 209–23.

——. "Nobiltà e chiese in Pisa durante i secoli XI e XII: Il monastero di S. Matteo (Prime ricerche)." In *Adel und Kirche: Gerd Tellenbach zum 65. Geburtstag dargebracht von Freunden und Schülern*, edited by Josef Fleckenstein und Karl Schmid, pp. 259–79. Fribourg: Herder, 1968.

——. *La pataria milanese e la riforma ecclesiastica. I. Le premesse*. Rome: Istituto storico italiano per il medio evo, 1955.

——. *La società milanese nell'età precomunale*. Rome, 1953. Reprinted, Rome: Laterza, 1974.

——. *Studi sulla cristianità medievale: Società, istituzioni, spiritualità*. Edited by Piero Zerbi. Milan: Vita e Pensiero, 1972.

*La vita comune del clero nei secoli XI e XII*. 2 volumes. Atti della Settimana di studio, Mendola, settembre 1959. Milan: Vita e Pensiero, 1962.

Viviani, Giuseppe Franco and Brugnoli, Pierpaolo. *Bibliografia veronese (1966–1970)*. Verona: Accademia di agricoltura, scienze, e lettere di Verona, 1971.

Viviani, Olindo. "La fine delle controversie per l'esenzione giurisdizionale del capitolo veronese." *AMAV* 130 (1953–54): 239–309.

Volpe, Gioacchino. *Toscana medievale; Massa Marittima, Volterra, Sarzana*. Florence: G. C. Sansoni, 1964.

Wallace-Hadrill, J. M. *The Frankish Church*. Oxford: Clarendon Press, 1983.

Weigle, Fritz. "Il processo di Raterio di Verona." *Studi storici veronesi* 4 (1953): 29–44.

——. "Ratherius von Verona im Kampf um das Kirchengut 961–968." *Quellen und Forschungen aus italienischen Archiven und Bibliotheken* 28 (1937–38): 1–35.

Wickham, Chris. *Early Medieval Italy: Central Power and Local Society 400–1000*. Totowa, N.J.: Barnes and Noble, 1981.

Zarpellon, Agostino. *Verona e l'agro veronese in età romana*. Verona: Nova historia, 1954.

Zerbi, Piero. "I monasteri cittadini di Lombardia." In *Il monachesimo e la riforma ecclesiastica (1049–1122)*, pp. 285–314. Atti della quarta Settimana internazionale di studio, Mendola, 23–29 agosto 1968. Miscellanea di Centro di studi medioevali 6. Milan: Vita e Pensiero, 1971.

Zielinski, Herbert. *Der Reichsepiskopat in spätottonischer und salischer Zeit (1002–1125)*. Stuttgart: Franz Steiner, 1984.

Zimmerman, Harald. "Die 'gregorianische Reform' in deutschen Landen." *Studi gregoriani* 13 (1989): 263–79.

Zivelonghi, Giuseppe. "Strumenti e spunti di ricerca nei documenti dell'Archivio Capitolare di Verona." In *Verona dalla caduta dei Carolingi al libero comune*, pp. 117–76. Atti del convegno del 24–26 maggio 1985. Verona: Accademia di agricoltura, scienze, e lettere di Verona, 1987.

Zumkeller, Adolar. *Augustine's Ideal of the Religious Life*. Translated by Edmund Colledge. New York: Fordham University Press, 1986.

# GENERAL INDEX

Adelard, Bishop (876–915), 146
Adige (river), 14–15, 22, 24, 29, 76n, 79–80, 128, 130, 150, 186
Agino, Bishop (844–847), 124n
Aistulf, Bishop (866–875), 148
Albaredo, 37
Angiari, 24–25, 37, 130, 131n, 150
Anno, Bishop (750–780), 17, 156
Ansa, Queen (c. 759?–774?), 26n, 65
Aquileia, 45n, 58n, 122–23, 139, 164
Arbizzano, 33, 37, 150n
Arcè, 36
Arcole, 149n
Arena, 18, 20
artisans, 85–86, 103–6, 173
Arzere, 37
Asti, 129n, 130n
Audibert, Abbot of S. Maria in Organo (831–845), 27, 66, 121
Audo, Bishop (860–866), 49, 101, 117, 151
Avesa, 37
Avio, 36, 130

Badia, 25, 35
Balsemate, 149
Bardolino, 25, 26, 34, 36
Begosso, 149
Belfiore d'Adige. *See* Porcile
Benedictines. *See* monasticism
Berengar I, King (888–924) and Emperor (915), 26, 46, 131
Bergamo, 94n, 161n
Bernard, Bishop (1122-1135), 151, 164–66, 169, 171n; and reform of S. Giorgio in Braida, 70, 81–82, 135, 160
Billongus, Bishop (847–850), 101, 106n, 151, 154
Bionde, 37

bishops of Verona, 12, 15–17, 142–74; authority of, 39–40, 45, 49, 118, 120, 122–38, 163n; control of trade, 19, 37; foundations by, 71n, 72, 74, 107, 115, 134; sources for, 180
Bologna, 58
Bonavigo, 25, 37, 71, 76n, 149
Bonefisio, 37
Bonferraro, 37, 137–38
Bovolone, 54, 130, 150
Brentonico, 36, 130, 186
Brenzone, 25–26, 36
Brescia, 124n, 150, 154, 159n, 165, 182
Bruno, Bishop (1072–1080), 77, 146–47, 159
bulls, papal, 39–40, 126–30, 137–38, 187n
Bussolengo, 24–25, 36

Cadalus (Pope Honorius II, 1061–1064), 74–76, 80–81, 139n, 148, 181n
Calavena, 37, 72–73
Caldiero, 37, 150n
Calmano, 74n
Calmasino, 127, 129
Camaldoli, 69, 93
Campalano, 150
Campanea (maior, minor), 28–30
Campomarzo, 18–20, 186
canons, cathedral. *See* cathedral chapter
canons regular, 69, 82–86, 92, 99; *see also* S. Giorgio in Braida *in the Index of Ecclesiastical Institutions*
Canossa, house of, 76–78
capitanei, 102–3
Caprino, 24–25, 36, 130
care of souls, 41, 59–60, 62, 121, 126, 132, 136, 177
Carpi, 76n
Casale [Alto], 25, 36

# INDEX OF ECCLESIASTICAL INSTITUTIONS

Placenames of institutions located outside the city of Verona and its immediate suburbs are indicated in parentheses. Untitled institutions are listed at the end.

Library of Congress Cataloging-in-Publication Data

Miller, Maureen C. (Maureen Catherine), 1959–
    The formation of a medieval church : ecclesiastical change in Verona, 950–
1150 / Maureen C. Miller.
        p.   cm.
    Includes bibliographical references and index.
    ISBN 0-8014-2837-8
    1. Catholic Church. Diocese of Verona (Italy)—History.    2. Verona Region
(Italy)—Church history.    I. Title.
BX1547.V44M55    1993
282'.4534'09021—dc20                                                    92-54971